AI for Humanitarianism

This book explores the transformative potential of artificial intelligence (AI) in addressing critical humanitarian challenges. It examines AI's role in enhancing emergency responses, poverty alleviation, and healthcare.

Chapters authored by a diverse group of international contributors cover topics such as AI's application in disease prediction, ethical AI practices, and innovative resource distribution. This book uniquely blends theoretical insights with practical case studies, providing a road map for leveraging AI in humanitarian efforts. Readers will benefit from detailed explorations of AI's capabilities and challenges, gaining insights into how AI can drive social change and improve global humanitarian outcomes.

Targeted at policymakers, researchers, practitioners, and anyone interested in the intersection of AI and humanitarianism, this book offers valuable perspectives on ensuring AI technologies are both advanced and ethically sound.

AI for Humanitarianism
Fostering Social Change
Through Emerging Technologies

Edited by
Adeyemi Abel Ajibesin and
Narasimha Rao Vajjhala

CRC Press
Taylor & Francis Group
Boca Raton London New York

CRC Press is an imprint of the
Taylor & Francis Group, an **informa** business

First edition published 2025
by CRC Press
2385 NW Executive Center Drive, Suite 320, Boca Raton FL 33431

and by CRC Press
4 Park Square, Milton Park, Abingdon, Oxon, OX14 4RN

CRC Press is an imprint of Taylor & Francis Group, LLC

© 2025 selection and editorial matter, Adeyemi Abel Ajibesin and Narasimha Rao Vajjhala; individual chapters, the contributors

Library of Congress Cataloging-in-Publication Data
Names: Ajibesin, Adeyemi Abel, editor. | Vajjhala, Narasimha, 1978- editor.
Title: AI for humanitarianism : fostering social change through emerging
technologies / edited by Adeyemi Abel Ajibesin and Narasimha Rao Vajjhala.
Description: 1. | Boca Raton, FL : CRC Press 2025. |
Includes bibliographical references and index.
Identifiers: LCCN 2024029997 (print) | LCCN 2024029998 (ebook) |
ISBN 9781032765716 (hardback) | ISBN 9781032748399 (paperback) |
ISBN 9781003479109 (ebook)
Subjects: LCSH: Humanitarianism—Technological innovations. |
Humanitarian assistance—Technological innovations.
Classification: LCC BJ1475.3 .A43 2025 (print) | LCC BJ1475.3 (ebook) |
DDC 361.7/40285—dc23/eng/20241011
LC record available at https://lccn.loc.gov/2024029997
LC ebook record available at https://lccn.loc.gov/2024029998

ISBN: 9781032765716 (hbk)
ISBN: 9781032748399 (pbk)
ISBN: 9781003479109 (ebk)

DOI: 10.1201/9781003479109

Typeset in Times
by codeMantra

Contents

Foreword

In an era where technology is rapidly reshaping our world, the transformative potential of artificial intelligence (AI) is undeniable. This forward-thinking book, *AI for Humanitarianism: Fostering Social Change Through Emerging Technologies*, edited by Adeyemi Abel Ajibesin and Narasimha Rao Vajjhala, is a pioneering effort to explore how AI can address some of the most pressing humanitarian challenges of our time. The authors, hailing from esteemed institutions such as the Cape Peninsula University of Technology and the University of New York Tirana, bring a wealth of knowledge and a diverse range of perspectives to this critical discourse.

This book embarks on its journey with an insightful "Introduction to AI in Humanitarian Work", laying the foundation for understanding AI's significant role in enhancing humanitarian efforts. From optimizing data collection and analysis to improving emergency preparedness and response, AI is presented as a game-changer in the humanitarian sector. The authors examine AI's potential to alleviate poverty, promote sustainable development, and revolutionize healthcare access and disease management.

One of the standout aspects of this book is its balanced approach to the ethical implications of AI. The chapters on "Ethical AI in Humanitarian Contexts" and "Ethical Considerations in AI for Humanitarian Contexts" provide a thorough examination of the moral challenges and responsibilities that come with deploying AI in vulnerable settings. By addressing these concerns, the authors emphasize the necessity of responsible AI practices that prioritize transparency, accountability, and human rights.

Moreover, this book highlights the importance of collaboration between public and private sectors to drive social innovation and create lasting impact. The chapter on "Public and Private Partnerships: Merging the Best of Both Worlds for Social Change" is particularly enlightening, showcasing successful initiatives and offering a road map for future collaborations.

In the realm of healthcare, AI's applications are explored extensively, from improving informal mobile health (mHealth) systems to pioneering digital hospitals and enhancing disease prediction and management. The innovative use of AI in diagnosing and predicting cardiovascular diseases and Alzheimer's disease demonstrates the potential for AI to transform patient care and medical research.

As we look to the future, *AI for Humanitarianism* also discusses the evolving trends and future directions of AI. The concluding chapter, "Future Directions and Responsible AI for Social Impact", serves as a call to action for policymakers, researchers, and practitioners to embrace AI's potential while ensuring it is used ethically and responsibly.

This book is an essential guide for anyone interested in the intersection of AI and humanitarianism. It provides both theoretical insights and practical case studies, making it a valuable resource for policymakers, practitioners, researchers, and students. By exploring the various applications of AI and addressing the ethical considerations involved, *AI for Humanitarianism* offers a comprehensive road map for leveraging emerging technologies to foster social change and improve the lives of those most in need.

I commend the authors and editors for their visionary work in compiling this volume and for their commitment to advancing the field of AI in ways that are both innovative and ethically sound. This book is not just a testament to the power of technology but also a reminder of our collective responsibility to use it wisely and for the greater good.

FOREWORD AUTHOR BIO

Etemi Joshua Garba is a professor of computer science. He is also a consultant in software engineering, digital economy, and multimedia data analytics (in data science and artificial intelligence) and an expert in the analysis and design (modeling and simulation) of software. He is the CEO and co-founder of a tech startup Ethereal.ng.

Professor Etemi Joshua Garba
Modibbo Adama University, Nigeria
August 10, 2024

Acknowledgments

To my beloved wife, Mrs. Olajumoke Olufemi Ajibesin, and my cherished children, Wisdom and Eunice Ajibesin, your unwavering support is my greatest treasure. Thank you for being my constant inspiration and the heartbeat of our family. I would also like to express my sincere gratitude to Professor Tiko Iyamu at the Faculty of Informatics & Design, Cape Peninsula University of Technology, South Africa, for his kind support.

Assoc. Prof. Adeyemi Abel Ajibesin

I want to thank my family members, particularly my mother, Mrs. Rajeswari Vajjhala, for her blessings and for instilling in me the virtues of perseverance and commitment.

Assoc. Professor Narasimha Rao Vajjhala

About the Editors

Adeyemi Abel Ajibesin is a distinguished academic scholar with over two decades of extensive experience in research, teaching, and leadership, particularly in electrical engineering and computer science. He is currently serving as a visiting professor in the Department of IT at Cape Peninsula University of Technology in South Africa, and he previously held positions such as the Chair/HoD of Software Engineering at the School of IT & Computing (SITC) at the American University of Nigeria, the founding Interim Dean of the School of Engineering, the Interim Dean of the School of IT & Computing, and the Director of the African Centre for ICT Innovation and Training. He has also served in various capacities at Simon Fraser University in Canada, the University of Cape Town in South Africa, and the Pan African University Institute for Basic Sciences, Technology Innovation in Kenya, among other institutions. His areas of research are data science, broadband networks, frontier analysis, and AI. His prolific research portfolio is reflected in numerous articles published in reputable peer-reviewed conference proceedings, journals, and books, alongside patents for engineering products and copyrighted computing software, showcasing his innovative contributions to his field. His leadership and academic excellence have been recognized through numerous awards and grants, including esteemed accolades such as Google Research (exploreCSR), AIMS, CSIR, and IEEE.

Narasimha Rao Vajjhala currently serves as the Dean of the Faculty of Engineering and Architecture at the University of New York Tirana in Albania. He previously held the position of Chair for the computer science and software engineering programs at the American University of Nigeria. He is a senior member of both the ACM and IEEE. He is the Editor-in-Chief of the *International Journal of Risk and Contingency Management* (IJRCM) and a member of the Risk Management Society (RIMS) and the Project Management Institute (PMI). With over 23 years of experience, he has taught programming and database-related courses across Europe and Africa at both graduate and undergraduate levels. He has also worked as a consultant for technology firms in Europe and participated in EU-funded projects. He holds a Doctorate in Information Systems and Technology from the United States, a Master of Science in Computer Science and Applications from India, and a Master of Business Administration specializing in Information Systems from Switzerland.

Contributors

Bashir Eseyin Abdullahi
Computer Science Department
Federal University Lokoja
Lokoja, Nigeria

Adeyemi Abel Ajibesin
Department of Information Technology,
    Faculty of Informatics and Design
Cape Peninsula University of Technology
Cape Town, South Africa

Taiwo Abiodun
Computer Science Department
Federal University Lokoja
Lokoja, Nigeria

Jyoti Batra
School of Computer Applications
Lovely Professional University
Punjab, India

Murat Tahir Çaldağ
Technology and Information
    Management Program
Başkent University
Ankara, Turkey

Eriona Çela
Department of Psychology, Faculty of
    Law and Social Sciences
University of New York Tirana
Tirana, Albania

Neelatphal Chanda
Department of Media Studies
Christ University
Bangalore, India

Philip Eappen
Shannon School of Business
Cape Breton University
Sydney, Canada

Azubuike Erike
Federal University of Technology
Owerri, Nigeria

Tarcízio Ferrão
Electrical Engineering Department
Rovuma University
Nampula, Mozambique

Ebru Gökalp
Mühendislik Fakültesi
Hacettepe University
Ankara, Turkey

Ishayu Gupta
Department of Media Studies
Christ University
Bangalore, India

Radha Srinivasan Iyer
SEC Centre for Independent Living
Pune, India

Yusuf Kabir Kasum
Computer Science Department
Federal University Lokoja
Lokoja, Nigeria

Christian Kaunert
International Security (Law and
    Government) Department
Dublin City University
Dublin, Ireland

Manju Khari
School of Computer and System Sciences
Jawaharlal Nehru University
New Delhi, India

Munir Maharazu Kubau
Information Systems Department, School
of IT and Computing
American University of Nigeria
Yola, Nigeria

Devender Kumar
School of Computer Applications
Lovely Professional University
Phagwara, India

Bashir Malgwi
Family Health International
Lagos, Nigeria

Yusuf Mshelia
Data Aid
Plateau, Nigeria
and
Nile University of Nigeria
Abuja, Nigeria

Yerzhan B. Mukashev
Business School
Kazakh-British Technical University
Almaty, Kazakhstan

Emeka Ogbuju
Computer Science Department
Federal University Lokoja
Lokoja, Nigeria

Francisca Oladipo
Computer Science Department
Thomas Adewumi University
Oko, Nigeria

Edoghogho Olaye
University of Benin
Benin, Nigeria

Bamidele Oluwade
Research and Development (R&D)
Department
Dewade Systems Limited
Bosso, Nigeria

Rajasekhara Mouly Potluri
Business School
Kazakh-British Technical University
Almaty, Kazakhstan

Babatunde Dauda Raheem
Computer Science Department
Federal University Lokoja
Lokoja, Nigeria

Md Mahfujur Rahman
Islamic Business School
Universiti Utara Malaysia
Sintok, Malaysia

Santhosh Kumar Rajamani
MIMER Medical College
Pune, India
And
Dr BSTR Hospital
Talegaon Dabhade, India

Selene Roldán Ruiz
Universidad Autónoma del Estado de
México
Toluca de Lerdo, Mexico

Arturo Roman Cesar Sanjuan
Universidad Autónoma del Estado de
México
Toluca de Lerdo, Mexico

Anjana Sharma
School of Computer Applications
Lovely Professional University
Phagwara, India

Pooja Sharma
School of Physical Sciences
Banasthali Vidyapith
Vanasthali, India

Bhupinder Singh
Sharda School of Law
Sharda University
Greater Noida, India

Hussein Umar
Computer Science Department
Federal University Lokoja
Lokoja, Nigeria

Samuel C. Avemaria Utulu
Information Systems Department, School
    of IT and Computing
American University of Nigeria
Yola, Nigeria

Narasimha Rao Vajjhala
Computer Science Department, Faculty
    of Engineering and Architecture
University of New York Tirana
Tirana, Albania

Ayush Verma
Department of Electrical Engineering
Jawaharlal Nehru University
New Delhi, India

Abraham Zirra
Data Aid
Abuja, Nigeria
and
Food & Agriculture Organization (FAO)
Abuja, Nigeria

Overview
AI for Humanitarianism

1

Adeyemi Abel Ajibesin and
Narasimha Rao Vajjhala

OVERVIEW OF THIS BOOK

AI for Humanitarianism: Fostering Social Change Through Emerging Technologies offers a comprehensive exploration of how AI can revolutionize humanitarian efforts across various sectors. This book brings together insights from experts across multiple disciplines, addressing the transformative potential of AI in enhancing disaster response, healthcare, education, and poverty alleviation. Each chapter examines specific applications of AI, from predictive analytics and data collection methodologies to ethical considerations and public-private partnerships. By examining real-world case studies and innovative AI technologies, the authors explore the ways in which AI can optimize resource distribution, improve logistical efficiency, and support sustainable development goals. This book also emphasizes the importance of ethical AI practices, transparency, and accountability to ensure that AI-driven solutions benefit vulnerable populations and promote social equity. Through a blend of theoretical frameworks and practical applications, this book aims to guide researchers, practitioners, policymakers, and stakeholders in leveraging AI to drive meaningful social change and humanitarian progress.

This book provides a comprehensive exploration of the transformative potential of AI in addressing critical humanitarian challenges. A total of 49 proposals were received before the deadline for submission of proposals. After a rigorous initial screening, eight proposals were rejected. From the remaining 41 submitted chapters, a meticulous double-blind review process was undertaken to ensure the highest quality and relevance of the content. This process culminated in the acceptance of 15 outstanding papers.

DOI: 10.1201/9781003479109-1

These accepted papers represent a combined effort of 39 distinguished authors hailing from ten different countries, showcasing a rich diversity of perspectives and expertise in the field. Chapters such as "Data Collection and Analysis for Humanitarian Action" and "The Humanitarian-AI Interface: Field Perspectives to Innovative Emergency Preparedness and Response" examine the mechanisms by which AI optimizes data utilization and improves emergency response strategies. This book examines "AI's Role in Alleviating Poverty during the Fourth Industrial Revolution" and extends this discussion to "The Role of Artificial Intelligence in Poverty Alleviation toward Sustainable Development", highlighting AI's capacity to foster economic growth and social equity. Healthcare applications are extensively covered, with chapters on "Exploring the Intersection of Artificial Intelligence and Informal mHealth Use for Healthcare Access in Humanitarian Contexts" and "AI in Healthcare: Social-Legal Impact and Innovations in Digital Hospitals and mHealth". The potential of AI in disease management is further explored in "Artificial Intelligence Applications in Human Disease Prediction", "Exploring Humanitarian Applications of Artificial Intelligence in Cardiovascular Disease Diagnosis", and "Advancing Humanitarian Efforts in Alzheimer's Diagnosis Using AI and MRI Technology". Addressing operational efficiency, "A Fair Resource-Sharing AI Algorithm for Humanitarian Camps" presents innovative approaches to resource distribution in crisis settings. Ethical considerations are a central theme, with "Ethical AI in Humanitarian Contexts: Challenges, Transparency, and Safety" and "Ethical Considerations in AI for Humanitarian Context – A Case Study of the Palestine-Israel Conflict" examining the moral implications and the need for responsible AI practices. "Public and Private Partnerships: Merging the Best of Both Worlds for Social Change" explores the collaborative potential between sectors to drive social innovation. "Halal Food Safety in the AI Era: New Horizons for Humanitarian Action" discusses the role of AI in ensuring ethical and safe food practices. Chapters like "Future Directions and Responsible AI for Social Impact" provide future research directions and action points for policymakers. By combining theoretical insights with practical case studies, this book offers a road map for leveraging AI technologies to enhance humanitarian efforts, ensuring they are both technologically advanced and ethically sound. This book serves as an essential guide for policymakers, practitioners, researchers, and anyone interested in the intersection of AI and humanitarianism.

In Chapter 2, "Data Collection and Analysis for Humanitarian Action", Devender Kumar, Jyoti Batra, and Anjana Sharma emphasize the pivotal role of information in humanitarian efforts, where timely and accurate data is crucial to alleviating suffering and improving the lives of those in vulnerable situations. At the heart of effective humanitarian action is a complex web of data that guides decision-making, shapes initiatives, and ensures that resources are directed where they are most needed. This chapter examines the methodologies of data collection and analysis that underpin successful humanitarian operations, highlighting how advances in technology, particularly AI, are revolutionizing these processes. From traditional methods like surveys and censuses to modern techniques utilizing satellites, drones, and social media, the landscape of data collection has evolved. The authors examine how these tools not only provide extensive geospatial information to swiftly aid in disaster response but also offer real-time insights through crowdsourcing, enhancing the ability to respond promptly and effectively to crises.

In Chapter 3, "The Humanitarian-AI Interface: Field Perspectives to Innovative Emergency Preparedness and Response", Yusuf Mshelia, Bashir Malgwi, Azubuike Erike, Abraham Zirra, and Edoghogho Olaye examine the crucial interface between humanitarian efforts and AI, focusing on enhancing AI adaptability to dynamic crises such as natural disasters, conflicts, and public health emergencies. Traditional humanitarian methods often struggle with resource optimization, decision-making, and timely aid delivery due to the vast and complex data generated during crises. These challenges are compounded by inefficiencies and delays inherent in conventional approaches, alongside unresolved ethical concerns regarding AI deployment in vulnerable contexts. This chapter addresses the need to bridge the gap between traditional humanitarian practices and the transformative potential of AI. The authors offer a comprehensive road map for AI integration in humanitarian activities, exploring case studies, AI technologies, algorithms, and data handling techniques. Emphasizing collaboration with policymakers, aid organizations, governments, and AI tool developers, this road map proposes innovative strategies for evaluation, metrics for success, and measures of effectiveness. This chapter also highlights opportunities and future directions for implementing AI-humanitarian collaborations, ensuring ethical considerations are at the forefront.

In Chapter 4, "AI's Role in Alleviating Poverty during the Fourth Industrial Revolution", Emeka Ogbuju, Bash Abdullahi, Husseini Umar, Babatunde Raheem, Yusuf Kabir, Taiwo Abiodun, and Francisca Oladipo explore the transformative potential of AI during the Fourth Industrial Revolution (4IR) in addressing global challenges, particularly poverty alleviation. AI presents a powerful tool to bridge socio-economic gaps, empower marginalized communities, and foster inclusive growth. This chapter examines AI's impact on poverty mitigation across various domains, revealing its significant potential in enhancing processes such as poverty mapping, education transformation, agricultural modernization, healthcare improvement, and financial sector advancement. For instance, researchers are utilizing satellite images to identify poverty-concentrated regions and developing AI programs to boost agricultural productivity through improved crop yields, detection of scarcity-prone areas, and disease management. The findings underscore the necessity for governmental bodies and private organizations to invest in and integrate AI into their poverty alleviation strategies, highlighting the numerous benefits AI offers in combating poverty during the 4IR.

In Chapter 5, "The Role of Artificial Intelligence in Poverty Alleviation toward Sustainable Development", Murat Tahir Çaldağ and Ebru Gökalp posit that poverty remains a significant challenge for many nations, but the integration of AI technologies has the potential to transform the fight against it. This chapter explores how AI can address the first Sustainable Development Goal (SDG) set by the United Nations: poverty alleviation. By categorizing the underlying roots of poverty into educational, economic, quality of life, environmental, social, and political factors, this study provides detailed explanations of AI-based solutions for each area. While the advantages of AI in combating poverty are substantial, this chapter also addresses important concerns such as biased training data, safety, privacy, financial costs, sustainability, overreliance, and the knowledge and skill requirements necessary for effective AI implementation. Through a comprehensive discussion of both the benefits and drawbacks of AI in poverty alleviation, this chapter offers a road map for government institutions and other stakeholders working toward this critical goal.

In Chapter 6, "Exploring the Intersection of Artificial Intelligence and Informal mHealth Use for Healthcare Access in Humanitarian Contexts", Munir Maharazu Kubau and Samuel Avemaria Utulu examine the dynamic intersection of AI and informal mobile health (mHealth) to enhance healthcare access in humanitarian contexts. Humanitarian settings often face crises, displacements, and limited healthcare services, making the integration of AI and informal mHealth practices crucial for addressing healthcare gaps and improving the well-being of vulnerable populations. The authors examine the foundational aspects of AI in healthcare, the prevalence of mobile technologies in these settings, and the practices and potential synergies of informal mHealth, while also addressing the challenges of integration. Utilizing an extensive literature review, this study provides a detailed understanding of the current knowledge on AI and informal mHealth in humanitarian contexts, offering actionable insights for policymakers and humanitarian efforts. This chapter envisions a future where AI and informal mHealth collaboratively provide resilient and accessible healthcare solutions for vulnerable populations.

In Chapter 7, "AI in Healthcare: Social-Legal Impact and Innovations in Digital Hospitals and mHealth", Bhupinder Singh and Christian Kaunert posit that AI is at the forefront of a healthcare revolution, transforming how medical services are perceived and utilized. As the digital era progresses, AI has become an essential tool in healthcare, encompassing applications such as digital hospitals, mobile health (mHealth) apps, predictive analytics, personalized medicine, telemedicine, and remote patient monitoring. AI's ability to predict disease outbreaks by analyzing historical data enables health authorities to respond swiftly and allocate resources efficiently, which is crucial during pandemics and public health emergencies. This chapter examines AI's role in forecasting illness outbreaks and resource allocation, paving the way for a more effective and adaptable healthcare system. Additionally, this chapter examines the social and legal implications of integrating AI into healthcare delivery, particularly within digital hospitals and mHealth applications.

In Chapter 8, "Artificial Intelligence Applications in Human Disease Prediction", Santhosh Kumar Rajamani and Radha Srinivasan Iyer provide a comprehensive exploration of AI applications in human disease prediction and healthcare. Beginning with an introduction to fundamental AI concepts, this chapter covers the various types of AI—narrow, general, and super AI—as well as key machine learning (ML) and deep learning (DL) principles. This chapter then highlights AI's diverse applications in disease prediction, including the forecasting of outbreaks, early detection and diagnosis, and the development of predictive models for personalized medicine. The authors examine ML approaches for disease prediction, discussing supervised learning techniques like classification and regression, unsupervised learning techniques such as clustering and dimensionality reduction, and reinforcement learning for optimizing treatment strategies. This chapter also explores DL architectures for disease prediction, including convolutional neural networks (CNNs) for medical image analysis, recurrent neural networks and long short-term memory for time-series data, and autoencoders and generative adversarial networks for disease detection. Furthermore, it addresses the challenges and opportunities of integrating AI into healthcare systems, examining ethical considerations, potential biases, and strategies for effective integration into healthcare workflows. Concluding with future directions and opportunities for AI in disease prediction, this chapter aims to equip readers with a thorough understanding of AI's potential to enhance healthcare outcomes and drive innovation in disease prediction.

In Chapter 9, "A Fair Resource-Sharing AI Algorithm for Humanitarian Camps", Bamidele Oluwade explores ML, with a focus on pattern recognition algorithms. These algorithms facilitate ML by utilizing a training set and a test set. Referencing the 1993 United States Patent 5267332, which introduced a pattern recognition procedure for visual images of the English alphabet, this chapter presents an alternative method for representing these alphabets as linked structures. This novel approach uses the qualitative equivalence of autonomous ordinary differential equations to enhance machine recognition. The development of this innovative pattern recognition algorithm for uppercase English letters has significant potential applications, particularly in the unique identification of individuals in emergency humanitarian settings such as refugee camps.

In Chapter 10, "Exploring Humanitarian Applications of Artificial Intelligence in Cardiovascular Disease Diagnosis", Tarcízio Ferrão and Adeyemi Abel Ajibesin explore the application of recurrent convolutional neural networks (RCNNs) for diagnosing and predicting cardiovascular diseases (CVDs) within the healthcare sector. This chapter identifies key DL algorithms used for CVD diagnosis and prediction and establishes ethical principles for their use in patient care. Beginning with a systematic review of DL applications in CVD detection and prediction, this chapter highlights the most recent, efficient, and functional models. The authors draw on recent studies using DL for CVD diagnosis, noting a common trend of employing CNNs and ML algorithms such as random forest (RF) and support vector machine (SVM). This chapter also proposes ethical guidelines for integrating AI into healthcare based on current medical and technological trends and discusses the selection of appropriate metrics for evaluating ML and DL models. The analysis indicates that RCNN has the potential to deliver superior results on medical datasets compared to commonly used models. Aimed at healthcare professionals, AI researchers, and those interested in the impact of emerging technologies on society, this chapter presents new ethical principles for AI integration in healthcare and consolidates key topics related to DL applications in CVD diagnosis and prediction. The authors provide valuable insights and suggest new research directions, contributing to a comprehensive understanding of AI's transformative potential in healthcare.

In Chapter 11, "Advancing Humanitarian Efforts in Alzheimer's Diagnosis Using AI and MRI Technology", Pooja Sharma, Ayush Verma, and Manju Khari state that Alzheimer's disease (AD) is a severe neurodegenerative condition that leads to dementia, characterized by the irreversible loss of memory. With no known cure, AD continues to claim numerous lives each year, predominantly affecting individuals aged 65 and older. Early detection and diagnosis are crucial for clinical intervention and management of the disease. This chapter introduces a novel approach using CNN for identifying the stages of AD from brain magnetic resonance imaging (MRI) images. The research involved classifying MRI images into categories of very mild, mild, moderate, and severe AD. Data preprocessing between unbalanced categories was performed using SMOTE and other image augmentation techniques. The proposed method achieved a testing accuracy of 95.16% and a training accuracy of 99.68%, surpassing the performance of the Inception-v3 model. Comparative analysis with standard image recognition models, including AlexNet, GoogLeNet, VGG-16, and ResNet-18, revealed that the GoogLeNet model provided the best results, with a training accuracy of 99.84% and a testing accuracy of 98.25%. This chapter aims to provide valuable insights into the application of CNN in the early detection and classification of Alzheimer's disease, highlighting its potential to significantly enhance diagnostic accuracy and improve patient outcomes.

In Chapter 12, "Ethical AI in Humanitarian Contexts: Challenges, Transparency, and Safety", Ishayu Gupta and Neelatphal Chanda explore how emerging AI technologies can drive social change and address global challenges. This chapter emphasizes the importance of ethical considerations and responsible AI practices to prevent exacerbating existing inequalities among vulnerable populations. The authors examine AI's role in ensuring access to quality education for all, innovative approaches to alleviating poverty, and amplifying human rights advocacy for marginalized groups. By presenting a comprehensive view of AI's impact on humanitarianism, the authors highlight new horizons while stressing the necessity for responsible and inclusive applications. This chapter offers valuable insights and recommendations for researchers, practitioners, policymakers, and stakeholders dedicated to leveraging new technologies to create a fairer and more sustainable world. This chapter aims to enhance understanding of the AI-humanitarianism nexus while advocating for safety measures and transparency to promote social progress.

In Chapter 13, "Ethical Considerations in AI for Humanitarian Context – A Case Study of the Palestine-Israel Conflict", Selene Roldán and Arturo Cesar critically explore the ethical considerations of using AI in humanitarian contexts, with a focus on the ongoing Palestine-Israel conflict as a case study. Through extensive analysis of philosophical perspectives from thinkers like Susan Sontag, Simone Weil, and Slavoj Žižek, this chapter unravels the ethical challenges and opportunities associated with AI in warfare. This chapter aims to propose a comprehensive ethical framework for developing and deploying AI in humanitarian settings, emphasizing key principles such as transparency, neutrality, intersectionality, and adherence to human rights and international law. This examination provides a thorough ethical critique, aiming to guide responsible AI practices in complex humanitarian scenarios.

In Chapter 14, "Public and Private Partnerships: Merging the Best of Both Worlds for Social Change", Rajasekhara Mouly Potluri and Yerzhan B. Mukashev posit that in recent years, civilization has faced significant challenges due to both human-made and natural events, including conflicts, natural disasters, displacements, mass exoduses, epidemics, and other crises that are reshaping our world. These disruptive forces are expected to intensify in the new millennium, necessitating substantial social interventions to mitigate their effects. Addressing these societal and humanitarian needs requires the collaboration of public and private sector partnerships, which possess the necessary resources and innovative capabilities to drive meaningful social change. This chapter highlights the critical insights from these partnerships, exploring how they function, their advantages and disadvantages, and the importance of sustainable collaborations. The authors examine the extensive research and initiatives by the Kazakhstan government to promote public-private partnerships, showcasing successful social impact projects. Through these examples, this chapter illustrates how competitive advantages, technological innovation, and effective resource management can achieve significant social impact within budget and on time.

In Chapter 15, "Halal Food Safety in the AI Era: New Horizons for Humanitarian Action", Md Mahfujur Rahman explores the transformative impact of AI on Halal food safety, emphasizing its global significance and contribution to broader humanitarian goals. Through comprehensive analysis, this chapter reveals how AI applications in Halal food safety can drive inclusive social and environmental change. By enhancing transparency, traceability, and efficiency in the Halal supply chain, AI technologies address long-standing challenges in food safety and ethical consumerism. This chapter also discusses the socio-economic benefits of AI in the Halal food industry, such as improved food security, reduced waste, and increased consumer trust. The authors underscore AI's role in promoting responsible consumption and supporting global efforts toward sustainable food systems. Through this detailed examination, this chapter presents AI's role in Halal food safety as a catalyst for positive humanitarian and societal transformation.

In the concluding Chapter 16, "Future Directions and Responsible AI for Social Impact", Adeyemi Abel Ajibesin, Eriona Çela, Narasimha Rao Vajjhala, and Philip Eappen explore the future trajectory of AI and its capacity to drive positive social change, emphasizing the essential role of responsible AI practices. The authors examine the emerging AI technologies and their applications across various sectors, including healthcare, education, and environmental sustainability. They highlight the ethical considerations and challenges associated with AI deployment, advocating for frameworks that ensure transparency, fairness, and accountability. This chapter presents strategies for integrating AI in ways that maximize social benefits while minimizing risks and providing actionable recommendations for policymakers, practitioners, and researchers. These strategies aim to encourage AI innovations that are both technologically advanced and ethically sound, ensuring AI's contributions to a more equitable and sustainable future.

Data Collection and Analysis for Humanitarian Action

2

Devender Kumar, Jyoti Batra, and Anjana Sharma

INTRODUCTION

Nowadays, the only global forces that already interact and influence humanitarian response are natural disasters, conflicts, untouchable crises of socioeconomic character, and catastrophes, which heighten the urgency for effective humanitarian aid. Humanitarian organizations are at the service of rescuing the people who experience suffering, saving lives, and restoring their dignity during and after crises and disasters. They are present in the countries around the globe where emergencies take place. Key to the effective implementation of these objectives is the collection and processing of information, which is the basis for the proper determination of appropriate measures and the most relevant interventions.

Definition of Humanitarian Action

The process termed "supplying aid" is aiding or assisting people. Assisting people has always been a necessity for individuals throughout human history. Direct assistance aid will be provided in the form of food or material provisions during times of famine,

DOI: 10.1201/9781003479109-2

drought, or natural calamities. Yet, the modern idea and the system of humanitarian assistance, which we commonly acknowledge as the impartial, autonomous, and neutral provision of help to people in immediate danger, are distinct phenomena of the second half of the 20th century. Although the concept of the system of international aid was first introduced after World War I in the Treaty of Versailles, a broadly accepted definition and conceptualization of humanitarian aid have only been part of tacit knowledge since the 1990s (Calhoun, 2008).

Importance of Data in Humanitarian Work

Across the humanitarian response cycle – preparedness and assessment, response, recovery, and long-term development – there is a growing reliance on data. This requires a cycle of data collection, analysis, and dissemination. Data enables more focused and effective responses by identifying the most pressing needs of impacted communities, such as food, housing, healthcare, water, and sanitation. Insights derived from data feed strategic decision-making, resource allocation, and operational planning, allowing humanitarian actors to deploy resources where required and react in real time as situations change. Monitoring important indicators and assessing initiatives help organizations ensure accountability, learn from successes and mistakes, and enhance humanitarian programs. Data may help advocate for legislative changes, mobilize resources, and increase awareness about the needs of impacted communities, increasing the effect of humanitarian action.

REVIEW OF LITERATURE

Overview of Humanitarian Crises

Humanitarian crises take many forms, including natural catastrophes like earthquakes, floods, storms, and wildfires, as well as complex situations like armed conflicts, diseases, and displacement crises. These disasters may have disastrous consequences for communities, resulting in relocation, loss of life, infrastructure devastation, and interruption of critical services. Understanding the complex and dynamic nature of humanitarian emergencies is critical for successful response and recovery efforts (Spiegel, 2017). Data relevant to humanitarian action can be broadly categorized into three main types. Geographic information systems (GISs), satellite photography, and aerial surveys offer vital insights into the geographical scope and severity of crises, allowing organizations to map impacted regions, estimate damage, and identify vulnerable people. Operational data, such as logistics, supply chain management, and real-time situational reporting, help the effective coordination and delivery of humanitarian aid on the ground, ensuring resources reach people in need in a timely way (Benini et al., 2003).

Data-Driven Decision-Making

Data-driven decision-making has led to numerous successful interventions in humanitarian action, including early warning systems that analyze meteorological data and historical patterns to anticipate natural catastrophes, including hurricanes, floods, and droughts. This allows people to prepare, evacuate, and lessen the damage. Socioeconomic data and vulnerability assessments enable humanitarian organizations to focus aid on the most disadvantaged communities, ensuring that resources are given where they are most needed and have the biggest impact. Real-time data on disease outbreaks and epidemiological patterns helps health officials discover, respond to, and limit infectious illnesses like Ebola, cholera, and COVID-19, ultimately saving lives.

Challenges in Decision-Making without Adequate Data

Decision-making without adequate data poses significant challenges in humanitarian action. Without accurate and timely data, humanitarian organizations may struggle to distribute resources efficiently, resulting in service gaps and missed chances to address important needs. In the absence of trustworthy data, humanitarian actors may make judgments based on assumptions or insufficient knowledge, increasing the likelihood of erroneous actions that fail to address the underlying causes of the crisis or worsen existing vulnerabilities (Egger & Schopper, 2022). Without data to track and evaluate the effects of interventions, humanitarian organizations may struggle to demonstrate responsibility to funders, beneficiaries, and other stakeholders, weakening confidence and credibility in their efforts (Hernandez & Roberts, 2020).

Ethical Considerations

When collecting data for humanitarian purposes, privacy and secrecy are of the highest priority. Humanitarian organizations must guarantee that impacted persons' personal information is protected and used exclusively for its intended purposes. This includes putting in place strong data protection mechanisms like encryption, anonymization, and secure data storage to reduce the risk of unauthorized access or disclosure. In addition, explicit rules for dealing with sensitive data should be created, including procedures for getting consent, exchanging information with other parties, and responding to data breaches.

Obtaining informed permission is critical for protecting the rights and dignity of those involved in data collection operations. Humanitarian organizations must adequately describe the goal, dangers, and advantages of data gathering to impacted communities, so that they may make voluntary and informed decisions regarding their involvement. This may include adopting accessible language, providing alternate communication channels for persons with inadequate reading or language abilities, and adhering to cultural norms and preferences about permission (Paulus et al., 2023).

METHODS

Quantitative data in humanitarian action is information that can be quantified and reported quantitatively. It offers objective and standardized parameters for evaluating the size, extent, and impact of humanitarian emergencies, as well as the efficacy of response activities. Quantitative data is frequently acquired through systematic surveys, evaluations, and statistical analyses, which enable quantitative comparisons, trend analysis, and data-driven decision-making (Spiegel, 2017). Quantitative data provides information on the number, composition, and distribution of people impacted by humanitarian crises. This may include age, gender, ethnicity, household size, and socioeconomic status, which can provide information on impacted communities' demographics as well as their special needs and vulnerabilities (Hilhorst et al., 2021). Health data provides information on illness prevalence, incidence, and dispersion among afflicted populations. Data on morbidity, mortality, immunization coverage, disease outbreaks, and access to healthcare services might be used to guide public health measures and healthcare delivery in humanitarian circumstances (Haak et al., 2018). Indicators of malnutrition, stunting, wasting, and micronutrient deficiencies are used to assess the dietary needs of afflicted populations. This information is essential for developing and monitoring food aid programs, nutrition initiatives, and mother and child health services in humanitarian settings (Spiegel, 2017). It evaluates the availability, accessibility, and quality of housing, shelter, and essential services, including water, sewage, and power, in humanitarian circumstances. This may include information on displacement, shelter types, housing conditions, availability of clean water and sanitation facilities, and infrastructure damage, which will help guide shelter and infrastructure interventions and humanitarian logistics. Food security and livelihoods data looks at the availability, access, and use of food and livelihood options among impacted communities. This may include information on food production, consumption, pricing, market access, income sources, and livelihood assets, which may be used to improve food security assessments, livelihood programming, and economic recovery efforts in humanitarian settings (Paulus et al., 2018). Data on education and child protection analyzes access, quality, and protection requirements for children and youth affected by humanitarian situations. Data on school enrollment, attendance, learning results, child safety risks, and incidences of violence might be used to guide education and child protection programs and advocacy activities. Quantitative data in humanitarian action serves as a quantitative foundation for needs assessment, program planning, monitoring and evaluation, and advocacy, allowing humanitarian organizations to prioritize resources, measure progress, and advocate for impacted populations' rights and well-being. By properly collecting, analyzing, and using quantitative data, humanitarian actors may better serve the immediate and long-term needs of crisis-affected people, lessen catastrophic damage, and promote resilience and sustainable development.

Surveys and questionnaires are commonly used in humanitarian efforts to acquire quantitative data from individuals or families impacted by disasters. These tools use standardized questionnaires with closed-ended or Likert scale questions to collect data on a variety of issues, such as demographics, health, nutrition, housing, food security, livelihoods, and education. Surveys can be carried out via face-to-face interviews, phone interviews, paper-based questionnaires, or digital data collection systems, depending on the context and available resources. They enable humanitarian organizations to swiftly and cost-effectively collect massive volumes of quantitative data, allowing for statistical analysis, trend detection, and evidence-based decision-making (Paulus et al., 2018). Remote sensing and GIS technologies play a critical role in collecting and analyzing spatial data for humanitarian action. Remote sensing techniques, such as satellite imagery, aerial photography, and unmanned aerial vehicles (UAVs), capture high-resolution images of the Earth's surface, allowing for the mapping and monitoring of environmental conditions, natural hazards, and changes in land use and land cover. GIS software enables the integration, visualization, and analysis of spatial data layers, including topography, infrastructure, population distribution, and vulnerability indicators. By combining remote sensing data with ground-based information, such as surveys and demographic data, humanitarian organizations can assess the geographical extent and severity of crises, identify at-risk populations, prioritize interventions, and facilitate informed decision-making in emergency response and disaster preparedness efforts.

Interviews and focus groups are effective techniques for gathering qualitative data in humanitarian action. Interviews are one-on-one interactions between a researcher and a crisis-affected individual that allow for a thorough assessment of their experiences, viewpoints, and needs. In contrast, focus groups bring together a small number of people from the impacted community to explore specific humanitarian concerns. Both strategies allow participants to tell their own stories, perceptions, and ideas, resulting in rich qualitative data that supports quantitative findings. Interviews and focus groups are especially useful for gathering complex information, establishing cultural context, and collecting varied community opinions (Fadiya et al., 2014). Case studies and narratives provide a better grasp of both individual experiences and the larger context of humanitarian disasters. Case studies, on the one hand, usually focus on specific people, families, or communities affected by a disaster, recording their experiences, problems, coping methods, and resilience. Narratives, on the other hand, use a variety of narrative strategies, such as personal experiences, testimonies, and oral histories, to depict the human effect of events and the complex dynamics at play. These qualitative data sources reveal important insights into impacted people's lived experiences, offering light on their needs, goals, and agency (Beduschi, 2022).

Field surveys are an essential means of gathering primary data in humanitarian intervention. They entail dispatching trained individuals or enumerators straight into the field to collect data from impacted populations. Surveys can be structured to obtain quantitative or qualitative data, depending on the study goals and the nature of the situation. Quantitative surveys often employ structured questionnaires with predetermined response options to collect numerical data on many elements of the humanitarian situation, such as demographics, needs assessments, health indicators, and service accessibility. In contrast, qualitative surveys may include open-ended questions or semi-structured interviews to delve deeper into individuals' experiences, perceptions, and coping methods (Riedler & Lang, 2022).

Interviews with impacted communities are another main data collection approach utilized in humanitarian aid. These interviews entail speaking directly with individuals or groups impacted by a crisis to acquire qualitative data on their experiences, perceptions, and needs. Interviews can be performed in person, over the phone, or via digital communication channels, depending on logistics and access to the impacted areas. They can take several forms, including structured interviews with predetermined questions, semi-structured interviews that allow for flexibility and exploration of pertinent themes, and unstructured interviews that foster open-ended discourse and storytelling. Interviews with impacted people give vital personal descriptions of the impact of crises on individuals and communities, emphasizing their perspectives, worries, and priorities. This qualitative data helps humanitarian organizations better understand the context, dynamics, and complexities of the humanitarian situation, informing more responsive and contextually appropriate interventions.

Secondary Data Collection

Utilizing existing databases and reports is an important aspect of secondary data collection in humanitarian intervention. These resources provide a wide range of data obtained by numerous organizations, governments, and research institutes before, during, and after a crisis. Existing databases may contain demographic data, health statistics, socioeconomic indicators, and geographic information gathered via national surveys, censuses, or administrative records. Reports from humanitarian agencies, non-governmental organizations (NGOs), United Nations (UN) agencies, and academic institutions give significant insights into the humanitarian situation, such as needs assessments, response plans, evaluations, and research findings. By accessing and analyzing these existing sources of data and information, humanitarian organizations can supplement their primary data collection efforts, fill gaps in knowledge, and gain a broader understanding of the context and challenges faced by affected populations. This enables more informed decision-making, resource allocation, and coordination of humanitarian response activities.

Collaboration with local authorities and NGOs is another significant technique for collecting secondary data in humanitarian operations. Local governments, civil society organizations, and community-based groups frequently have vital information and insights on the humanitarian situation in their various areas of operation. Collaboration with these stakeholders allows humanitarian organizations to have access to local knowledge, experience, and networks, allowing data exchange, validation, and contextualization. Local governments may give access to administrative information, official statistics, and catastrophe response plans, whereas NGOs might provide field reports, needs assessments, and community input acquired via their ongoing programs. Collaborative data gathering activities promote trust, improve coordination, and guarantee that humanitarian interventions are based on local realities and goals. They also promote ownership and sustainability by empowering local actors to actively participate in data-driven decision-making processes and contribute to the design, implementation, and evaluation of humanitarian interventions (Bell et al., 2021).

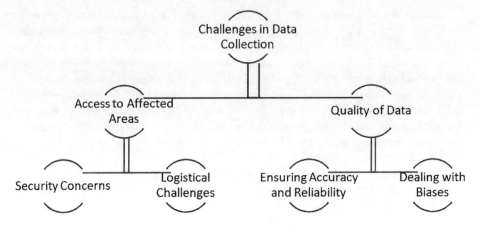

FIGURE 2.1   Challenges in data collection for humanitarian action.

Challenges in data collection for humanitarian action

A distinct set of difficulties arise when gathering precise and trustworthy data in humanitarian contexts, as shown in Figure 2.1. These difficulties may make it more difficult to make well-informed decisions, allocate resources efficiently, and ultimately protect the welfare of the impacted community (Spainhour Baker et al., 2020).

Challenges Faced during Data Collection

Access to some areas or populations inside a crisis area may be restricted, which may result in partial datasets that may not fully represent the needs and risks. Accessible populations are frequently underrepresented in data gathering, which may cause their unique needs and crucial solutions to be overlooked (Deb & Baudais, 2022).

Data collectors face serious safety risks when operating in violent or conflict-ridden areas, which may make it more difficult for them to access certain populations and lower the quality of the data they gather. When gathering data in conflict zones or communities hit by natural catastrophes, humanitarian workers may come under bodily threat from things like assault, theft, or kidnapping. It is critical to ensure field workers' safety. Personal identifiable information (PII) and other sensitive information are frequently included in humanitarian data. To keep the confidence of the impacted communities, it is crucial to maintain compliance with data protection laws like the General Data Protection Regulation (GDPR) and ethical data privacy practices.

Access to remote places may be constrained by logistical constraints, such as inadequate infrastructure or movement restrictions brought on by security concerns, which will impede data collection operations even more. Humanitarian crises often unfold in places that are hard to reach: conflict zones, remote communities, or areas devastated by natural disasters. Damaged infrastructure and a lack of transportation create major obstacles to access. Aid organizations struggle with limited resources – not enough money, people, or equipment. Prioritizing data collection can be difficult when faced with urgent needs for food, shelter, and medical care, especially in underfunded or long-lasting crises. Reaching communities in crisis poses significant challenges, and ensuring the accuracy of the collected data is even more daunting. With damaged infrastructure, scarce resources, and safety risks, there's a heightened risk of incomplete information and biases. This makes it challenging to grasp the genuine needs of affected populations and to provide aid effectively.

Ensuring precise and dependable data collection amid humanitarian operations is a multifaceted challenge. Accessing affected populations in remote regions or conflict areas is hindered by impaired infrastructure, safety considerations, and resource constraints. This obstacle often results in incomplete data, potentially overlooking critical details regarding specific needs and vulnerabilities within the affected community. Furthermore, data bias can emerge from various sources, such as sampling limitations, respondent concerns about stigmatization or manipulation, and the urgency to gather data swiftly in time-critical scenarios. These hurdles impede the ability of humanitarian organizations to attain a comprehensive understanding of actual needs on the ground, thereby obstructing their capacity to deliver targeted and efficient aid to those most in need. Gathering impartial data in humanitarian emergencies poses a distinct obstacle. Data collectors may inadvertently harbor biases, impacting their choice of participants or how they interpret responses. Moreover, affected communities might be reluctant to disclose accurate information due to concerns about stigma, the urgency for immediate aid, or cultural considerations. These dynamics have the potential to influence data toward demographics or overlook specific needs, thereby impeding the efficacy of focused interventions.

DATA ANALYSIS TECHNIQUES

Data analysis plays a crucial role in humanitarian action, informing decision-making, resource allocation, and program evaluation. By collecting and analyzing data effectively, humanitarian organizations can gain valuable insights into the needs of affected populations, measure the impact of their interventions, and improve their overall effectiveness (Kim De Boeck et al., 2023). Descriptive statistics provide summaries of the sample and the measures collected. It helps in understanding the basic features of the data, for instance, mean, median, mode, and standard deviation, as shown in Figure 2.2 (Spainhour Baker et al., 2020).

In humanitarian endeavors, inferential statistics play a pivotal role in analyzing data. By extrapolating insights from sample data to draw conclusions about broader populations, inferential statistics enable humanitarian organizations to make well-informed decisions and craft targeted interventions. This is particularly beneficial when faced with resource constraints and time limitations, as it enables a deeper understanding of the needs and vulnerabilities of affected populations based on the collected data. Utilizing techniques like hypothesis testing, confidence intervals, and regression analysis, inferential statistics aid in identifying significant relationships, trends, and patterns within humanitarian datasets. Data analysis is fundamental in humanitarian action for

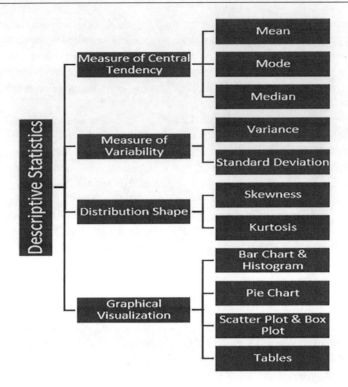

FIGURE 2.2   Role of data analysis in humanitarian action.

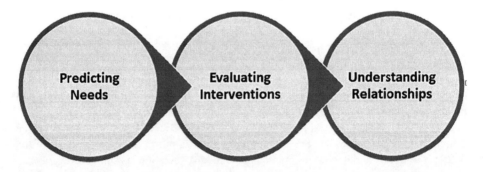

FIGURE 2.3   Steps for prediction and interferences.

comprehending needs, efficiently allocating resources, and assessing intervention out-comes. Inferential statistics are integral to this endeavor, facilitating predictions and drawing inferences about larger populations using data sampled from specific subsets, as shown in Figure 2.3.

Utilizing inferential statistics, a humanitarian organization conducting a sample survey on children's nutritional status in a refugee camp can estimate the prevalence of malnutrition across the entire camp population. This estimation aids in the more efficient allocation of resources, such as food aid and medical care, to address the identified needs. Information is gathered regarding variables such as water accessibility, sanitation infrastructure, and healthcare availability across various conflict-affected regions. Through statistical analyses, relationships between these variables and the occurrence of diseases can be inferred. This understanding guides the implementation of focused interventions aimed at enhancing living standards and mitigating the risk of outbreaks. In humanitarian action, where decisions have significant consequences for vulnerable populations, the concept of statistical significance is essential for interpreting results derived from inferential statistics. While inferential statistics enable us to make inferences about a broader population using sampled data, statistical significance serves as a metric to evaluate the reliability of these inferences.

Statistical tests produce a p-value, which signifies the likelihood of obtaining the observed outcomes (or more extreme) assuming the null hypothesis holds true. Conventional convention dictates that a p-value below 0.05 (typically indicated as "$p<0.05$") indicates statistical significance. This suggests a minimal probability (less than 5%) that the observed disparity is solely attributable to chance, allowing us to reject the null hypothesis in favor of the alternative hypothesis (H1). Technology is crucial in humanitarian data collection, facilitating efficient and precise gathering and analysis. Mobile devices with data collection apps empower field workers to gather data directly from affected populations, including remote areas. GISs assist in mapping and visualizing data, enhancing decision-making and resource allocation. Moreover, cloud-based platforms and databases offer secure storage and accessible data for analysis. Advanced analytical tools and statistical software aid in processing and interpreting data, enabling organizations to extract actionable insights and guide targeted humanitarian efforts.

Mobile Data Collection

Mobile data collection (MDC) technology has emerged as an indispensable tool for humanitarian organizations in recent years, presenting numerous advantages compared to conventional paper-based approaches (Chandola, 2023). The advantages of MDC are given as follows:

- Mobile phones are prevalent even in remote or resource-constrained environments, ensuring broader access to data collection.
- Data collection, transmission, and analysis occur at a significantly faster pace compared to paper-based methods, expediting decision-making processes.
- Embedded features such as GPS and data validation tools mitigate errors and enhance data precision.
- MDC eliminates expenses associated with paper, printing, and transportation, offering a more economical alternative.
- Data can be gathered and analyzed instantaneously, enabling swift responses to evolving needs and circumstances.
- Many mobile apps incorporate data visualization tools, simplifying the interpretation and communication of findings.

Apps and platforms

MDC has emerged as a crucial tool in humanitarian endeavors, offering benefits such as accessibility, efficiency, and real-time data insights. Some widely utilized apps and platforms for MDC applications are given below:

Real-time monitoring

Real-time monitoring plays a crucial role in enhancing MDC for humanitarian action. Numerous MDC platforms feature cloud-based dashboards that offer real-time data visualization and analytics capabilities. Combining SMS responses with data collection tools enables immediate reporting and analysis of data. Linking MDC platforms with other tools facilitates instantaneous data transfer and integration with current systems for enhanced analysis.

Machine Learning and Artificial Intelligence

The integration of artificial intelligence (AI) and machine learning (ML) is revolutionizing the way humanitarian organizations gather and interpret data to enhance their decision-making processes. These technologies automate the collection of data from various sources, including text, images, and sensors, enabling the analysis of large datasets to identify trends and make predictions. Additionally, they facilitate communication with affected communities. However, challenges such as data scarcity, potential biases, and ethical dilemmas necessitate thoughtful deliberation and responsible deployment to ensure equitable benefits for all those in need (Comes, 2016).

Predictive analytics, driven by ML (as shown in Figure 2.4) and AI, is transforming data analysis within humanitarian action, facilitating proactive and precise interventions. Its pivotal role can be outlined as follows:

- AI algorithms leverage historical data on weather patterns, environmental conditions, and past disasters to forecast the probability and severity of natural calamities such as floods, droughts, or earthquakes.
- ML models scrutinize data on demographics, health indicators, and social determinants to pinpoint populations most susceptible to specific events, such as children, the elderly, or individuals residing in geographically precarious areas.
- By predicting future needs, AI aids in optimizing resource distribution, identifying areas likely to require urgent aid such as food, water, or medical supplies. This enables pre-positioning of resources and more efficient deployment during emergencies.
- Predictive models facilitate the creation of early warning systems that notify communities and authorities about potential threats, enabling preemptive actions to minimize potential harm.

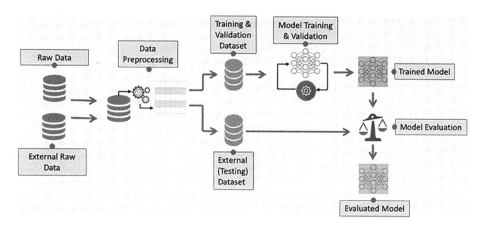

FIGURE 2.4   Steps for applying machine learning.

TABLE 2.1   Features for increasingly leveraging the power of automation

FEATURE	DESCRIPTION	EXAMPLE
Predictive analytics	Analyzing data to anticipate future needs and potential crises	Predicting droughts to pre-position food and resources
Automating repetitive tasks	Using AI to handle routine data processing tasks	Automating data cleaning and generating reports
Improving efficiency and scalability	Analyzing large datasets and generating real-time insights	Scaling analysis for diverse data sources and providing a faster turnaround

Examples in Practice

The World Food Programme (WFP) employs AI to predict droughts and other climate extremes, enabling the proactive placement of food and resources in vulnerable regions before hunger crises occur. The UN Children's Fund (UNICEF) utilizes AI to forecast the potential spread of diseases, enabling the timely deployment of vaccination campaigns and other preventive measures.

As shown in Table 2.1, the integration of ML and AI for data analysis presents considerable promise for humanitarian organizations to enhance their efficiency and effectiveness. However, it is essential to exercise caution and address potential challenges to ensure responsible implementation. This approach is crucial for unlocking the full potential of these technologies in improving the delivery of humanitarian aid and, ultimately, saving lives.

Successful Examples of Data-Driven Humanitarian Interventions

COVID-19 pandemic response (global, 2020-present)

- *Challenges*: Addressing the global COVID-19 pandemic's rapid transmission, limited understanding of the virus, and the strain on healthcare systems (Chang et al., 2022).

Approach using data

- Platforms such as Worldometer and Johns Hopkins University provided current data on case numbers, fatalities, and vaccination rates, aiding decision-making worldwide.
- Utilization of mobile phone and location tracking data monitored population movement patterns and predicted potential outbreaks.
- AI models forecasted future caseloads and resource requirements, facilitating proactive resource allocation and readiness.

Outcomes

- Data-driven insights guided public health measures, including lockdowns, travel restrictions, and vaccination drives. Real-time monitoring enabled healthcare systems to adapt resources and prioritize care for vulnerable groups.

Cyclone Idai response in Mozambique

- *Challenges*: Addressing the devastating impacts of Cyclone Idai, which caused widespread destruction and displacement and hindered access to affected regions (Kielwein 2023).

Approach using data

Satellite data assessed the extent of damage, identified flood zones, and aided in planning rescue and relief missions. Drones with cameras surveyed flooded areas, assisting search and rescue teams in locating stranded individuals. Analysis of social media posts provided insights into urgent needs, requests for assistance, and potential hazards.

Outcomes

Data-driven analysis facilitated targeted search and rescue operations, enabling swift aid delivery to affected communities. Real-time information enhanced coordination among aid agencies and optimized resource allocation.

Ukraine conflict response (2022-present)

- *Challenges*: Responding to the complex humanitarian crisis stemming from the ongoing conflict in Ukraine, including mass displacement, service disruptions, and escalating humanitarian needs.

Approach using data

High-resolution satellite imagery monitored ground situations, evaluated infrastructure damage, and tracked population movements. Social media analysis helped to identify refuge-seeking locations, understand community needs, and coordinate responses accordingly. Mobile data analysis helped to analyze mobile network data to discern population displacement patterns and guide focused aid distribution.

Outcomes

Data-driven insights guided the delivery of humanitarian aid, including provisions like food, shelter, and medical assistance, to displaced populations and impacted communities. Real-time monitoring facilitated a coordinated and effective response to the evolving situation and emerging needs, as shown in Table 2.2.

While the examples of data-driven humanitarian interventions (such as the response to the COVID-19 pandemic, Cyclone Idai, and the conflict in Ukraine) have demonstrated the potential of this approach, there are also significant insights to be gleaned from shortcomings in data collection and analysis within these scenarios: The efficacy of data-driven interventions heavily relies on the quality, accuracy, and comprehensiveness of the data. Overcoming data limitations necessitates cooperation among humanitarian organizations, local communities, and governments to establish dependable data collection methods and facilitate access to pertinent information. Ethical considerations and data privacy play a critical role in data-driven humanitarian endeavors. Prioritizing informed consent, transparent data practices, and robust security measures is essential for fostering trust with affected communities and mitigating potential harm. Developing local capacity, which includes training and empowering local communities

TABLE 2.2 Case studies of data-driven humanitarian interventions

CASE STUDY	CHALLENGE	DATA-DRIVEN APPROACH
COVID-19 pandemic response (global, 2020-present)	Rapid transmission, limited knowledge, and strain on healthcare systems	Real-time case tracking, mobility data analysis, and predictive modeling
Cyclone Idai response in Mozambique (2019)	Widespread destruction, displacement, and limited access	Satellite imagery analysis, drone technology, and social media monitoring
Ukraine conflict response (2022-present)	Displacement, service disruptions, and increasing aid needs	High-resolution satellite imagery, social media analysis, and mobile data analysis

in data collection and analysis, is pivotal for ensuring the sustainability and efficacy of data-driven interventions. Appreciating local contexts and integrating diverse perspectives are indispensable for accurate data interpretation and culturally sensitive responses. Transparency and accountability are fundamental for fostering trust and guaranteeing the ethical use of data in humanitarian interventions. Involving affected communities throughout the entire process, spanning from data collection to analysis and decision-making, nurtures trust and upholds responsible data practices.

CONCLUSION

The effective use of data collection and analysis is paramount in humanitarian action. As highlighted throughout this chapter, data serves as the backbone for informed decision-making, efficient resource allocation, and impactful interventions. Humanitarian organizations rely on diverse data sources, from traditional surveys and censuses to modern technologies such as satellite imagery, drones, and social media analytics, to gain comprehensive insights into crises. The integration of AI and ML has further revolutionized data collection and analysis, enabling the prediction of disasters, optimization of resource distribution, and enhancement of real-time decision-making. These technological advancements have proven instrumental in various humanitarian scenarios, from disaster response and public health crises to conflict zones. However, the deployment of data-driven approaches in humanitarian contexts is not without challenges. Issues such as data quality, access to affected areas, and ethical considerations regarding privacy and informed consent must be addressed to ensure the effectiveness and integrity of humanitarian efforts. Ethical data collection practices and the inclusion of vulnerable groups are essential to maintaining trust and accountability within affected communities. Enhancing local capacity for data collection and analysis, promoting transparency, and prioritizing cultural sensitivity will be crucial in maximizing the benefits of data-driven humanitarian interventions. In conclusion, while the challenges are significant, the opportunities presented by advanced data collection and analysis techniques offer a promising path toward more efficient, effective, and equitable humanitarian action. By leveraging these tools responsibly and ethically, humanitarian organizations can better meet the needs of vulnerable populations, improve the outcomes of their interventions, and contribute to a more resilient global society.

REFERENCES

Beduschi, A. (2022). Harnessing the potential of artificial intelligence for humanitarian action: Opportunities and risks. *International Review of the Red Cross, 104*(9), 1149–1169.

Bell, D., Lycett, M., Marshan, A., & Monaghan, A. (2021). Exploring future challenges for big data in the humanitarian domain. *Journal of Business Research, 131*(1), 453–468.

Benini, A. A., Conley, C. E., Shdeed, R., Spurway, K., & Yarmoshuk, M. (2003). Integration of different data bodies for humanitarian decision support: An example from mine action. *Disasters*, *27*(4), 288–304.

Calhoun, C. (2008). The imperative to reduce suffering: Charity, progress, and emergencies in the field of humanitarian action. In Michael Barnett, and Thomas G. Weiss, (eds.), *Humanitarianism in Question: Politics, Power, Ethics* (pp. 73–97). Cornell University Press, Ithaca, NY.

Chandola, B. (2023). Promoting principles-based use of technology in humanitarian assistance. *Observer Research Foundation*, *58*(4), 23–45.

Chang, V., Ali, M. A., & Hossain, A. (2022). Chapter 2- Investigation of COVID-19 and scientific analysis big data analytics with the help of machine learning. In Victor Chang, Mohamed Abdel-Basset, Muthu Ramachandran, Nicolas G. Green, and Gary Wills (eds.), *Novel AI and Data Science Advancements for Sustainability in the Era of COVID-19* (pp. 21–66). Springer, Singapore.

Comes, T. (2016). Technology innovation and big data for humanitarian operations. *Journal of Humanitarian Logistics and Supply Chain Management*, *6*(3), 23–51.

Deb, S., & Baudais, V. (2022). The challenges of data collection in conflict affected areas: A case study in the Liptako-Gourma region. *SIPRI Insights on Peace and Security*, *22*(7), 11–18.

Egger, C., & Schopper, D. (2022). Organizations involved in humanitarian action: Introducing a new dataset. *International Studies Quarterly*, *66*(2), 34–48.

Fadiya, S. O., Saydam, S., & Zira, V. V. (2014). Advancing big data for humanitarian needs. *Procedia Engineering*, *78*(1), 88–95.

Haak, E., Ubacht, J., Van den Homberg, M., Cunningham, S., & Van de Walle, B. (2018, May). A framework for strengthening data ecosystems to serve humanitarian purposes. In *Proceedings of the 19th Annual International Conference on Digital Government Research: Governance in the Data Age* (pp. 1–9). Delft.

Hernandez, K., & Roberts, T. (2020). Predictive analytics in humanitarian action: A preliminary mapping and analysis. *K4D Emerging Issues Report*, *33*(1), 27–34.

Hilhorst, D., Melis, S., Mena, R., & van Voorst, R. (2021). Accountability in humanitarian action. *Refugee Survey Quarterly*, *40*(4), 363–389.

Kielwein, C. (2023, November 24). Can we make better use of humanitarian data for an impartial and humane response to crisis? *Humanitarian Practice Network*, *12*(5), 165–187.

Kim De Boeck, M., Besiou, C., Decouttere, C., Rafter, S., Vandaele, N., Van Wassenhove, L. N., & Yadav, P. (2023). Data, analytical techniques and collaboration between researchers and practitioners in humanitarian health supply chains: A challenging but necessary way forward. *Journal of Humanitarian Logistics and Supply Chain Management*, *13*(3), 127–155.

Paulus, D., Meesters, K., & Van de Walle, B. A. (2018). Turning data into action: Supporting humanitarian field workers with open data. In *Proceedings of the 15th ISCRAM Conference (pp. 1030–1039)*. Kristiansand.

Paulus, D., de Vries, G., Janssen, M., & Van de Walle, B. (2023). Reinforcing data bias in crisis information management: The case of the Yemen humanitarian response. *International Journal of Information Management*, *72*(1), 102–133.

Riedler, B., & Lang, S. (2022). Integrating geospatial datasets for urban structure assessment in humanitarian action. *ISPRS Annals of the Photogrammetry, Remote Sensing and Spatial Information Sciences*, *4*(3), 293–300.

Spainhour Baker, L., Hailey, P., Kim, J., & Maxwell, D. (2020). The challenges of humanitarian information and analysis: Evidence from Yemen. *Humanitarian Practice Network*, *76*(7), 583–612.

Spiegel, P. B. (2017). The humanitarian system is not just broke, but broken: Recommendations for future humanitarian action. *The Lancet*, *135*(2), 475–498.

The Humanitarian-AI Interface

Field Perspectives to Innovative Emergency Preparedness and Response

3

Yusuf Mshelia, Bashir Malgwi,
Azubuike Erike, Abraham Zirra,
and Edoghogho Olaye

INTRODUCTION

In recent years, the intersection of humanitarian aid and artificial intelligence (AI) has emerged as a promising frontier in the quest for more effective, efficient, and innovative approaches to disaster preparedness and response (Marić et al., 2022; Toorajipour et al., 2021). The convergence of these two domains has the potential to revolutionize the way humanitarian organizations anticipate, mitigate, and address the impact of natural disasters, conflicts, and other humanitarian crises worldwide. This research endeavors to explore the critical path forged by the humanitarian-AI interface, illuminating its transformative potential in bolstering humanitarian preparedness and response efforts.

Traditional humanitarian practices have often been challenged by the scale, complexity, and unpredictability of modern crises, leading to gaps in timely response, resource allocation, and coordination (Thow et al., 2013). Despite the tireless efforts

DOI: 10.1201/9781003479109-3

of aid organizations and frontline responders, the ever-evolving nature of emergencies necessitates a paradigm shift in the way we conceptualize and approach humanitarian action. In this context, AI technologies present a compelling opportunity to augment human capabilities, enhance decision-making processes, and better understand different contexts for which you previously had little or no knowledge and optimize resource allocation in humanitarian contexts (Younis et al., 2022).

The urgency of addressing global humanitarian challenges has propelled the integration of AI into various aspects of disaster management, ranging from early warning systems and risk assessment to logistics optimization and needs analysis. AI-driven solutions hold the promise of not only improving the speed and accuracy of response efforts but also enabling proactive measures to prevent crises before they escalate. By harnessing the power of machine learning, predictive analytics, and data-driven insights, humanitarian actors can gain a deeper understanding of complex emergencies, identify vulnerable populations, and tailor interventions to meet their specific needs.

However, the convergence of humanitarian aid and AI also raises important ethical, social, and operational considerations that must be carefully navigated (Grass et al., 2023; Lohiya et al., 2017). Concerns regarding data privacy, algorithmic bias, and the potential for unintended consequences underscore the need for robust governance frameworks and ethical guidelines to govern the development and deployment of AI in humanitarian settings (Imran et al., 2020). Moreover, the digital divide and unequal access to AI technologies pose challenges to ensuring equitable and inclusive humanitarian assistance, particularly in marginalized and underserved communities.

THE HUMANITARIAN-AI INTERFACE

The humanitarian-AI interface refers to the intersection and interaction between humanitarian aid efforts and AI technologies. It involves the utilization of AI tools, techniques, and methodologies to enhance various aspects of humanitarian operations, including preparedness, response, and recovery in the face of natural disasters, conflicts, and other humanitarian crises. This interface encompasses a wide range of AI applications, such as predictive analytics, machine learning, natural language processing, computer vision, and robotics. These technologies enable humanitarian organizations to analyze vast amounts of data, generate actionable insights, automate tasks, and optimize resource allocation in dynamic and challenging environments.

Importance of Innovative Humanitarian Preparedness and Response

In crises, time is often of the essence. Firstly, innovative approaches to preparedness and response can enable humanitarian organizations to anticipate, detect, and respond to emergencies more quickly, thereby saving lives and reducing the impact of disasters.

Secondly, humanitarian actors can enhance the effectiveness of their response efforts. This might include using data analytics to identify areas at high risk of disasters, deploying drones for rapid damage assessment, or employing AI-powered chatbots for real-time communication with affected populations. Thirdly, innovative approaches will help humanitarian organizations optimize the allocation and utilization of resources, ensuring that aid reaches those who need it most in a timely and cost-effective manner. This might involve using blockchain technology for transparent and efficient supply chain management or deploying autonomous robots for logistics and distribution tasks.

Owing to the unpredictable and dynamic nature of crises, requiring humanitarian organizations to be agile and adaptable in their response, innovative preparedness and response strategies can help organizations better anticipate and respond to evolving challenges, whether they are natural disasters, conflict-related emergencies, or public health crises like pandemics. Lastly, communities can become more resilient to future disasters and crises. This might involve building infrastructure that can withstand natural hazards, establishing early warning systems to alert residents of impending threats, or implementing community-based disaster risk reduction initiatives.

The Humanitarian Landscape

Integration of AI brings both potential and problems in the constantly changing field of humanitarian aid. Understanding current humanitarian preparedness and response techniques and procedures is essential to successfully navigating this confluence. With a focus on their advantages, disadvantages, and potential areas for improvement, this chapter offers a perceptive analysis of various approaches. Traditional humanitarian preparedness and response methods have long relied on expert judgment, manual processes, and historical data analysis. The distribution of resources by humanitarian organizations is determined by previous experiences, established protocols, and field worker assessments. Although these techniques have proven invaluable in saving lives and reducing suffering, they frequently have flaws, especially in quickly changing emergency circumstances.

Technology advancements have revolutionized the humanitarian sector by providing new tools and techniques to improve response and readiness (Smith et al., 2016). Humanitarian operations can improve efficiency, accuracy, and outreach via the use of modern algorithms for predictive analytics and robotics for quick evaluations. However, obstacles such as lack of funding, poor infrastructure, and a lack of skilled workers can make it difficult to integrate these advances (Navaz et al., 2021). Considering this, the integration of AI has enormous potential to improve humanitarian preparedness and response (Pandey et al., 2023). AI systems can analyze massive volumes of data at previously unheard-of rates, spot patterns and abnormalities, and produce useful insights instantly. AI can completely transform the humanitarian response cycle at every point, from anticipating natural catastrophes to allocating resources optimally. However, to make sure that AI is used responsibly and fairly, issues like algorithmic accountability, biases in algorithms, and ethical considerations need to be properly addressed.

Analysis of the Limitations and Challenges Faced in Traditional Approaches

Traditional humanitarian preparedness and response methods, while valuable, are not without limitations and challenges. Understanding these drawbacks is crucial for identifying areas where innovation, such as the integration of AI, can offer improvements. Manual data gathering and analysis is a common feature of traditional systems, which can be laborious. Delays in acquiring information and making decisions can cause significant harm to the affected populations in quickly changing crisis circumstances. In addition, a key component of traditional humanitarian activities is expert judgment. Nevertheless, this subjectivity may add biases and contradictions to the systems used to make decisions, which might affect the effectiveness and equity of aid delivery. Even with advancements in data gathering, many humanitarian organizations find it difficult to make the most of the data collected. Challenges, including deficient data management procedures, limited analytical capabilities, and poor incorporation of data into decision-making procedures, impede the effective utilization of available information (Marić et al., 2022). Humanitarian organizations have significant challenges due to resource limits, which include limited money, a scarcity of manpower, and logistical difficulties (Cross, 2019). These limitations hinder their ability to organize efficient responses to widespread situations and aid all affected individuals.

AI APPLICATIONS IN HUMANITARIAN PREPAREDNESS AND RESPONSE

An Overview of AI Technologies Applicable to Humanitarian Contexts

AI technologies offer a wide range of applications in humanitarian contexts, contributing to more effective, efficient, and innovative approaches to disaster preparedness, response, and recovery. Some of the applications are listed below:

1. *Predictive Analytics and Early Warning Systems*: Predictive analytics uses historical data, machine learning algorithms, and statistical models to forecast future events, enabling early warning systems for natural disasters and other emergencies to reduce risk (Ahmet, 2022).
2. *Remote Sensing and Image Analysis*: Remote sensing technologies, combined with AI algorithms, allow for the analysis of satellite imagery and aerial photographs to assess the extent of damage, monitor environmental changes, and identify vulnerable areas (Bushnaq et al., 2022).

3. *Natural Language Processing (NLP)*: NLP techniques enable the analysis of textual data, social media feeds, and communication channels to extract relevant information, identify emerging trends, and understand community needs during emergencies (Mhlanga, 2022; Rocca et al., 2023).
4. *Robotics and Drones*: Robotics and drones equipped with AI capabilities are used for search and rescue operations, damage assessment, and delivery of medical supplies and aid packages to remote or inaccessible areas (Dhamija et al., 2021).
5. *Chatbots and Virtual Assistants*: Chatbots and virtual assistants powered by AI technology provide real-time information, support, and assistance to affected populations, facilitating communication and access to essential services (Ahmet, 2022).

Case Studies Showcasing Successful Implementations of AI in Disaster Response and Preparedness

Some case studies showcasing successful implementations of AI in disaster response and preparedness are listed below:

Case Study 1: Predictive Analytics for Flood Early Warning System

In Bangladesh, studies conducted by Ganguly et al. (2019) and Islam (2019) showed that the International Centre for Diarrheal Disease Research, Bangladesh, in collaboration with local authorities and international partners, uses historical weather data, river levels, soil moisture levels, and satellite imagery with machine learning algorithms to forecast floods in vulnerable regions with high accuracy. When the risk of flooding exceeds a certain threshold, automated alerts are sent to local communities via Short Message Service (SMS), radio broadcasts, and mobile apps, enabling timely evacuation and preparedness measures.

Case Study 2: UAVs for Damage Assessment and Search and Rescue in Earthquake Response

Following a major earthquake in Nepal, the World Food Programme (WFP), in collaboration with the Government of Nepal and humanitarian partners, deployed unmanned aerial vehicles (UAVs) equipped with AI-powered image analysis capabilities for rapid damage assessment and search and rescue operations (Pangeni et al., 2020; Wang, 2020). The UAVs captured high-resolution aerial imagery of affected areas, which was then processed using AI algorithms to identify damaged buildings, infrastructure, and potential survivor locations. This information enabled responders to prioritize their efforts, allocate resources effectively, and coordinate rescue operations in the most severely affected areas.

Case Study 3: Machine Learning for Disease Outbreak Prediction and Monitoring

In Uganda, the Ministry of Health, in partnership with the World Health Organization (WHO) and academic institutions, implemented a machine learning-based system for disease outbreak prediction and monitoring[1]. The system analyzes various data sources, including health records, environmental data, and social media feeds, to detect early signs of disease outbreaks such as Ebola, cholera, and malaria. By leveraging machine learning algorithms, the system can identify patterns and trends indicative of potential outbreaks, enabling public health authorities to deploy resources and implement preventive measures in high-risk areas.

Case Study 4: Chatbots for Information Dissemination and Crisis Communication

In the aftermath of Cyclone Idai in Mozambique, the United Nations Development Programme (UNDP), in collaboration with local partners, deployed AI-powered chatbots for information dissemination and crisis communication and translation. The chatbots, accessible via SMS, social media platforms, and mobile apps, provided real-time updates on weather conditions, emergency shelter locations, relief distribution points, and health advisories. Additionally, the chatbots facilitated two-way communication, allowing affected populations to request assistance, report emergencies, and access personalized support services (Peña-Cáceres et al., 2024; Piccolo et al., 2018).

In Cyprus, the use of chatbots in news media platforms, although relatively recent, offered many advantages to journalists and media professionals and, at the same time, facilitated users' interaction with useful and timely information. The study conducted by Maniou and Veglis (2020) shows the usability of a news chatbot during a crisis, employing the 2020 COVID-19 pandemic as a case study.

Evaluating the Impact of AI on Humanitarian Interventions

Evaluating AI systems in humanitarian settings is crucial to ensuring that they effectively address the needs of vulnerable populations without further exposing their vulnerability. While evaluating the general AI system is necessary, the evaluation indicators for AI systems in such contexts should uniquely incorporate some of these indicators and the corresponding assessment metrics, as described below:

1. *Impact Assessment*: This includes measuring how effectively the AI system delivers aid, facilitates decision-making, or improves the overall efficiency of humanitarian operations.

2. *Ethical Considerations*: This includes evaluating the AI system's fairness, transparency, accountability, and the mitigation of biases, especially concerning vulnerable populations.

3. *Accuracy and Reliability*: This evaluates the accuracy and reliability of the AI system in performing its intended tasks by assessing its ability to correctly identify and respond to humanitarian needs.

4. *Scalability*: This assesses the scalability of the AI system to ensure it can handle increasing volumes of data and adapt to changing humanitarian situations.

5. *Accessibility and Inclusivity*: This evaluates the accessibility and inclusivity of the AI system to ensure it can be used effectively by all stakeholders, including those with limited resources or technological literacy.

6. *Human-in-the-Loop and User Feedback*: By involving a human factor in the assessment and gathering of feedback from users, including humanitarian workers and affected populations, this assesses their satisfaction with the AI system and identify areas for improvement.

7. *Data Privacy and Security*: This evaluates the AI system's data privacy and security measures to ensure that sensitive information is protected and that the system complies with relevant regulations and standards.

8. *Interoperability*: This evaluates the AI system's interoperability with other humanitarian tools and systems to ensure seamless integration and data sharing.

9. *Cultural Sensitivity and Contextual Awareness*: This assesses the AI system's cultural sensitivity and contextual awareness to ensure it can effectively operate in diverse humanitarian settings without causing unintended harm or offense.

CHALLENGES AND ETHICAL CONSIDERATIONS

Key Challenges in Integrating AI into Humanitarian Practices

- *Infrastructure:* In humanitarian settings, there are several issues that stem from inadequate power supply and poor internet access, which are crucial for AI technology to function. AI systems' deployment and operation are hampered by weak infrastructure, which reduces the systems' effectiveness in such environments (Garcia, 2022). Limited access to technology infrastructure and resources poses a significant obstacle to the scalability of AI technologies in less developed regions. Inadequate internet connectivity, unreliable power supply, and outdated hardware/software systems constrain the deployment and utilization of AI tools and applications in humanitarian operations. Bridging the digital divide and enhancing access to technology infrastructure are essential steps toward ensuring the widespread adoption of AI in underserved communities.

- *Accessibility:* The accessibility of extensive, high-quality datasets significantly influences the effectiveness of AI systems. Nevertheless, the validation processes of AI models encounter substantial challenges in humanitarian contexts, primarily stemming from issues such as incomplete, inconsistent, or invalid data, as well as other data quality issues (Edo, 2020). To ensure the seamless integration of AI technology into humanitarian operations, it is imperative to confront these limitations in data and ensure the reliability of available data for decision-making.

- *Adherence to Humanitarian Principles:* AI systems must adhere to humanitarian principles such as independence, impartiality, humanism, and neutrality. The use of AI systems in humanitarian settings, however, raises concerns regarding these principles' compatibility and the potential for these principles to either strengthen or weaken humanitarian principles and values.

- *Cultural and Social Issues:* AI systems may find it difficult to comprehend and adjust to the numerous cultural subtleties and contextual dynamics of humanitarian contexts (Crawford & Calo, 2016). Inaccurate or unsuitable results from AI technology might exacerbate already existing problems if local cultures, languages, and sociopolitical processes are not thoroughly understood.

- *Funding:* The problem of funding is a significant barrier to the scaling of AI technology in humanitarian situations (Cheng et al., 2021). Large sums of money are frequently needed for AI projects' deployment, maintenance, research, and development. Allocating funds to AI projects in less developed areas, however, may be hampered by donor preferences, competing priorities, and financial constraints. Because of this, it is difficult for humanitarian groups to get enough money to finance AI-driven initiatives and maintain them over the long run.

- *Resistance to Change:* The implementation of AI technology in humanitarian situations is significantly hampered by resistance to change resulting from ingrained traditions, religious beliefs, and cultural norms (Cadden et al., 2022). It's possible for stakeholders and local communities to be skeptical of or reluctant to adopt AI-driven solutions because of worries about ethical dilemmas, privacy problems, or job displacement. It takes extensive community participation, stakeholder meetings, and initiatives to develop trust and understanding about the advantages of AI technology to overcome opposition to change.

- *Lack of Technical Capacity:* Lack of ability for efficient application of AI technology is one of the main obstacles to its implementation in less developed areas (Bell et al., 2021). A major obstacle to the adoption and application of AI solutions in humanitarian situations is the lack of technical know-how and funding. Humanitarian practitioners have an additional obstacle in their efforts to fully utilize AI technologies and applications due to inadequate training and skill development programs.

Ethical Considerations

The integration of AI into humanitarian initiatives raises several ethical considerations that must be carefully addressed, which are given as follows:

- *Bias and Fairness*: AI algorithms can perpetuate biases present in the data used to train them, leading to unfair or discriminatory outcomes. Biases in AI systems may disproportionately impact vulnerable populations, exacerbating existing inequalities and injustices (Barocas & Selbst, 2016).
- *Privacy and Data Protection*: AI technology must abide by stringent privacy and data protection rules to preserve the confidentiality and rights of affected populations, since humanitarian contexts frequently contain sensitive data pertaining to people's health, safety, and socioeconomic position (Patel, 2024).
- *Transparency and Accountability*: The opacity of AI algorithms poses challenges for transparency and accountability in humanitarian interventions. Humanitarian organizations must ensure that AI systems are transparent, explainable, and accountable, enabling affected populations to understand how decisions are made and to hold responsible parties accountable for their actions (Veale et al., 2018).

Partnerships between Humanitarian Organizations, Governments, and AI Developers

Potential partnerships between humanitarian organizations, governments, and AI developers hold significant promises for leveraging AI technologies to address humanitarian challenges effectively. Opportunities and benefits that exist in partnerships are given as follows:

1. Humanitarian organizations often collect vast amounts of data related to disasters, conflicts, and humanitarian needs. Partnering with AI developers allows for the responsible sharing of data, enabling developers to train AI algorithms on relevant datasets and develop predictive models for early warning systems, risk assessment, and decision support tools. Governments can facilitate data sharing agreements and provide access to authoritative datasets, while humanitarian organizations contribute domain expertise and contextual insights to ensure the relevance and accuracy of AI solutions.
2. Governments and humanitarian organizations can partner with AI developers to transfer technology and build local capacity in AI-driven solutions. This can involve training local staff in AI technologies, supporting the development of locally relevant AI applications, and fostering innovation hubs and centers of excellence in AI for humanitarian purposes. By empowering local actors to develop and deploy AI solutions tailored to their specific contexts and needs, partnerships can enhance the sustainability and scalability of AI interventions in humanitarian settings.

3. Governments play a crucial role in shaping policies, regulations, and ethical guidelines for the responsible use of AI in humanitarian contexts. Collaborating with humanitarian organizations and AI developers allows governments to develop informed policies that balance innovation with ethical considerations, privacy concerns, and human rights principles. By engaging in multi-stakeholder dialogs and consultations, partnerships can foster consensus building, knowledge sharing, and the development of best practices for AI governance in humanitarian settings.

4. Governments and humanitarian organizations can collaborate with AI developers to field test and validate AI solutions in real-world humanitarian settings. This involves conducting pilot projects, trials, and evaluations to assess the effectiveness, usability, and impact of AI technologies in addressing specific humanitarian challenges. By partnering with governments and humanitarian organizations, AI developers gain access to field data, feedback from end users, and opportunities to iterate and improve their solutions based on real-world insights and experiences.

FUTURE RESEARCH DIRECTIONS AND RECOMMENDATIONS

The intersection of AI and humanitarian efforts is poised for continued growth and evolution, with several future trends and developments expected to shape the landscape. Future developments in AI will focus on enhancing decision support systems for humanitarian organizations. This includes the integration of AI algorithms with real-time data streams, advanced analytics, and predictive modeling techniques to provide decision-makers with actionable insights and recommendations for more effective and efficient response strategies. As AI becomes increasingly integrated into humanitarian operations, there will be a growing emphasis on explainable AI (XAI) techniques that enhance transparency, accountability, and trust in AI-driven decision-making processes. Future developments will focus on developing interpretable AI models and techniques that enable users to understand how AI algorithms reach their conclusions and recommendations.

AI technologies will increasingly be used to address climate-related challenges and enhance disaster risk reduction efforts. Future developments will focus on leveraging AI-driven climate models, satellite imagery analysis, and predictive analytics to assess climate risks, develop early warning systems for extreme weather events, and inform adaptive strategies for building resilience in vulnerable communities. Future trends in the intersection of AI and humanitarian efforts will involve increased partnerships and collaboration across sectors, including academia, government agencies, the private sector, and civil society organizations. Collaborative initiatives will focus on harnessing the collective expertise, resources, and networks of diverse stakeholders to develop and scale AI-driven solutions that address the most pressing humanitarian challenges.

Recommendations to Active Stakeholders

To maximize the potential of the humanitarian-AI interface, policymakers, humanitarian organizations, and AI developers should collaborate and take coordinated actions. The recommendations for each stakeholder group, including policymakers, humanitarian organizations, and AI developers, to maximize the potential of the humanitarian-AI interface are given as follows:

Policymakers

1. *Develop Ethical and Regulatory Frameworks*: Establish clear ethical guidelines, regulatory frameworks, and standards for the responsible design, deployment, and use of AI technologies in humanitarian contexts. Ensure that AI-driven solutions adhere to principles of transparency, accountability, fairness, privacy, and human rights.
2. *Facilitate Cross-Sector Collaboration*: Foster partnerships and collaboration between government agencies, humanitarian organizations, academia, and the private sector to leverage complementary expertise and resources in developing and implementing AI-driven solutions for humanitarian preparedness and response.

Humanitarian organizations

1. *Prioritize Needs and Contextual Relevance*: Ensure that AI-driven solutions are developed and implemented in close collaboration with affected communities, considering their needs, priorities, and contextual realities. Engage with local stakeholders, community leaders, and civil society organizations to co-design and co-create AI interventions that are culturally appropriate, inclusive, and responsive to local contexts.
2. *Invest in Innovation and Research*: Allocate resources and funding for research and innovation in AI technologies for humanitarian purposes. Foster a culture of innovation within humanitarian organizations, encouraging experimentation, learning, and adaptation to emerging technologies and best practices.
3. *Promote Knowledge Sharing and Collaboration*: Facilitate knowledge sharing, collaboration, and networking among humanitarian organizations, AI developers, and other stakeholders through platforms, events, and initiatives that promote the exchange of ideas, experiences, and lessons learned.

AI developers

1. *Design Ethical AI Solutions*: Embed ethical considerations into the design and development of AI-driven solutions for humanitarian purposes. Prioritize fairness, transparency, accountability, privacy, and human rights in the development and deployment of AI algorithms and systems.

2. *Build Contextually Relevant Solutions*: Tailor AI solutions to the specific needs and challenges faced in humanitarian contexts, taking into account the cultural, social, and environmental factors that may influence their effectiveness and adoption. Engage with humanitarian organizations and end users throughout the development process to ensure that AI solutions are contextually relevant and responsive to real-world needs.

3. *Promote Responsible AI Practices*: Advocate for responsible AI practices within the AI developer community, raising awareness about the potential risks and implications of AI technologies in humanitarian settings. Collaborate with policymakers, humanitarian organizations, and other stakeholders to develop guidelines, standards, and best practices for the responsible use of AI in humanitarian contexts.

CONCLUSION

In conclusion, the integration of AI offers a critical path to innovative humanitarian preparedness and response, revolutionizing how humanitarian organizations anticipate, assess, and address crises. By harnessing the power of AI technologies, stakeholders can enhance the efficiency, effectiveness, and scalability of humanitarian efforts, ultimately saving lives and alleviating suffering in vulnerable communities around the world. Innovative humanitarian preparedness and response through the integration of AI requires a concerted effort from all stakeholders to overcome challenges, foster collaboration, and promote responsible innovation. With the evaluation strategies, indicators, and metrics for successful AI interventions outlined in this work considering stakeholder engagement, we can harness the transformative potential of AI to build more resilient, sustainable, and inclusive humanitarian systems that respond effectively to the needs of those most in need.

NOTE

1 https://gcgh.grandchallenges.org/grant/using-artificial-intelligence-predict-disease-emergence-uganda

REFERENCES

Barocas, S., & Selbst, A. D. J. C. I. R. (2016). Big 'data's disparate impact. *California Law Review, 105*(2), 671–732.

Bell, D., Lycett, M., Marshan, A., & Monaghan, A. (2021). Exploring future challenges for big data in the humanitarian domain. *Journal of Business Research, 131*(1), 453–468.

Bushnaq, O. M., Mishra, D., Natalizio, E., & Akyildiz, I. F. (2022). Unmanned aerial vehicles (UAVs) for disaster management. In Adil Denizli, Marcelo S. Alencar, Tuan Anh Nguyen, David E. Motaung (eds.), *Nanotechnology-Based Smart Remote Sensing Networks for Disaster Prevention* (pp. 159–188). Amsterdam: Elsevier.

Cadden, T., Dennehy, D., Mantymaki, M., & Treacy, R. (2022). Understanding the influential and mediating role of cultural enablers of AI integration to supply chain. *International Journal of Production Research, 60*(14), 4592–4620.

Cheng, L., Varshney, K. R., & Liu, H. (2021). Socially responsible ai algorithms: Issues, purposes, and challenges. *Journal of Artificial Intelligence Research, 71*(2), 1137–1181.

Crawford, K., & Calo, R. J. N. (2016). There is a blind spot in AI research. *Nature, 538*(7), 311–323.

Cross, N. R. (2019). *Overlapping Vulnerabilities: The Impacts of Climate Change on Humanitarian Needs.* Oslo: Norwegian Red Cross.

Dhamija, P., Gupta, S., Bag, S., & Gupta, M. L. (2021). Humanitarian supply chain management: A systematic review and bibliometric analysis. *International Journal of Automation and Logistics, 3*(2), 104–136.

Edo, J. E. (2020). *The High Dimensional Data Components Needed by Big Data Specialists for Improving Decision Making in International Development and Humanitarian Organizations.* Colorado Springs: Colorado Technical University.

Ganguly, K. K., Nahar, N., & Hossain, B. M. (2019). A machine learning-based prediction and analysis of flood affected households: A case study of floods in Bangladesh. *International Journal of Disaster Risk Reduction, 34*, 283–294.

Garcia, E. V. (2022). Multilateralism and artificial intelligence: What role for the United Nations? In Maurizio Tinnirello (ed.), *The Global Politics of Artificial Intelligence* (pp. 57–84). New York: Chapman and Hall/CRC.

Grass, E., Ortmann, J., Balcik, B., & Rei, W. (2023). A machine learning approach to deal with ambiguity in the humanitarian decision-making. *Production and Operations Management, 32*(9), 2956–2974.

Imran, M., Ofli, F., Caragea, D., & Torralba, A. (2020). Using AI and social media multimodal content for disaster response and management: Opportunities, challenges, and future directions. *Information Processing & Management, 57*(5), 102–131.

Islam, A. S. (2010). Improving flood forecasting in Bangladesh using an artificial neural network. *Journal of Hydroinformatics, 12*(3), 351–364.

Lohiya, R., Mandowara, A., & Raolji, R. (2017). Privacy preserving data mining: A comprehensive survey. *International Journal of Computer Applications, 97*(5), 88–97.

Maniou, T. A., & Veglis, A. (2020). Employing a chatbot for news dissemination during crisis: Design, implementation and evaluation. *Future Internet, 12*(7), 109.

Marić, J., Galera-Zarco, C., & Opazo-Basáez, M. (2022). The emergent role of digital technologies in the context of humanitarian supply chains: A systematic literature review. *Annals of Operations Research, 319*(1), 1003–1044.

Mhlanga, D. (2022). Human-centered artificial intelligence: The superlative approach to achieve sustainable development goals in the fourth industrial revolution. *Sustainability, 14*(13), 7804.

Navaz, A. N., Serhani, M. A., El Kassabi, H. T., Al-Qirim, N., & Ismail, H. (2021). Trends, technologies, and key challenges in smart and connected healthcare. *IEEE Access, 9*(2), 74044–74067.

Pandey, D. K., Hunjra, A. I., Bhaskar, R., & Al-Faryan, M. A. S. (2023). Artificial intelligence, machine learning and big data in natural resources management: A comprehensive bibliometric review of literature spanning 1975–2022. *Resources Policy, 86*(2), 104–112.

Pangeni, B., Pudasaini, U., Pudasaini, D., & Pradhan, S. (2020). Evolution of unmanned aerial vehicles in Nepal. *Journal on Geoinformatics, Nepal, 19*(1), 17–29.

Patel, K. (2024). Ethical reflections on data-centric AI: Balancing benefits and risks. *International Journal of Artificial Intelligence Research and Development, 2*(1), 1–17.

Peña-Cáceres, O., Tavara-Ramos, A., Correa-Calle, T., & More-More, M. (2024). Integral chatbot solution for efficient incident management and emergency or disaster response: Optimizing communication and coordination. *TEM Journal, 13*(1), 49–67.

Piccolo, L. S., Roberts, S., Iosif, A., & Alani, H. (2018). Designing chatbots for crises: A case study contrasting potential and reality. In *Paper Presented at the Proceedings of the 32nd International BCS Human Computer Interaction Conference*, Belfast, 32.

Rocca, R., Tamagnone, N., Fekih, S., Contla, X., & Rekabsaz, N. (2023). Natural language processing for humanitarian action: Opportunities, challenges, and the path toward humanitarian NLP. *Frontiers in Big Data, 6*(2), 108–132.

Smith, C. E., Fullerton, S. M., Dookeran, K. A., Hampel, H., Tin, A., Maruthur, N. M., … & Ordovás, J. M. (2016). Using genetic technologies to reduce, rather than widen, health disparities. *Health Affairs, 35*(8), 1367–1373.

Thow, A., Young, L., Kluser, S., & Broadley, D. (2013). *World Humanitarian Data and Trends 2013*. Genève: Université de Genève.

Toorajipour, R., Sohrabpour, V., Nazarpour, A., Oghazi, P., & Fischl, M. J. J. O. B. R. (2021). Artificial intelligence in supply chain management: A systematic literature review. *Journal of Business Research, 122*, 502–517.

Veale, M., Van Kleek, M., & Binns, R. (2018). Fairness and accountability design needs for algorithmic support in high-stakes public sector decision-making. In *Paper Presented at the Proceedings of the 2018 CHI Conference on Human Factors in Computing Systems*, Montreal.

Wang, N. (2020). "We Live on Hope…": Ethical considerations of humanitarian use of drones in post-disaster Nepal. *IEEE Technology and Society Magazine, 39*(3), 76–85.

Younis, H., Sundarakani, B., & Alsharairi, M. (2022). Applications of artificial intelligence and machine learning within supply chains: Systematic review and future research directions. *Journal of Modelling in Management, 17*(3), 916–940.

The Role of Artificial Intelligence in Poverty Alleviation during the Fourth Industrial Revolution

4

Emeka Ogbuju, Bashir Eseyin Abdullahi,
Hussein Umar, Babatunde Dauda Raheem,
Yusuf Kabir Kasum, Taiwo Abiodun,
and Francisca Oladipo

INTRODUCTION

The Fourth Industrial Revolution (4IR) is a focal point of contemporary discourse with societal impact at the forefront of discussions, and it is poised to reshape human existence by altering how our economies function, how governance operates, and how we live (Luo, 2023). Originating in the 17th century, the industrial revolutions, starting with Britain as a major player, significantly transformed the world economy (Dunga, 2019).

DOI: 10.1201/9781003479109-4

The 1st Industrial Revolution marked a shift from agrarian to industrial livelihoods, replacing hand tools with steam engines and initiating a move toward mechanization. This revolution, which began in Britain in the 18th century, spurred urbanization and social change (Schwab, 2016). The 2nd Industrial Revolution introduced the expansion of petroleum, electricity, and steel industries and scientific advancement (Ooi et al., 2018). The 3rd Industrial Revolution, which was in the 1950s, introduced the use of computers and digital technology, thereby automating manufacturing and disrupting industries such as banking, communication, and energy (Ooi et al., 2018). These technological advancements also open doors in areas such as space research and biotechnology.

Industry 4.0 represents the convergence of the physical, digital, and biological realms, fueled by advances in AI, the Internet of Things (IoT), robots, quantum computing, machine learning, deep learning, and a variety of other novel technologies. This epoch represents a significant shift in how cultures interact with technology, erasing the distinction between the physical and virtual worlds and ushering in a new era of connection and possibilities. Traditional industries undergo significant change within the Industry 4.0 ecosystem, as digitization pervades every aspect of economic activity. The effects of Industry 4.0 are felt across industries and borders, from smart factories that optimize manufacturing processes to healthcare systems that use data analytics for individualized treatment. Furthermore, the confluence of AI, IoT, and robots not only improves efficiency and production but also produces creative solutions to long-standing societal concerns, such as poverty reduction. This transformational period provides unparalleled opportunity for innovation and equitable progress, but it also raises significant ethical, social, and economic issues. As societies negotiate the landscape of Industry 4.0, fundamental challenges arise about equity, access, and benefit distribution. Accepting the potential of Industry 4.0 necessitates not only technological innovation but also a commitment to promoting a more equitable and sustainable future for everyone.

The 4IR is not only a technological phenomenon but also a multifaceted transformation that intersects with various disciplines and domains of human endeavor (McKinsey, 2022). Beyond its technological innovations, this revolution challenges the prevailing paradigms in economics, governance, ethics, and culture. For instance, questions about the ethical use of AI, data privacy, and algorithmic bias demand interdisciplinary insights that draw upon fields such as philosophy, law, and social science. Despite global planning and preparation for the impact of 4IR on humanity and business, there remains a limited depth on its impact on the overall society, including the effects of AI on poverty (Mhlanga, 2021). Each industrial revolution has prompted adaptation and transition from agrarian to industrial and post-industrial societies, with associated challenges (Mhlanga, 2021). The anticipated impact of 4IR on society extends beyond job loss to a fundamental shift in the delivery of public and private goods and services (Dunga, 2019). Notably, AI's potential in agriculture as mentioned by Smith (2018) holds promise for improving productivity and addressing challenges. This study delves into the specific impact of AI on poverty within the context of the ongoing 4IR, examining its role in alleviating societal challenges.

LITERATURE REVIEW

Brief History of AI

The concept of AI traced its roots back to the mid-20th century, when John Cathy proposed the idea that machine simulation could encompass various facets of learning and intelligence (Mhlanga & Ndhlovu, 2020). Wisskirchen et al. (2017) defined AI as what revolves around the investigation of intelligent problem-solving behavior and the development of intelligent computer systems. AI is categorized into weak AI and strong AI: Weak AI simulates intelligence in the cognitive process, while strong AI involves computers in intellectual and self-learning abilities and optimizes experience-based behavior abilities. Strong AI comprises automatic networking, contributing to a scaling effect across various economic disciplines like machine learning, deep learning, dematerialization, robotization, the gig economy, and autonomous driving (Wisskirchen et al., 2017).

Despite decades of study, AI remains a complex and elusive subject within the field of computer science. Its application ranges from the capability of machines to carry out advanced thinking to search algorithms for board games, influencing various aspects of society, including marking decisions through the analysis of purchase histories (Haenlein & Kaplan, 2019). The public perception of intelligent computers often involves robots, but early robotics efforts were more focused on mechanical engineering than intelligent control. However, the synergy of AI and robotics is transforming into a powerful tool for testing ideas globally about intelligent behavior (Haenlein & Kaplan, 2019).

Theoretical Definition of Poverty

Traditionally, poverty has been narrowly defined with a focus on financial aspects. However, contemporary scholars are broadening these perspectives, acknowledging poverty as a multiple-dimension phenomenon encompassing factors like income, education, and social exclusion (DAIA, 2018). The shift underscores that poverty is not just attributed to a factor but also arises from a complex interplay of several elements. The United Nations introduced a nuanced understanding of poverty, distinguishing between absolute poverty and overall poverty. On the one hand, absolute poverty signifies the deprivation of fundamental human needs such as food, water (safe drinking), sanitation facilities, shelter, health, information, and education (Mhlanga & Moloi, 2020). On the other hand, overall poverty extends beyond income, encapsulating elements like hunger, ill-health, malnutrition, limited access to education, unsafe environment, mortality, housing shortage, social exclusion, increased morbidity, and discrimination (The World Bank, 2022). In addition, overall poverty encompasses a lack of participation in decision-making across social, civil, and cultural domains. The UN further introduced the Multidimensional Poverty Index in 2020, which incorporates diverse elements like health, education, and standard of living. The Joseph Rowntree Foundation (JRF) in 2013 defined poverty as a state where material resources are not sufficient to meet the minimum requirement (Mhlanga & Moloi, 2020). The World Bank emphasized consumption and income as key variables defining poverty, particularly if an individual falls below a specific income as the poverty datum line (The World Bank, 2022). Considering these various definitions, this chapter aims to explore the various impacts of AI on poverty, with consideration of its implications across different domains.

Global Poverty Statistics

The global war against poverty continues, with a noble but sluggish decline in extreme poverty in the whole world. The proportion of the global population that is living in extreme poverty reduced in 2015 to 10%, from 16% in 2010 and a significant 36% in 1990 (The World Bank, 2023). However, the current trajectory indicates a shortfall in achieving the goal of reducing extreme poverty to below 6% by 2030 (The World Bank, 2023).

People grappling with extreme poverty continue to face enduring deprivation and are vulnerable to disasters. While the argument for robust social protection systems and substantial government spending on essential services is recognized, there's a pressing need to strengthen and scale up these interventions (Guterres, 2019). Notably, in 2018, 8% of households living in extreme poverty were employed, underscoring the complex nature of poverty despite being employed (Guterres, 2019). The World Bank echoes the concentration of poverty in sub-Saharan Africa; they estimated that more than half of people living in extreme poverty reside in the region. Despite the decline of the global rate of poverty, progress is uneven, and the World Bank notes that sub-Saharan Africa continues to face significant poverty challenges (The World Bank, 2023). The sub-Saharan African region witnessed about four hundred and thirteen million people surviving on less than 1.90 US dollars per day, which is more than the combination of poor people in the other regions (Mhlanga & Moloi, 2020). Alarming projections suggest that by 2030, nearly 9/10 individuals in extreme poverty will be in the sub-Saharan African region. The ongoing effort to eradicate extreme poverty is facing challenges due to the low development rate in different parts of the world, especially in the sub-Saharan African region (The World Bank, 2023).

Empirical Literature Review

While the empirical literature on the impact of AI on poverty is at a nascent stage, recent studies have illuminated the transformative potential of AI, particularly in the agriculture sector. Smith (2018) contended that AI, fueled by relevant data, advanced algorithms, and computation, is starting to gain its abilities by enhancing agricultural productivity. The paper emphasized the role of AI applications in disease detection, automation, and measurement precision, thus reducing the need for human decision and eventually optimizing farm efficiency. Dharmaraj and Vijayanand (2018) underscored the increasing global population, which is estimated to attain nine billion by 2050, as a driving force behind the necessity for AI in the field of agriculture. The researchers emphasized AI's role in revolutionizing farming practices, thus enabling farmers to achieve more with less. Vincent et al. (2019) further emphasized the global challenge of population growth against limited arable land. The researchers advocated for smart and efficient farming equipment that is powered by AI and machine learning to improve productivity in agriculture. The researchers highlighted the integration of wireless sensor networks with AI systems like multilayer perception (MLP) and neural networks (NNs), to gain access to suitable land for agriculture. Bajuwa et al. (2021) explored the transformative potential of AI in healthcare, aiming to address challenges like population health improvement, patient experience enhancement, caregiver satisfaction, and cost reduction. It emphasized the importance of AI in navigating healthcare's complexities and responding to global health crises. It advocated a human-centered approach in building reliable AI systems and envisioning AI-driven precision medicine and connected care as the future of healthcare. Despite challenges, AI stands poised to revolutionize diagnostics, therapeutics, and healthcare delivery, fostering a data-driven and personalized approach to medicine. Eli-Chukwu (2019) identified different challenges in agriculture that can be solved with the adoption of AI. These challenges include disease control, soil treatment, low impute, big data requirements, and the knowledge gap between technology and farmers. The study underscored the flexibility, cost-effectiveness, accuracy, and high performance of AI in addressing the listed challenges. Zavadskaya's (2017) study aimed to explore the application of AI in the financial sector, specifically in trading, prediction of exchange rates, credit rating, prediction of bankruptcy, and portfolio management. The study found that artificial neural networks (ANNs) as proxies for AI offer more accurate forecasting results, especially when combined with big data and sentiment analysis through Google Trends. Wahi et al. (2018) acknowledged the historical development of AI and its prevalent use in countries with high incomes. The study identified the challenges of the application of AI in countries with low incomes but recognized the promising role of AI in the transformation of healthcare in these countries.

RESEARCH METHODOLOGY

This study aims to evaluate the role of AI in poverty alleviation within the context of the 4IR. Through a comprehensive review of existing literature and scholarly works, we investigate various facets of AI's impact on poverty reduction. The methodology employed in this study is designed to provide a thorough examination of AI's potential contributions to addressing poverty challenges within the evolving technological landscape of the 4IR.

Research Approach and Data Collection

In this research, a secondary research approach was adopted, utilizing existing literature and scholarly works as the primary sources of data. Secondary research allows for the exploration of diverse perspectives and insights from a wide range of sources such as academic papers, reports, and reputable online repositories. Data collection for this research involved a systematic review of relevant literature on AI and poverty alleviation. We identified and selected sources through comprehensive searches of academic databases, relevant journals, and reputable online repositories. The inclusion criteria for sources were based on their relevance to the research objectives and the quality of their methodology and findings.

Methodological Strategy for Data Analysis

The main methodological strategy for data analysis in this study is content analysis. This approach enables a systematic examination of textual content to identify themes, trends, and insights related to AI's potential to reduce poverty. To ensure rigor in our analysis, we employed a multi-stage process. Initially, we conducted open coding to identify key concepts and ideas present in the literature. Next, we performed axial coding to establish connections between codes and develop overarching themes. Finally, we conducted selective coding to refine and validate our identified themes, ensuring that they accurately reflected the data and addressed the research objectives.

Research Question and Parameters

The research question guiding this study is "What is the role of AI in poverty alleviation during the Fourth Industrial Revolution?" The parameters of our research include the following:

1. Identifying key concepts and trends in the literature related to AI and poverty alleviation.
2. Evaluating the effectiveness of AI-driven interventions in addressing poverty challenges.
3. Exploring the ethical, social, and economic implications of AI's role in poverty reduction efforts.

The methodology employed facilitates a comprehensive examination of AI's potential to alleviate poverty during the 4IR. We aim to provide insights into the complex interplay between AI technologies and poverty reduction efforts. This chapter seeks to contribute valuable insights to policymaking, strategic actions, and future research efforts in this critical field through systematic data analysis and interpretation.

RESULTS AND DISCUSSION

Data Collection and Poverty Maps

The global estimate of extreme poverty by the World Bank reveals that 736 million people are currently living in extreme poverty, with concentrations notably high in five countries: Nigeria, India, the Democratic Republic of Congo, Ethiopia, and Bangladesh.

The pivotal role of research and data in measuring progress in the fight against poverty is evident in the joint efforts of the United Nations and the World Bank (Weber, 2019). Location emerges as a fundamental variable in the pursuit of global poverty eradication, as emphasized by DAIA (2018). Traditional approaches to identifying impoverished populations, such as household surveys, often pose financial challenges for many nations. However, the adoption of AI presents a transformative solution to this issue. Cutting-edge research, like the study at Stanford University, utilizes advanced machine learning algorithms and satellite imagery to precisely map poverty in African nations such as Nigeria, Rwanda, Malawi, Uganda, and Tanzania, showcasing AI's evolving role in poverty eradication efforts (Schmidt, 2019). AI facilitates accurate predictions by analyzing satellite images in correlation with survey data. It offers an efficient means to map poverty.

The integration of AI into data gathering and poverty mapping serves as a potent tool, providing novel solutions to poverty-related challenges. Through advancements in technology such as machine learning and satellite photo analysis, accurate predictions and mapping of impoverished areas are now possible. These developments not only enhance accuracy but also contribute to the creation of more efficient resource allocation systems. AI-driven data gathering and mapping furnish policymakers and stakeholders with significant insights into poverty dynamics, enabling targeted interventions and resource allocation where they are most needed. Ultimately, the incorporation of AI into poverty mapping signifies a significant advancement in the global effort to combat poverty and promote sustainable development.

In large areas of sub-Saharan Africa, India, and Bangladesh, more than 61% of the population lives in poverty. Unfortunately, obtaining reliable data from regions such as North Korea, where the population experiences prolonged periods of starvation, presents significant challenges. Individuals living in poverty face a higher risk of disability and illness, which can have profound implications for their well-being and livelihoods. Illness can impair learning ability, reduce productivity, deplete household savings, and significantly diminish the quality of life, perpetuating the cycle of poverty or exacerbating existing deprivation. International agencies often define poverty in terms of income thresholds, with thresholds such as earning less than $2 per day or $1.25 per day being commonly used. However, the consequences of poverty extend beyond mere income levels and are experienced on a relative scale, as highlighted by the World Health Organization (WHO).

To further emphasize the integration of AI into public policymaking, we recommend the development of robust policy frameworks that govern the ethical use of AI technologies in poverty mapping. These frameworks should prioritize equitable access to AI-driven insights and ensure that marginalized communities would benefit from data-driven interventions. Additionally, policymakers should collaborate with AI experts and stakeholders to design strategies for scaling AI solutions sustainably, particularly in low-resource environments where traditional data collection methods may be insufficient.

AI's Impact on Agriculture in Rural Areas

As stated earlier, poverty is a multiple-dimension phenomenon encompassing factors like income, education, and social exclusion (DAIA, 2018). The impact of poverty is mainly pronounced in rural areas where a significant portion of the population lives in extreme poverty. The World Bank identifies agriculture as a primary livelihood source in regions with high rates of poverty. Thus, these regions become a focal place for AI-driven intervention (Sunjoyo, 2023). According to DAIA, AI can address poverty through the enhancement of soil cultivation practices for livestock rearing and crop growth. Effective harvesting of crops and optimal crop cultivation can be achieved through automation. Schmidt (2019) focused on the pivotal role of AI through robotics in the war against world hunger.

Ongoing collaborative initiatives between tech giants like Google and leading academic institutions such as Stanford University are continuously advancing AI programs tailored for agricultural purposes, demonstrating the latest strides in AI-driven solutions for rural farming communities. These programs are contributing to disease detection and crop yield production. For instance, in a ground-breaking study that was conducted at Federal University, Lokoja, Nigeria, Ahmed et al. (2023) explored seasonal crop yield prediction with the use of machine learning techniques. The research does not only signify a notable contribution to the field of computer science but also an important aspect of enhancing crop yield prediction in Nigeria. Simultaneously, another significant investigation conducted by Oluwole et al. (2023) aimed to integrate soil nutrients and location weather variables for crop yield prediction, focusing on developing a recommendation system and utilizing data from the Agricultural Development Program (ADP) Kogi State in Nigeria. The researchers employed a machine learning approach to recommend suitable crops based on input soil and climate statistics. Both emerged as pivotal efforts in leveraging AI to revolutionize agricultural practice in rural areas. The studies collectively contribute to the advancement of quality crop yield among farmers in the region. These endeavors signify a positive step toward harnessing technology for sustainable and efficient agricultural development, underscoring the transformative impact of AI in rural farming communities.

In the domain of agricultural policy, there is a growing need to integrate AI-driven solutions into existing frameworks to enhance productivity and alleviate poverty in rural areas. Policymakers should consider incentives for the adoption of AI technologies among smallholder farmers, including subsidies for AI-powered tools and equipment. Moreover, public-private partnerships can facilitate the development and deployment of low-cost AI solutions that are easily deployable in remote regions, thus ensuring that even the most marginalized farmers can benefit from technological advancements.

AI's Impact on Education

Poverty is often intertwined with limited access to education; as highlighted by the World Bank, an estimated 39% of the poorest people in the world lack the essential foundation. The region with a high poverty rate faces barriers like low institutional capacity, financial limitations, and low access to education (Wong, 2020). However, the integration of AI holds transformative potential in elevating education opportunities for poor children.

AI facilitates adaptive learning techniques through computer algorithms, fostering interactive and customized education experiences tailored to the unique needs of the learner (DAIA, 2018). By discerning individual learning requirements, AI can effectively address access issues, providing a personalized education that transcends financial constraints. Intelligent chat boards serve as virtual tutors, democratizing access to education for public areas with economic disadvantages, thereby contributing to the mitigation of educational inequalities.

Recent research by Mhlanga and Moloi (2020) highlighted AI's educational impact, particularly amid challenges posed by COVID-19, showcasing how technology remains pivotal in expanding educational access and opportunities; even in times of crisis, technology emerged as a catalyst to enable a wild range of access to different classes through online education. The shift from the physical class to the virtual class not only surmounts spatial limitations but also enhances educational accessibility.

For education policymakers, the integration of AI technologies presents an opportunity to address disparities in access to quality education. To ensure equitable access to AI-powered educational platforms, governments should prioritize investments in digital infrastructure and teacher training programs. Additionally, policy frameworks should be developed to safeguard student data privacy and mitigate algorithmic bias in AI-driven learning systems. By adopting inclusive policies and scaling AI solutions responsibly, education systems can better serve underserved communities and promote lifelong learning opportunities for all.

AI's Impact on Healthcare

Poverty and limited access to quality healthcare are frequently intertwined, as underscored by the World Bank. Regions with restricted healthcare access often exhibit high poverty rates (Ubi & Ndem, 2019). Nevertheless, the 4IR has ushered in transformative advancements, with AI emerging as a pivotal force reshaping various sectors, including healthcare. Amid its multifaceted influence, AI's role in alleviating poverty within the realm of healthcare stands as a beacon of hope. This section explores the profound impact of AI on health and its contribution to poverty alleviation during the 4IR, drawing upon relevant literature and empirical evidence.

Cutting-edge AI-powered technologies have transformed healthcare accessibility, especially in regions with limited resources, demonstrating the latest advancements in AI's role in bridging healthcare gaps and alleviating poverty-related health disparities. Through telemedicine platforms and AI-driven diagnostic tools, individuals from underserved communities gain access to timely medical consultations and diagnostic services, transcending geographical barriers. By democratizing healthcare access, AI empowers marginalized populations to receive essential medical care, thereby mitigating the adverse effects of poverty on health outcomes. AI-driven predictive analytics and machine learning algorithms enable healthcare practitioners to identify disease trends, anticipate outbreaks, and personalize treatment regimens effectively. By harnessing vast datasets encompassing demographic, environmental, and clinical variables, AI facilitates early disease detection and intervention, thereby preventing disease progression and reducing healthcare costs (Bajuwa et al., 2021). Consequently, individuals from impoverished backgrounds benefit from proactive healthcare interventions, averting the financial burden associated with prolonged illness and hospitalization. The advent of precision medicine, fueled by AI-driven genomic sequencing and bioinformatics, has revolutionized disease management paradigms. By discerning genetic predispositions and molecular signatures, AI facilitates the development of tailored treatment protocols tailored to individual patient's unique genetic makeup and disease profiles (Quazi, 2022). This personalized approach not only enhances treatment efficacy but also minimizes adverse drug reactions and treatment-related complications, thereby optimizing healthcare resource utilization and reducing the economic burden on impoverished individuals. AI-powered analytics and predictive modeling empower public health authorities to formulate evidence-based interventions targeting endemic diseases and health disparities prevalent in impoverished communities (Syrowatka et al., 2021). By analyzing disparate data sources encompassing socioeconomic indicators, environmental factors, and health outcomes, AI facilitates the identification of high-risk populations and the formulation of targeted intervention strategies. By optimizing resource allocation to implement preventive health campaigns, AI-driven public health initiatives enhance healthcare equity and resilience, thereby mitigating the adverse impact of poverty on population health.

AI's Role in Enhancing Financial Inclusion through Digital Means

Digital financial inclusion serves as a means to reach households that are financially inactive, especially people who are not able to gain access to formal financial services designed to meet their needs (Alameda, 2018). Those who are excluded from the formal financial sector are always the youth, the women, and the people at a disadvantage economically, mostly in rural areas. The emergence of digital financial inclusion gained prominence with success stories like M-PESA, which is an innovative payment system that originated in Kenya (Wang & He, 2020). The significance of digital finance lies in its ability to leverage information and communications technology (ICT) to expand the reach and usage of financial services among the poor (Mhlanga & Moloi, 2020).

The integration of AI and ICT into the financial sector has transformed financial inclusion into a digital domain, showcasing the latest frontier in leveraging technology to empower marginalized populations and promote economic resilience, thereby enabling vulnerable populations to access financial services. Digital financial inclusion, augmented by AI, diverges from traditional financial inclusion by significantly reducing transaction costs, most especially in rural areas (Wang & He, 2020). Online products and services underpin digital financial inclusion by providing extensive information to customers that would have been inaccessible without digital services (Mhlanga & Moloi, 2020). One of the benefits of digital financial inclusion includes gaining access to formal financial services. The use of AI facilitates transactions in irregular small amounts, assisting individuals in managing their uneven incomes (Mhlanga & Moloi, 2020). Another benefit of digital financial inclusion is that digital financial services mitigate the risks that are associated with cash-based transactions, by reducing the possibility of theft, loss, and many other forms of financial crime (Mhlanga & Moloi, 2020).

Individuals and organizations gain from improved security standards and fraud detection methods when they digitize transactions, which protects their financial assets and promotes faith in the formal financial system. In this vein, Ogbuju et al. (2020a) developed a system that would help to detect counterfeit banknotes and contribute to curbing the menace of currency counterfeiting in lower currencies in Nigeria. In essence, the convergence of AI, ICT, and financial inclusion marks a paradigm shift in how financial services are supplied and accessed. Governments, financial institutions, and development practitioners may expedite progress toward inclusive and sustainable economic growth and ensure that no one falls behind in the digital era by leveraging technology for both inclusivity and currency security.

CONCLUSION

This study investigated the transformative influence of AI on poverty reduction in agriculture, education, and financial inclusion. It demonstrated AI's ability to use accessible and relevant data to handle poverty-related issues thoroughly. AI's growing importance is evidenced by its capacity to transform old ways and empower marginalized communities. AI emerges as a potent tool for fostering inclusive and sustainable development, with applications ranging from crop production prediction to improved educational access and financial inclusion. This study, which examined diverse industries, emphasized AI's critical role in redefining policies and developing resilience against poverty in today's scenario. However, to fully realize AI's potential in poverty alleviation, concerted efforts are imperative to address ethical, regulatory, and equity considerations, ensuring equitable access to AI-driven healthcare innovations for all segments of society. AI stands as a beacon of hope, bridging the gap between healthcare haves and have-nots and heralding a future of improved health equity and resilience. Furthermore, incorporating AI into financial inclusion projects improves the accessibility and use of financial services, particularly among marginalized people. AI-driven financial inclusion projects help vulnerable populations achieve economic resilience and empowerment by lowering transaction costs, eliminating cash-based transaction hazards, and expanding access to credit and savings mechanisms.

Furthermore, it is critical to emphasize the vital role that public policy plays as we consider the broader implications of AI in reducing poverty. The creation of thorough frameworks that regulate the moral application of AI technology, guaranteeing fair access and avoiding its abuse, must be given top priority by policymakers. Governments, tech companies, and other pertinent parties can work together to establish policies that will allow AI solutions to be scaled sustainably, especially in contexts with limited resources. This involves investigating low-cost AI solutions that are simple to implement in isolated or developing areas, democratizing access to AI's revolutionary potential for a range of groups. To fully realize artificial intelligence's transformative potential as we traverse the complexity of poverty in the 21st century, deliberate integration of AI into public policy frameworks is essential.

REFERENCES

Ahmed, A., Adewumi, S. E., & Yemi-Peters, V. (2023a). Seasonal crop yield prediction in Nigeria using machine learning techniques. *Journal of Applied Artificial Intelligence, 4*(1), 9–20.

Alameda, T. (2018, June 14). Data, AI and financial inclusion: The future of global banking. Retrieved November 9, 2023, from BBVA: https://www.bbva.com/en/data-ai-financial-inclusion-future-globalbanking/

Bajuwa, J., Munir, U., Nori, A., & Williams, B. (2021). Artificial intelligence in healthcare: Transforming the practice of medicine. *Future Healthcare Journal, 8*(2), 188–194.

DAIA. (2018, November 9). Artificial intelligence and global challenges—No poverty. Retrieved November 5, 2023, from Medium: https://medium.com/daia/artificial-intelligence-and-global-challengesa-plan-for-progress-fecd37cc6bda

Dharmaraj, V., & Vijayanand, C. (2018). Artificial intelligence (AI) in agriculture. *International Journal of Current Microbiology and Applied Science, 7*(12), 2022–2128.

Dunga, H. (2019). The impact of the technological revolution on poverty: A case of South Africa. In *Proceedings of International Academic Conferences* (pp. 47–57). International Institute of Social and Economic Science.

Eli-Chukwu, N. C. (2019). Applications of artificial intelligence in agriculture: A review. *Engineering Technology and Applied Science Research, 9*(4), 4377–4383.

Guterres. (2019). *Report of the Secretary-General on SDG Progress 2019*: Special Edition. United Nations Publisher. Retrieved November 5, 2023, from https://sustainabledevelopment.un.org/content/documents/24978Report_of_the_SG_on_SDG_Progress_2019.pdf

Haenlein, M., & Kaplan, A. (2019). A brief history of artificial intelligence: On the past, present and future of artificial intelligence. *California Management Review, 61*(4), 1–10.

Luo, J. (2023). Designing the future of the fourth industrial revolution. *Journal of Engineering Design, 34*(10), 779–785.

McKinsey. (2022). *What Are Industry 4.0, the Fourth Industrial Revolution, and 4IR?* McKinsey & Company (Issue August).

Mhlanga, D. (2021). Artificial intelligence (AI) and poverty reduction in the fourth industrial revolution (4IR). *Sustainability, 13*(11), 5788.

Mhlanga, D., & Moloi, T. (2020). COVID-19 and the digital transformation of education: What are we learning on 4IR in South Africa? *Education Sciences, 10*(7), 180.

Mhlanga, D., & Ndhlovu, E. (2020). Socio-economic implications of COVID-19 for smallholder livelihoods in Zimbabwe. *Preprint*.

Ogbuju, E., Adetayo, A. P., & Obilikwu, P. (2020a). A face recognition system for attendance records in a Nigerian university. *Journal of Scientific Research and Development, 19*(2), 38–45.

Ogbuju, E., Usman, W. O., Obilikwu, P., & Yemi-Peters, V. (2020b). Deep learning for genuine naira banknotes. *FUOYE Journal of Pure and Applied Sciences, 5*(1), 56–67.

Oluwole, O. E., Edgar, O. O., & Fredrick, B. D. (2023). Integrating soil nutrients and location weather variables for crop yield prediction. *International Journal of Innovative Science and Research Technology, 8*(3), 2317–2323.

Ooi, K.-B., Lee, V.-H., Tan, G. W.-H., Hew, T.-S., & Hew, J.-J. (2018). Cloud computing in manufacturing: The next industrial revolution in Malaysia? *Expert Systems with Applications, 93*(1), 376–394.

Quazi, S. (2022). Artificial intelligence and machine learning in precision and genomic medicine. *Springer Nature, 29*(8), 120.

Schmidt, L. (2019, July 29). AI improves farming with Google's TensorFlow. Retrieved November 9, 2023, from The Borgen Project: https://borgenproject.org/tag/artificial-intelligence-and-poverty/

Schwab, K. (2016). The fourth industrial revolution. *Pocketbook4you*. Retrieved November 4, 2023, from https://books.google.com/books

Smith, M. J. (2018). Getting value from artificial intelligence in agriculture. *Animal Production Science, 60*(1), 46–54.

Sunjoyo, N. (2023). *Agriculture Overview: Development News, Research, Data.* The World Bank.

Syrowatka, A., Kuznetsova, M., Alsubai, A., Beckman, A. L., Bain, P. A., Craig, K. J., et al. (2021). Leveraging artificial intelligence for pandemic preparedness and response: A scoping review to identify key use cases. *NPJ Digital Medicine, 4*(96), 1–14.

The World Bank. (2022). *Global Progress in Reducing Extreme Poverty Grinds to a Halt.* IBRD-IDA.

The World Bank. (2023). *Understanding Poverty Overview.* IBRD IDA.

Ubi, P., & Ndem, B. (2019). Poverty and health outcome in Nigeria. *International Journal of Economic and Financial Issues, 9*(6), 12–141.

Vincent, D. R., Deepa, N., Elavarasan, D., Srinivasan, K., Chauhdary, S. H., & Iwendi, C. (2019). Sensors-driven AI-based agriculture recommendation model for assessing land suitability. *Sensors, 19*(17), 3667.

Wahi, B., Cossy-Gantner, A., Germann, S., & Schwalbe, N. (2018). Artificial intelligence (AI) and global health: How can AI contribute to health in resource-poor settings? *BMJ Global Health, 3*(4), 798.

Wang, X., & He, G. (2020). Digital financial inclusion and farmers. *Sustainability, 12*(4), 1668.

Weber, I. (2019, October 17). How AI is being used to map poverty. Retrieved November 9, 2023, from Electronic Specifier: https://www.electronicspecifier.com/products/artificial-intelligence/how-ai-is-being-used-to-map-poverty

Wisskirchen, G., Biacabe, B. T., Bormann, U., Muntz, A., Niehause, G., Solar, G. J., & Brauchitsch, B. V. (2017). *Artificial Intelligence and Robotics and Their Impact on the Workplace.* IBA Global Employment Institute.

Wong, M. (2020, May 22). Stanford researchers harness satellite imagery and AI to help fight poverty in Africa. Retrieved November 9, 2023, from Stanford News: https://news.stanford.edu/2020/05/22/using-satellites-ai-help-fight-poverty-africa/

Zavadskaya, A. (2017). Artificial intelligence in finance: Forecasting stock market returns using artificial neural networks. *Business, 12*, 1–154.

The Role of Artificial Intelligence in Poverty Alleviation toward Sustainable Development

5

Murat Tahir Çaldağ and Ebru Gökalp

INTRODUCTION

As society continues to push toward technological advancements such as general artificial intelligence (AI) and fully automated war machines, it's important to remember that basic issues like poverty, hunger, education access, and inequality still persist from the earliest days of human civilization. The Sustainable Development Goals (SDGs) that the United Nations (2015) presented are the most important areas that require improvement soon. The first SDG is named "No Poverty" in the resolution. Although poverty has several different descriptions and varies according to context, it can be defined as *an individual's lack of essential needs and resources* (Haughton & Khandker, 2009). In recent decades, global poverty has been decreasing, but the COVID-19 pandemic caused a major setback to the SDGs for 2030 (Kharas & Dooley, 2022; World Bank, 2020).

DOI: 10.1201/9781003479109-5

AI has proven to be a useful tool for addressing various problems related to poverty. Several studies have demonstrated the effectiveness of AI-based solutions in tackling issues such as predicting water quality, anti-corruption measures, healthcare education, K-12 curriculum evaluation, and disaster monitoring. For instance, a case study conducted by Hameed et al. (2017) in tropical regions showed that using artificial neural networks can yield more accurate and less time-consuming results in predicting water quality. Another study conducted by Odilla (2023) in Brazil developed an AI-based anti-corruption tool that helped in criminal investigations, tracking public resources, and identifying misuse of public assets. Chow et al. (2023) designed an AI-based chatbot for supporting healthcare education in the context of radiotherapy. In Hong Kong, a study conducted by Yau et al. (2023) evaluated K-12 school teachers on AI curriculum, providing insights for developers and policymakers. Lastly, Sufi and Khalil (2022) created an automated disaster monitoring system using social media posts to provide fast and location-based knowledge. Such examples of AI applications in different domains can help address poverty-related issues and eventually alleviate poverty.

AI has the potential to address many root causes of poverty. It is an emerging technology that can make significant progress in poverty reduction by providing benefits such as management, automation, and improvement of poverty data governance. To effectively address poverty, it is crucial to identify and address its underlying causes. These root causes may include factors such as inadequate education, social conflict, inequality, discrimination, insufficient infrastructure, inadequate healthcare systems, climate change, limited job opportunities, restricted access to clean water resources, lack of government support, physical or mental disabilities, social injustice, corruption, absence of strong role models, natural disasters, exploitative lending practices that exacerbate poverty, inaccessible healthcare, insufficient safety nets, low wages, unequal distribution of wealth, and unsafe living conditions (de Bruijn & Antonides, 2022; Haughton & Khandker, 2009; Mueller & Techasunthornwat, 2020; Ridley et al., 2020; Siddiqui et al., 2020).

This study aims to analyze the impact of AI technologies on the root causes of poverty through sustainable development. The possible opportunities that AI can provide to alleviate poverty are reviewed and mapped for each root cause of poverty. Also, the drawbacks of the utilization of AI technologies are discussed. Lastly, a feasible road map for countries suffering from poverty to utilize AI technologies is suggested.

REVIEW OF LITERATURE

Artificial Intelligence

The idea of AI can be seen throughout history from the mythological tales of intelligent automations and half-human, half-machine cyborgs (Akgün Çomak & Pembecioğlu, 2022). The theoretical foundations of AI can be linked to the electronic brain concept addressed by McCulloch and Pitts (1943) and the idea of creating thinking machines addressed by Turing (1950). The use of AI as a term for intelligent machines was recognized in the proposal of the Dartmouth Summer Research Project in 1956 (McCarthy et al., 2006). The founding father of AI defined the term as "the science and engineering of making intelligent machines, especially intelligent computer programs" (McCarthy, 2004, p. 2).

The advent of cyber-physical systems, big data, the Internet of Things, cloud computing, and numerous other emerging technologies has revolutionized the way in which businesses, industries, and societies have presented new opportunities for AI. This has opened up new prospects for AI, enabling a blend of these technologies to solve problems that arise in various domains. For instance, the integration of AI, digital twin technologies, and the Internet of Things has led to the development of intelligent optimization and automation systems for managing the energy in residential districts (Agostinelli et al., 2021); similarly, cloud-based finance and technology (fintech) applications use AI for enhanced security (Kunduru, 2023). The use of AI-based technologies in healthcare can provide benefits such as diagnosis and treatment of diseases with a reduction of human errors (Yeasmin, 2019), while in the educational context, AI has facilitated personalized learning, feedback gathering, and interactive learning (Baïdoo-Anu & Ansah, 2023). While AI offers great potential for benefits, it also poses certain risks that can impede its full utilization. Such risks include security and privacy concerns, insufficient awareness and knowledge about AI, bias in training data and among developers, and an excessive reliance on AI. If the risks are not addressed properly, they can lead to negative consequences (Prather et al., 2023; Valový & Buchalcevova, 2023).

The utilization of AI to address modern-day challenges has emerged as a significant factor in its widespread adoption. Hence, directing AI-powered solutions toward some of the world's most pressing issues, such as poverty, climate change, sustainability, and education, has become a necessity. By leveraging the capabilities of AI, we can develop innovative solutions that can help overcome these challenges and contribute toward building a better world. The aim of this study is to show how AI can be utilized to alleviate poverty.

Sustainable Development Goals

SDGs were introduced by the United Nations in 2015 as a framework to guide countries, businesses, and societies toward a more sustainable future. The SDGs consist of 17 critical objectives that address the urgent challenges we face today. These goals are based on the principles of people, planet, prosperity, peace, and participation, highlighting the importance of working together to create a better world for all. A comprehensive list of the SDGs and their respective targets, given below, outlines significant challenges that require immediate action.

- Goal 1   No poverty
- Goal 2   Zero hunger
- Goal 3   Good health and well-being

- Goal 4   Quality education
- Goal 5   Gender equality
- Goal 6   Clean water and sanitation
- Goal 7   Affordable and clean energy
- Goal 8   Decent work and economic growth
- Goal 9   Industry, innovation, and infrastructure
- Goal 10   Reduced inequalities
- Goal 11   Sustainable cities and communities
- Goal 12   Responsible consumption and production
- Goal 13   Climate action
- Goal 14   Life below water
- Goal 15   Life on land
- Goal 16   Peace, justice, and strong institutions
- Goal 17   Partnerships for the goals

SDG1 named "No Poverty" has been updated lately as ending poverty in all its forms everywhere. This SDG aims to eradicate extreme poverty, improve the quality of life of the poor by providing access to basic services and rights, and build the resilience of the poor who are vulnerable to natural disasters, climate change, and crises (United Nations, 2015). The United Nations recognizes the importance of tackling natural disasters, climate change, and crises to ensure the provision of basic services and rights to vulnerable populations. The overarching goal of poverty eradication is to secure a better future for all of humanity. In this regard, it is imperative to explore new avenues for alleviating poverty. The present study endeavors to shed light on the potential of AI technologies to achieve this objective. The following section delves into the opportunities for leveraging these technologies to address poverty-related challenges.

Artificial Intelligence Applications to Alleviate the Underlying Causes of Poverty

To effectively combat poverty, it is imperative to comprehensively understand the complex and multifaceted nature of the issue. Poverty is a phenomenon that is directly and indirectly influenced by a variety of economic, societal, and environmental factors. Common causes of poverty include the lack of basic needs, inadequate education, corruption, digital divide, lack of financial resources, unemployment, and the aftermath of natural disasters. Gweshengwe and Hassan (2020) categorized poverty dimensions from the literature as financial, economic, material, social, and seasonal factors, while an additional study conducted by Addae-Korankye (2014) presented significant factors creating poverty in Africa such as poor governance, corruption, lack of job opportunities, conflicts, poor infrastructure, and inefficient resource management. Given the extensive and varied causes of poverty, the effects of AI-based applications on poverty can also be diverse, both direct and indirect (Raghavendra et al., 2023). In this context, this study categorizes the underlying roots of poverty into *educational, economic, quality of life, environmental, social,* and *political factors,* providing a detailed explanation of AI-based solutions for each category. A comprehensive understanding of these dimensions and the potential for AI-based solutions to address them is essential to effectively alleviate poverty and enhance the quality of life for those affected.

Educational factors

The present discourse delves into the issue of educational factors that contribute to poverty, which refers to unequal access to education due to a range of factors including accessibility, economic, social, environmental, and governance issues. The causes of inadequate education include a lack of school infrastructure, high education costs, underqualified teachers and staff, societal norms, insufficient resources, and a lack of IT infrastructure. The lack of proper education can have negative consequences on the quality of life of individuals and their families.

Education is a significant factor that can provide variable opportunities for people to escape poverty. Providing equal access, rights, and quality of education harms poverty. People acquire new skills and knowledge through education to improve their standards of living. Education can help individuals acquire knowledge in finance, accounting, strategic business management, supply chain management, digital transformation, programming, and other fields, which can raise awareness and help them reach their potential. The skills and knowledge acquired through education can provide stability for the entire family. The research conducted by Sedana et al. (2019) in Indonesia has taken into account education as a multifaceted factor that has a negative effect on poverty. Hofmarcher (2021) presented education as a fundamental tool that people use to escape poverty in a pan-European context.

The increasing trend in AI starting with generative AI tools such as ChatGPT (2024), Google Gemini (2024), and GitHub Copilot (2024) has peaked the interest in AI among the general public. This interest has been a motivating factor for students, teachers, and administrators to integrate AI-based tools for educational purposes. Therefore, the motivation and interactivity with AI-based educational tools will increase awareness of the benefits of using these tools for learning and improving skills and knowledge.

Economic factors

Economic inequalities have persisted as a complex and enduring issue throughout human history, stemming from limited resources, which can lead to conflicts at various scales. In addition to disparities in wealth distribution, factors such as unemployment rates, lack of job opportunities, low wages, and over-indebtedness contribute significantly to poverty. The research conducted by Ferreira et al. (2021) indicated that over-indebtedness stands as an underlying cause of poverty. This phenomenon arises when individuals or businesses accumulate more debt than their income can sustain, resulting in financial instability and eventual poverty. Utilizing AI-based practices to analyze financial data enables predictive risk analysis through machine learning models, thereby aiding in preventing over-indebtedness and facilitating timely interventions to circumvent poverty.

Another notable advantage of AI lies in identifying poverty to enhance the living standards of individuals affected. Income, expenditures, debts, risk factors associated with financial status, employment rates, and other economic indicators form the basis for identifying individuals in poverty. AI can effectively pinpoint individuals living in poverty, providing policymakers with valuable insights for poverty alleviation efforts. A study conducted by Alsharkawi et al. (2021) in Jordan presented a model for tracking poverty to generate effective improvements. Another study by Gao et al. (2020) offered a model identifying poverty-affected households in the context of food insecurity with an accuracy of 80%. These models leverage AI-based techniques to analyze data, delivering valuable insights to policymakers for poverty alleviation efforts.

Another benefit AI can provide is economic growth, which can be achieved by automating manual labor, increasing technological innovations, and improving productivity, which results in an increase in human capital and a reduction in poverty (Xian, 2023). The use of AI-based techniques can lead to more efficient and effective resource allocation, helping policymakers design better poverty alleviation programs. Therefore, AI is a promising tool for addressing the economic challenges faced by societies, including poverty, and has the potential to promote equitable and sustainable growth.

Quality of life factors

Access to necessities, such as nutritionally balanced food, clean water, reliable healthcare, sustainable energy, and standard living conditions, is a fundamental component necessary for the maintenance of overall well-being and the prevention of poverty. Failure to provide these basic needs can have significant impacts on individuals and communities, leading to poor health outcomes, malnutrition, disease, and suboptimal living conditions. For example, limited access to healthcare can result in a lack of preventative care, exacerbating chronic conditions and reducing overall life expectancy. Insufficient access to clean water and nutritionally balanced food can lead to malnutrition, stunting, and other related health issues that negatively impact quality of life. Additionally, inadequate access to energy and standard living conditions can impede the ability of individuals and communities to thrive, limiting economic opportunities and hindering overall progress. Therefore, prioritizing the provision of these essential quality of life factors is critical in reducing poverty and promoting sustainable development.

Inadequate infrastructure and substandard living conditions can limit individuals' access to essential services, ultimately contributing to poverty. Urban areas, in particular, face challenges such as transportation, communication, food and material logistics, crime, and societal conflicts. Achieving financial stability and satisfying fundamental needs while maintaining standard living conditions are vital to living above the poverty line. AI-based geographic mapping of poverty can identify the areas affected and target the investments accordingly (Gulyani et al., 2010). Additionally, utilizing satellite imagery for tracking significant factors such as crime, traffic jams, and communication problems can enhance the opportunities for new businesses, which will create new jobs.

Social and political factors

Social and political factors encompass a range of issues, including *poor governance, corruption, discrimination,* and *the digital divide. Poor governance* plays a critical role in managing resources and establishing strategies and decisions that can impact poverty levels. Effective governance plays a crucial role in managing resources and establishing strategies and decisions that can impact poverty levels. Poor governance, allocation of resources, and lack of vision have been identified as key factors contributing to poverty, according to research by Addae-Korankye (2014). To combat poverty, government institutions need to have a strong influence on regulating resources and distributing infrastructure. This requires collaboration and participation from both management and citizens, facilitated by effective communication channels and institutions. Creating the necessary communication channels and institutions will enhance governance by promoting collaboration and participation from the people, creating an open ecosystem focused on addressing the right problems. Zuiderwijk et al. (2021) highlighted the significant benefits of AI in public governance, including risk identification, improved performance, economic gains, sustainability, and collaboration. Projects such as Canada's immigration process control system, Poland's optimization of employment services, and Finland's assistant Aurora AI are examples of AI-based initiatives being developed for public services (Kuziemski & Misuraca, 2020).

One of the most important factors hindering the alleviation of poverty is *corruption*. Although corruption can be perceived as the allocation of resources and services for personal gains, it does have a greater effect on communities, countries, and the world as a whole (Jain, 2001). The most significant effect is the erosion of trust in bureaucrats, politicians, government officials, public workers, etc. Especially in developing countries, corruption can have devastating effects as increases in economic, social, educational, and environmental inequalities. Research on Nigeria presented that political corruption has a negative impact on income inequalities, which indirectly increases poverty (Ojo et al., 2020). The case study in China presented corruption in rural regions, mainly individuals, and the type is embezzlement of poverty funds that require immediate attention (Wu & Christensen, 2021). AI-based technologies can prevent corruption by finding the causes and identifying the sources. The advantages of AI-based anti-corruption tools are demonstrated in a study conducted by Odilla (2023) in Brazil. This study presented the advancement of AI-driven tools capable of analyzing extensive datasets and diverse information sources to monitor, detect, and report suspicious activities for further scrutiny.

Environmental factors

Environmental factors that contribute to poverty include *natural disasters, pollution, and climate change*. While these factors may be observed on a large scale, addressing their effects requires micro- to macro-level practices. *Natural disasters*, such as earthquakes, forest fires, and tsunamis, can have devastating effects on unprepared societies, pushing a larger number of people into poverty. Therefore, it is crucial to carefully plan and execute every countermeasure in a timely fashion. AI-based technologies offer solutions such as risk assessments, early warning and monitoring, search and rescue practices, emergency evaluation, and decision-making systems (Tan et al., 2021). Shan et al. (2019) developed a disaster damage assessment model based on AI using social media texts, while Wang and Zhang (2023) created a real-time earthquake monitoring

AI-based system in China. Smartphone early warning systems for different crises are also being used, as discussed by Xu & Xue (2024). Additionally, Yigitcanlar et al. (2020) explored the idea of building safer cities with AI-based modeling for disaster management.

Climate change is widely recognized as a root cause of poverty, exerting significant impacts on the world through rising sea levels, weather pattern alterations, and ecological transformations. Furthermore, pollution is intricately linked to climate change, as the resultant environmental damage carries long-term implications for human life. While the conservation of the environment in its entirety is imperative, the attainment of a global consensus among governments remains an aspirational goal. The integration of AI-based technologies across various sectors holds the potential to mitigate environmental harm by fostering the development and utilization of more eco-friendly tools, machinery, and transportation systems (Cowls et al., 2023). While the advantages of AI in poverty alleviation are noteworthy, some apprehensions must be considered. These drawbacks and potential solutions are explored in the following session.

DRAWBACKS OF THE UTILIZATION OF AI TECHNOLOGIES

AI technologies offer a lot of benefits, but they can also have some drawbacks that may impact their utilization. Some of the significant concerns include *biased training data, safety, privacy, financial costs, sustainability, overreliance,* and *prerequisites for proficiency and expertise.* AI has the potential to either prevent or perpetuate discrimination, as its *bias is rooted in the training data* used by developers to create the model. This can result in scenarios where the developer's own bias is reflected in the model, or the training data is incomplete, leading to misleading solutions that require further investigation. In sectors such as healthcare or defense, where the impact on human life is significant, the training of AI models requires heightened supervision. Therefore, it is essential to ensure that AI is developed and utilized responsibly to realize its potential benefits. In fields such as programming (Becker et al., 2023), crime prediction (Berk, 2021), and employment interviews (Mirowska & Mesnet, 2022), the usage of AI-based technologies should follow standards to reduce bias. Case studies have shown that AI-based solutions exhibit higher levels of racial biases in rental house markets (Wang et al., 2023) and gender-based biases in image-generative AI (Sun et al., 2024). Additionally, AI-based recruitment and law enforcement can have discriminatory effects (Stahl et al., 2023), especially due to the overrepresentation of some groups in training datasets, which can provide biased results.

Security and *privacy* are significant barriers to the adoption and usage of emerging technologies. The issues related to security in AI are based on the vulnerability of the systems to cyberattacks and the devastation AI can generate in the hands of others. Privacy issues in AI-based technologies include the acquisition, storage, and extraction of data. The perception of AI using unauthorized private data needs to be addressed by providing information or increasing transparency in AI systems (Li & Zhang, 2017).

The *financial cost* of AI technologies is also a significant barrier. The establishment of a technical infrastructure for AI-based systems and the expanse of the experts who are required to work create a financial strain on the government (Wirtz et al., 2019). The *sustainability of AI-based systems* presents a unique challenge due to various factors. One of the main issues is the potential impact of new technological advancements on the efficiency and effectiveness of poverty identification and prevention applications. For instance, advancements in AI technology could lead to more accurate and timely identification of poverty-stricken areas, enabling more targeted and effective interventions. However, this also raises concerns about the equitable distribution of these technological benefits and ensuring that the most vulnerable populations are not left behind. Another critical consideration is the allocation of resources required for these systems to function effectively.

Overreliance on AI presents a significant risk, as it could elevate AI to a position of indispensability. Over-dependence, characterized by excessive trust in AI methods and results (Ebert & Louridas, 2023), may result in complacency and inaction in future generations. This issue lies at the center of the ongoing discussion on AI-driven educational tools and the use of generative language models (Holstein & Doroudi, 2022). It is essential to adopt a balanced approach in leveraging AI for solutions to effectively tackle this challenge.

DISCUSSION

In today's global society, poverty continues to pose a significant challenge for many nations. However, the incorporation of AI-powered technologies has the potential to revolutionize the fight against poverty. By streamlining processes and optimizing decision-making, AI can help diminish poverty by generating more employment opportunities, increasing productivity, and providing greater access to vital services like healthcare and education. While the advantages of AI in poverty alleviation are noteworthy, some apprehensions must be considered. Concerns include the possibility that AI may widen the digital divide, particularly in low-income communities with limited technological access. Additionally, there are worries that AI may replace human jobs, exacerbating income inequality even further.

The potential of AI to revolutionize poverty reduction efforts on a global scale is immense. Advanced tracking mechanisms, geographically linked identification maps, data-driven decision-making systems, and innovative opportunities are just some of the ways AI can contribute to creating a better world for all. However, it's important to acknowledge and address the potential downsides of AI. To ensure that nations grappling with poverty can benefit from AI, we must follow a comprehensive road map by overcoming identified obstacles and embracing AI's potential.

- It is essential to identify and prioritize the root causes of poverty within the country's context to achieve sustainable development. Utilizing AI-based technological advancements can have a significant impact on critical areas.

- It is important to conduct a cost-benefit analysis to make informed AI invest-ment decisions within limited budgets.
- Establishing a robust technological infrastructure to support AI-based sys-tems will pave the way for transformative change.
- Developing comprehensive training programs for communities, government institutions, and businesses will empower them to effectively create, use, and maintain AI solutions.
- Implementing mechanisms for data collection, analysis, monitoring, and reg-ulation will ensure the responsible deployment of AI technologies.
- By fostering AI initiatives with government incentives, we can enhance the acceptance and integration of AI-based technologies.
- Analyzing community feedback and incorporating improvements are vital for ensuring that AI solutions meet the diverse needs of the population.
- Involving communities in the creation, design, and management of AI-based systems will foster a sense of ownership and inclusivity.
- Establishing clear ethical guidelines for AI and application development will ensure that technological advancements are aligned with societal values.

Lastly, encouraging and supporting local entrepreneurs will drive innovation and eco-nomic growth, creating a ripple effect of positive change.

CONCLUSION

When analyzing the potential impact of AI on poverty alleviation, it is essential to thor-oughly assess both its positive and negative aspects. AI has the capacity to influence poverty in various areas, including education, economics, quality of life, environment, and social and political factors. It's important to acknowledge that the use of AI also brings drawbacks, such as biased training data, financial costs, overreliance, knowledge and skill requirements, and security and privacy concerns. These downsides need to be carefully weighed before implementing any AI-based solutions. As AI continues to transform different sectors, it's crucial to recognize that there is no universal approach to using AI for poverty alleviation. Each community, society, and country has its unique considerations, and not every situation necessitates AI-based solutions. Therefore, the decision to utilize AI should be made by taking all relevant factors into consideration.

The recent progress in AI and emerging technologies provides numerous opportu-nities to alleviate poverty and create an environment for people to flourish. However, the absence of ethical standards, biased training datasets, and disregard for human factors in the design, development, and implementation of these technologies present new chal-lenges. In particular, the ethical dilemmas surrounding the training datasets of AI-based applications necessitate further qualitative and quantitative research. Ultimately, the insights from this study can offer valuable guidance for government institutions dedi-cated to poverty alleviation. By integrating AI where appropriate, we can ultimately enhance the quality of life for individuals and communities.

REFERENCES

Addae-Korankye, A. (2014). Causes of poverty in Africa: A review of literature. *American International Journal of Social Science*, 3(7), 147–153.

Agostinelli, S., Cumo, F., Guidi, G., & Tomazzoli, C. (2021). Cyber-physical systems improving building energy management: Digital twin and artificial intelligence. *Energies*, 14(8), Article 8. https://doi.org/10.3390/en14082338

Akgün Çomak, N., & Pembecioğlu, E. (2022). Yapay Zeka—Transhümanizim—Mitoloji. İn N. Bozbuğa, S. Gülseçen, V. Kamer, & B. Kurtuldu (Eds.), *Tıp Bilişimi II* (pp. 69–96). Istanbul: Istanbul University Press. https://doi.org/10.26650/B/ET07.2022.006

Alsharkawi, A., Al-Fetyani, M., Dawas, M., Saadeh, H., & Alyaman, M. (2021). Poverty classification using machine learning: The case of Jordan. *Sustainability*, 13(3), 1412.

Baidoo-Anu, D., & Ansah, L. O. (2023). Education in the era of generative artificial intelligence (AI): Understanding the potential benefits of ChatGPT in promoting teaching and learning. *Journal of AI*, 7(1), Article 1. https://doi.org/10.61969/jai.1337500

Becker, B. A., Denny, P., Finnie-Ansley, J., Luxton-Reilly, A., Prather, J., & Santos, E. A. (2023). Programming is hard-or at least it used to be: Educational opportunities and challenges of AI code generation. In *Proceedings of the 54th ACM Technical Symposium on Computer Science Education V.1* (pp. 500–506). New York: ACM.

Berk, R. A. (2021). Artificial intelligence, predictive policing, and risk assessment for law enforcement. *Annual Review of Criminology*, 4, 209–237.

ChatGPT. (2024). ChatGPT. https://chat.openai.com/

Chow, J. C. L., Sanders, L., & Li, K. (2023). Design of an educational chatbot using artificial intelligence in radiotherapy. *AI*, 4(1), Article 1. https://doi.org/10.3390/ai4010015

Cowls, J., Tsamados, A., Taddeo, M., & Floridi, L. (2023). The AI gambit: Leveraging artificial intelligence to combat climate change—Opportunities, challenges, and recommendations. *AI & Society*, 38, 283–307.

de Bruijn, E.-J., & Antonides, G. (2022). Poverty and economic decision making: A review of scarcity theory. *Theory and Decision*, 92(1), 5–37. https://doi.org/10.1007/s11238-021-09802-7

Ebert, C., & Louridas, P. (2023). Generative AI for software practitioners. *IEEE Software*, 40(4), 30–38.

Ferreira, M. B., Pinto, D. C., Herter, M. M., Soro, J., Vanneschi, L., Castelli, M., & Peres, F. (2021). Using artificial intelligence to overcome over-indebtedness and fight poverty. *Journal of Business Research*, 131, 411–425.

Github Copilot. (2024). https://github.com/features/copilot

Google Gemini. (2024). https://gemini.google.com/app

Gulyani, S., Talukdar, D., & Jack, D. (2010). *Poverty, living conditions, and infrastructure access: A comparison of slums in Dakar, Johannesburg, and Nairobi*. World Bank Policy Research Working Paper, 5388.

Guo, J., & Li, B. (2018). The application of medical artificial intelligence technology in rural areas of developing countries. *Health Equity*, 2(1), 174–181.

Gweshengwe, B., & Hassan, N. H. (2020). Defining the characteristics of poverty and their implications for poverty analysis. *Cogent Social Sciences*, 6(1), 1768669.

Hameed, M., Sharqi, S. S., Yaseen, Z. M., Afan, H. A., Hussain, A., & Elshafie, A. (2017). Application of artificial intelligence (AI) techniques in water quality index prediction: A case study in tropical region, Malaysia. *Neural Computing and Applications*, 28(1), 893–905. https://doi.org/10.1007/s00521-016-2404-7

Haughton, J., & Khandker, S. R. (2009). *Handbook on Poverty+ Inequality*. Washington, DC: World Bank Publications.

Hofmarcher, T. (2021). The effect of education on poverty: A European perspective. *Economics of Education Review*, *83*, 102124.

Holstein, K., & Doroudi, S. (2022). Equity and artificial intelligence in education. In W. Holmes, & K. Porayska-Pomsta (Eds.), *The Ethics of Artificial Intelligence in Education* (pp. 151–173). New York: Routledge.

Jain, A. K. (2001). Corruption: A review. *Journal of Economic Surveys*, *15*(1), 71–121.

Kharas, H., & Dooley, M. (2022). The *Evolution* of *Global Poverty*, 1990–2030. Center for Sustainable Development at Brookings.

Kunduru, A. R. (2023). Artificial intelligence advantages in cloud fintech application security. *Central Asian Journal of Mathematical Theory and Computer Sciences*, *4*(8), 48–53.

Kuziemski, M., & Misuraca, G. (2020). AI governance in the public sector: Three tales from the frontiers of automated decision-making in democratic settings. *Telecommunications Policy*, *44*(6), 101976.

Li, X., & Zhang, T. (2017). An exploration on artificial intelligence application: From security, privacy and ethic perspective. *2017 IEEE 2nd International Conference on Cloud Computing and Big Data Analysis (ICCCBDA)* (pp. 416–420). Chengdu. https://doi.org/10.1109/ICCCBDA.2017.7951949

McCarthy, J. (2004). *What Is Artificial Intelligence?* New York: Springer.

McCarthy, J., Minsky, M. L., Rochester, N., & Shannon, C. E. (2006). A proposal for the dartmouth summer research project on artificial intelligence, august 31, 1955. *AI Magazine*, *27*(4), 12–12.

McCulloch, W. S., & Pitts, W. (1943). A logical calculus of the ideas immanent in nervous activity. *The Bulletin of Mathematical Biophysics*, *5*, 115–133.

Mirowska, A., & Mesnet, L. (2022). Preferring the devil you know: Potential applicant reactions to artificial intelligence evaluation of interviews. *Human Resource Management Journal*, *32*(2), 364–383. https://doi.org/10.1111/1748-8583.12393

Mueller, H., & Techasunthornwat, C. (2020). *Conflict and Poverty*. The World Bank.

Odilla, F. (2023). Bots against corruption: Exploring the benefits and limitations of AI-based anti-corruption technology. *Crime, Law and Social Change*, *80*(4), 353–396. https://doi.org/10.1007/s10611-023-10091-0

Ojo, L. B., Eusebius, A. C., Ifeanyi, O. J., & Aderemi, T. A. (2020). Political corruption, income inequality and poverty in Nigeria. *Acta Universitatis Danubius. Relationes Internationales*, 13(1), 7–19.

Prather, J., Reeves, B. N., Denny, P., Becker, B. A., Leinonen, J., Luxton-Reilly, A., Powell, G., Finnie-Ansley, J., & Santos, E. A. (2023). "It's weird that it knows what I want": Usability and interactions with copilot for novice programmers. *ACM Transactions on Computer-Human Interaction*. arXiv Preprint arXiv:2304.02491. https://doi.org/10.1145/3617367.

Raghavendra, A. H., Majhi, S. G., Mukherjee, A., & Bala, P. K. (2023). Role of artificial intelligence (AI) in poverty alleviation: A bibliometric analysis. *VINE Journal of Information and Knowledge Management Systems*, *54*(4), 38–57.

Ridley, M., Rao, G., Schilbach, F., & Patel, V. (2020). Poverty, depression, and anxiety: Causal evidence and mechanisms. *Science*, *370*(6522), eaay0214. https://doi.org/10.1126/science.aay0214

Sedana, Y. I., Sri, B. M. K., Djinar, S. N., & Nyoman, S. I. A. (2019). Socio-economic factors affecting poverty in Bali Province, Indonesia. *Russian Journal of Agricultural and Socio-Economic Sciences*, *90*(6), 192–202.

Shan, S., Zhao, F., Wei, Y., & Liu, M. (2019). Disaster management 2.0: A real-time disaster damage assessment model based on mobile social media data—A case study of Weibo (Chinese Twitter). *Safety Science*, *115*, 393–413.

Siddiqui, F., Salam, R. A., Lassi, Z. S., & Das, J. K. (2020). The intertwined relationship between malnutrition and poverty. *Frontiers in Public Health*, 8. https://www.frontiersin.org/articles/10.3389/fpubh.2020.00453

Stahl, B. C., Schroeder, D., & Rodrigues, R. (2023). Unfair and illegal discrimination. In B. C. Stahl, D. Schroeder, & R. Rodrigues (Eds.), *Ethics of Artificial Intelligence: Case Studies and Options for Addressing Ethical Challenges* (pp. 9–23). Cham: Springer International Publishing. https://doi.org/10.1007/978-3-031-17040-9_2

Sufi, F. K., & Khalil, I. (2022). Automated disaster monitoring from social media posts using AI-based location intelligence and sentiment analysis. *IEEE Transactions on Computational Social Systems*, 1–11. https://doi.org/10.1109/TCSS.2022.3157142

Sun, L., Wei, M., Sun, Y., Suh, Y. J., Shen, L., & Yang, S. (2024). Smiling women pitching down: Auditing representational and presentational gender biases in image-generative AI. Journal of Computer-Mediated Communication, 29(1), zmad045. https://doi.org/10.1093/jcmc/zmad045

Tan, L., Guo, J., Mohanarajah, S., & Zhou, K. (2021). Can we detect trends in natural disaster management with artificial intelligence? A review of modeling practices. *Natural Hazards*, *107*, 2389–2417.

Turing, A. M. (1950). Mind. *Mind*, *59*(236), 433–460.

United Nations. (2015). Transforming our world: The 2030 agenda for sustainable development (A/RES/70/1). https://www.un.org/en/development/desa/population/migration/generalassembly/docs/globalcompact/A_RES_70_1_E.pdf

Valový, M., & Buchalcevova, A. (2023). The psychological effects of AI-assisted programming on students and professionals, *2023 IEEE International Conference on Software Maintenance and Evolution (ICSME)*, Bogotá (385–390). doi: 10.1109/ICSME58846.2023.00050.

Wang, H., & Zhang, J. (2023). A deep learning approach for suppressing noise in livestream earthquake data from a large seismic network. *Geophysical Journal International*, *233*(3), 1546–1559. https://doi.org/10.1093/gji/ggad009

Wang, X., Liang, C., & Yin, M. (2023). The effects of AI biases and explanations on human decision fairness: A case study of bidding in rental housing markets. *Proceedings of the Thirty-Second International Joint Conference on Artificial Intelligence*, Macao (pp. 3076–3084). https://doi.org/10.24963/ijcai.2023/343

Wirtz, B. W., Weyerer, J. C., & Geyer, C. (2019). Artificial intelligence and the public sector—Applications and challenges. *International Journal of Public Administration*, *42*(7), 596–615. https://doi.org/10.1080/01900692.2018.1498103

World Bank. (2020). *Poverty and Shared Prosperity 2020: Reversals of Fortune*. Washington, DC: The World Bank.

Wu, S., & Christensen, T. (2021). Corruption and accountability in China's rural poverty governance: Main features from village and township cadres. *International Journal of Public Administration*, *44*(16), 1383–1393.

Xian, F. (2023). Quantifying the economic benefits of artificial intelligence technology. *Proceedings of the 4th Management Science Informatization and Economic Innovation Development Conference, MSIEID 2022*, December 9–11, 2022, Chongqing, China.

Xu, C., & Xue, Z. (2024). Applications and challenges of artificial intelligence in the field of disaster prevention, reduction, and relief. *Natural Hazards Research*, *4*(1), 169–172. https://doi.org/10.1016/j.nhres.2023.11.011

Yau, K. W., Chai, C. S., Chiu, T. K. F., Meng, H., King, I., & Yam, Y. (2023). A phenomenographic approach on teacher conceptions of teaching Artificial Intelligence (AI) in K-12 schools. *Education and Information Technologies*, *28*(1), 1041–1064. https://doi.org/10.1007/s10639-022-11161-x

Yeasmin, S. (2019). Benefits of artificial intelligence in medicine. *2019 2nd International Conference on Computer Applications & Information Security (ICCAIS)*, Riyadh (pp. 1–6). https://doi.org/10.1109/CAIS.2019.8769557

Yigitcanlar, T., Butler, L., Windle, E., Desouza, K. C., Mehmood, R., & Corchado, J. M. (2020). Can building "artificially intelligent cities" safeguard humanity from natural disasters, pandemics, and other catastrophes? An urban scholar's perspective. *Sensors, 20*(10), 2988.

Zuiderwijk, A., Chen, Y.-C., & Salem, F. (2021). Implications of the use of artificial intelligence in public governance: A systematic literature review and a research agenda. *Government Information Quarterly, 38*(3), 101577.

Exploring the Intersection of Artificial Intelligence and Informal Mobile Health Use for Healthcare Access in Humanitarian Contexts

6

Munir Maharazu Kubau and
Samuel C. Avemaria Utulu

INTRODUCTION

The rapid advancement of technology has ushered in a new era of possibilities for transforming healthcare delivery, especially in the realms of mobile health (mHealth) and artificial intelligence (AI) (European Commission Joint Research Centre., 2020; Kuo, 2023; Sharma, 2023). mHealth and informal mHealth are subsets of e-health in

DOI: 10.1201/9781003479109-6

which people seek healthcare support, services, and solutions using mobile devices such as smartphones, tablets, and wearable devices (Hampshire et al., 2021a; Maharazu et al., 2022). The need for this transformation is critical in humanitarian contexts where resources are limited, geographic constraints exist, and suddenly unpredictable crises occur. We explored the synergies between informal mHealth and AI in this research study, shedding light on how they can revolutionize healthcare in areas with limited access to formal healthcare services or are bounded by circumstantial factors. The convergence of informal mHealth and AI offers hope for dynamic and often precarious solutions in humanitarian contexts (Legido-Quigley & Asgari-Jirhandeh, 2018; World Health Organization, 2022). This approach departs from conventional healthcare methodologies, providing innovative solutions capable of circumventing the barriers that have historically hampered effective medical treatment in these contexts. These solutions operate outside formal institutional frameworks in informal settings, beyond formal healthcare systems. It encompasses solutions that operate outside formal institutional frameworks and extend beyond formal healthcare systems.

In exploring the relationship between how technology and humanitarian healthcare overlap, we uncover a narrative of possibilities where mobile technologies and AI are combined to redefine healthcare delivery in crisis-stricken settings or regions. Exploring a humanitarian context is not simply a technical exercise; it is a journey into the heart of health-related issues. By harnessing informal mHealth and AI appropriately, informal healthcare has the potential to bridge gaps and barriers in healthcare accessibility related to poor contexts, special circumstances, individuals with fear of stigmatization, marginalized groups, humanitarian contexts, and many other health-related issues (Christie et al., 2018; Glenton et al., 2023a; Sam, 2021). Humanitarian contexts are circumstances that involve crises and a high level of vulnerability, such as events related to natural disasters, armed conflicts, displacement, or other disruptive events (Cobham & Newnham, 2018; Cross, 2019; Hilhorst et al., 2019). The resources that are available in these environments are limited, complex issues are prevalent, and international aid is urgently needed. In humanitarian settings, medical care and shelter are often scarce, and individuals are exposed to a variety of risks. In these complex contexts, a comprehensive approach is needed that not only addresses immediate needs but also upholds human rights, respects cultural considerations, and fosters collaboration among governments, non-governmental organizations (NGOs), and international organizations (Väyrynen, 2022). In addition to providing timely and life-saving assistance, fostering resilience, and supporting recovery and rebuilding, the overarching goal is to ensure communities can recover and rebuild.

THE EMERGENCE OF INFORMAL MHEALTH

It is imperative that we state that informal mHealth is a subset of mHealth. Initially, mHealth was introduced to allow patients to have access to medical services without having to meet with any medical practitioner face-to-face (Barbosa et al., 2020; Sudhinaraset et al., 2013). The aim is to try to transcend the geographical barriers hindering adequate access to medical services. However, mHealth requires formal registration with a particular healthcare facility before one can enjoy its services (Källander et al., 2013; Schmidt et al., 2019). Not only this, but it also requires one to book an appointment with a medical practitioner. In developed countries, this has been perfectly utilized given their preparedness in terms of available information technology and telecommunications infrastructure. Developed countries also benefit from the positive ratio of medical personnel and the number of those seeking healthcare services. In developing countries, the use of mHealth faces many technology-based and social challenges that make accessing treatment using mobile devices very difficult (Mustapha et al., 2024). Developing countries also face the challenges of equal distribution of healthcare service provision infrastructure among urban, sub-urban, and rural settlements and of defining and aligning traditional and Western medicine (Adeniyi et al., 2020; Utulu & Mustapha, 2023). This gave rise to the emergence of informal mHealth, given that it does not have to deal with the obstacles, namely, formal registration, a trained physician, alignment between traditional medicine and Western medicine, etc., that are associated with mHealth. The strategic use of mobile devices by people to access medical information informally is called informal mHealth, which was given by research scholars in the field. Hampshire et al. (2021) defined informal Health as "the spontaneous or bottom-up use of phones by…patients for healthcare purposes" (p. 2). Informal mHealth simply means accessing medical information through the use of a smartphone to have solutions about a particular illness or to remain aware of medication prescriptions without involving a trained medical practitioner (Maharazu et al., 2022).

Machine Learning (ML) in Healthcare

As AI advances in healthcare, machine learning (ML) is at the heart of AI's impact on healthcare services, which empowers systems to learn from data and improve their performance. In this section, the various types of ML including supervised and unsupervised learning as well as reinforcement learning are discussed. In the field of healthcare delivery, ML is becoming increasingly important through a variety of approaches tailored to specific needs. The use of ML models in AI-powered informal mHealth applications is integral to various tasks such as predictive analytics, diagnostic support, and personalized treatment recommendations. For example, in the case of health records, supervised learning algorithms can identify patterns and predict disease outcomes, enabling preventive and early intervention measures. The use of unsupervised learning techniques like clustering can facilitate resource allocation and intervention targeting based on the health traits of a patient population. Using reinforcement learning algorithms, treatment strategies can be optimized over time to improve patient outcomes and ease healthcare delivery service.

Natural language processing (NLP) in the healthcare sector

The use of natural language processing in mHealth applications enables speech recognition, language understanding, and text analysis to be performed. The effectiveness of communication in healthcare depends on natural language processing (NLP), which serves as an essential tool for extracting insights from unstructured data (Zhou et al., 2022). Personalized responses and recommendations are possible with language-understanding models that interpret user queries and extract relevant information from text inputs. We explore an overview of how NLP facilitates medical record analysis, literature reviews, and patient communication by enabling machines to comprehend and interpret human language and perform such tasks. Like, in the case of individuals who are using informal mHealth to search for medical information and get responses through such technological channels of communication. This is one of the properties of informal mHealth, which helps individuals have access to accurate healthcare information without involving any professionals. For example, social media posts and patient reviews can be analyzed using text analysis techniques like sentiment analysis to gain insight into public health trends and patient satisfaction, thereby improving healthcare services and decision-making.

HEALTHCARE SERVICE NEEDS IN HUMANITARIAN CONTEXTS

Humanitarian context refers to situations and environments where individuals and communities are affected by crises, disasters, conflicts, or other emergencies, and they require external assistance to meet their basic needs and protect their well-being (Churruca-Muguruza, 2018; Whittaker et al., 2021). In such contexts, the usual structures and systems that support communities may be disrupted or overwhelmed, necessitating humanitarian aid and intervention.

- In humanitarian contexts, vulnerable populations are disproportionately affected, including refugees, internally displaced people, and marginalized groups (Churruca-Muguruza, 2018). When you explore the unique healthcare challenges these groups face, you will understand that crises are not uniform and often exacerbate existing disparities. Cultural sensitivity, language barriers, and trauma are all considered critical disparities associated with individuals within the humanitarian context.
- In order to develop inclusive and equitable healthcare solutions, we need to understand and address the healthcare disparities among vulnerable populations (World Health Organization, 2010). Diverse cultural beliefs, customs, and practices are necessary for healthcare practices to be respectful of and aligned with these populations. It is possible for language barriers to impede effective communication, resulting in a lack of informed consent and compromised quality of care. It is additionally imperative that healthcare strategies incorporate trauma-informed care due to the widespread impact of trauma on vulnerable populations.
- The commitment to addressing the specific healthcare needs of vulnerable populations becomes a moral and strategic imperative during humanitarian crises (Hunt et al., 2018). This commitment lays the groundwork for

compassionate and effective healthcare responses by acknowledging and dissecting the multifaceted challenges these populations face. In addition to providing immediate medical interventions, it promotes empowerment and uplift for vulnerable communities, fosters resilience, and ensures that healthcare solutions are accessible while respecting the inherent dignity and diversity of all people.

Given the above discussion, it is evident that healthcare encounters several challenges that make access to medical services difficult. This enhances the suitability of informal mHealth and makes it a suitable tool for bridging healthcare gaps in the humanitarian context. Harnessing the power of AI, people constrained in the humanitarian context could have access to medical services without having to rely on what the stakeholders provide for them as healthcare services. This is particularly important given the uniqueness of their situations.

CONVERGENCE OF INFORMAL MHEALTH AND AI IN HUMANITARIAN CONTEXT

The intersection of informal mHealth and AI represents a symbiotic relationship, in which the inherent accessibility of healthcare information amplifies the impact of AI on tackling healthcare concerns, especially in humanitarian contexts. Individuals are connected to personalized healthcare recommendations using informal mHealth platforms (Hampshire et al., 2021). Despite this, this intersection goes beyond geographical barriers, enabling sophisticated healthcare capabilities to reach areas with limited or nonexistent formal healthcare infrastructure. Based on this background, we can understand how the fusion of informal mHealth and AI can reshape healthcare dynamics, especially in humanitarian contexts. In the field of humanitarian healthcare globally, organizations and partnerships have emerged to harness the power of technology for healthcare delivery and services (Gardner et al., 2007). Through collaborations between tech companies and NGOs, scalable, adaptable solutions can be rapidly deployed during crises. A collaborative, comprehensive approach is necessary to address complex healthcare challenges in humanitarian settings, and these initiatives emphasize the importance of leveraging technology, not as a standalone solution.

In addition, as stated earlier, some may have concerns about data privacy and infrastructure that need to be addressed. To address these challenges, it requires collaboration with stakeholders, which include governments, healthcare professionals, IT companies, informal mHealth researchers, and informal mHealth users, to establish clear guiding principles and standards, develop mechanisms for safeguarding data privacy and security, and ensure ethical and strategic use of informal mHealth technologies among individuals. However, data privacy within AI-enabled informal mHealth applications necessitates the deployment of robust technologies and methodologies to safeguard sensitive healthcare information, although not all websites and applications require such sensitive information.

INFORMAL MHEALTH PRACTICES WITHIN HUMANITARIAN CONTEXTS

In humanitarian contexts, technology plays an increasingly important role in shaping responsive and adaptive healthcare solutions in humanitarian crises, where chaos, displacement, and resource scarcity combine, among other health-related issues (Dubey et al., 2022). We begin with a brief overview of informal mHealth practices within the special context of humanitarian relief efforts. In the face of crises ranging from armed conflicts to natural disasters and outbreaks of infectious diseases, mobile technologies are emerging as a transformative force, while healthcare systems are struggling to overcome the challenges. Healthcare delivery is increasingly facilitated by mobile phones, smartphones, and widespread applications, which are ubiquitous in resource-constrained settings (Goldbach et al., 2014). A diverse range of informal mHealth practices have emerged in this dynamic environment, ranging from grassroots community-led interventions to sophisticated mobile applications and healthcare-related platforms.

In addition, these practices extend to the use of wearable devices, mobile apps, and sensor-based technology as means of monitoring and securing health (Mahmood et al., 2022). This supports early detection, surveillance, and response to health-related issues. However, as part of informal mHealth practices, individuals are provided and empowered with personalized information about treatment plans and medication schedules through mobile technology, such as educational apps, videos, and interactive AI apps (chatbot). Social media, messaging apps, and community support platforms play an important role in community-driven health initiatives in humanitarian contexts, fostering peer support, and disseminating localized health information (local remedies) through social media channels. The use of communication apps, location-based services, and crowd-sourced data in emergency response coordination enables healthcare services, aid organizations, and affected communities to coordinate more efficiently. Informal mHealth practices within humanitarian contexts leverage the versatility of mobile technologies to provide accessible and timely healthcare solutions, empowering individuals and communities in challenging and resource-constrained settings.

The Prevalence of Mobile Technologies in the Humanitarian Contexts

Humanitarian contexts are undergoing a paradigm shift as a result of the prevalence and adoption of mobile technologies in how healthcare services are conceptualized and provided (Kabra et al., 2017). The ubiquity of mobile phones and smartphones underscores their pervasive influence even in environments marked by limited resources, scarcity, and infrastructure challenges. In situations where formal healthcare infrastructure is compromised, mobile technologies are indispensable as personal, portable, and connective tools. Individuals are equipped with technological lifelines that transcend geographic barriers, bringing improved healthcare access to the fingertips of those in need, whether they are located in bustling urban centers or in remote and underserved regions affected by humanitarian crises (Gardner et al., 2007). It empowers individuals and communities to actively participate in their health and well-being with the emergence of mobile technologies as ubiquitous tools of connectivity and accessing information, especially when facing crises which disrupt healthcare services.

As a result of disasters or conflicts where physical infrastructure may be severely damaged, mobile technologies are emerging as resilient channels for facilitating communications, accessing healthcare information, and providing healthcare services. Health conditions, resource needs, and emergency response coordination can all be quickly updated through basic mobile phone use, facilitating direct communication through the use of that mobile technology to get all healthcare information and solutions (De Jongh et al., 2012). Furthermore, the increasing popularity of smartphones makes it possible to deploy sophisticated apps that extend beyond communication to feature health monitoring and educational health information. Mobile technologies, as a result, are ubiquitous not only due to their accessibility but also because of their transformative capabilities in overcoming geographical and logistical barriers, bringing healthcare closer and more accessible to the heart of humanitarian matters through mobile technologies.

Bridge Gaps in Healthcare Access

The imperatives (necessity) of healthcare access become starkly apparent within the tumultuous landscape of humanitarian crises, and it is in this context that informal mHealth practices play a transformative role in bridging critical gaps (Heymann et al., 2015). A crisis can disrupt supply chains, undermine infrastructure, and result in mass displacements of populations, all of which pose formidable challenges to formal systems of healthcare delivery. The emergence of informal mHealth practices in this context can be seen as catalysts for change, capable of overcoming barriers and offering a lifeline to communities in desperate need of healthcare services. In addition to delivering medical interventions, these practices serve as conduits to establish a resilient healthcare ecosystem that can adapt to crisis-specific needs.

INTEGRATING AI AND INFORMAL MHEALTH IN THE HUMANITARIAN CONTEXT

Integrating AI-driven informal mHealth solutions with the unique challenges faced by people in humanitarian contexts can have a profound impact. The benefits of integrating AI with informal mHealth have the potential to provide transformative welfare benefits for healthcare access, most especially in resource-restrained areas like humanitarian contexts. The combination of AI algorithms with informal mHealth apps improves diagnostic precision, enabling timely interventions and personalized healthcare. AI and informal mHealth enhance healthcare delivery efficiency and accessibility. It has the

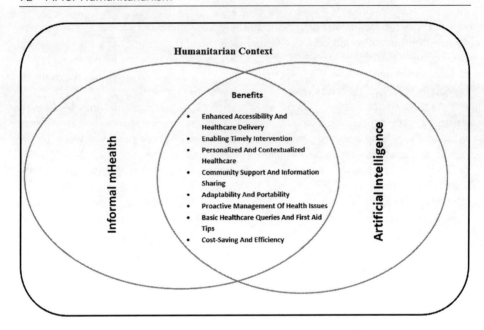

FIGURE 6.1   Integration of informal mHealth and AI in the humanitarian context.

benefit of cost reductions. AI-driven chatbots and virtual health assistants can provide immediate and accessible healthcare information and solutions, reducing the burden on formal healthcare systems. When integrated with informal mHealth, predictive analytics from AI empower individuals to manage their health proactively (see Figure 6.1).

Healthcare Information Accessible in Crisis Situations

In humanitarian contexts where access to formal healthcare infrastructure is limited, AI-powered chatbots and virtual health assistants can provide accessible health information (Efe, 2022; Xiao et al., 2023). AI health tools can provide guidance on basic health queries, provide first-aid tips, and disseminate information about prevalent health issues, allowing individuals in crisis situations to make informed decisions regarding their health and well-being.

Predictive and Analytics for Disease Surveillance

Humanitarian crises present significant threats to vulnerable populations due to disease outbreaks (Poole et al., 2020). Predictive analytics can help address these threats. Predictive analytics powered by AI can analyze health data from mobile devices to identify potential disease hotspots and prevent diseases from spreading (Sagner et al., 2017, p. 4). In resource-constrained environments, this proactive approach is crucial for managing health risks.

Tailored Health Education in Diverse Cultural Contexts AI-Powered

Humanitarian settings can provide tailored health education by using AI-powered content delivery technology (Efe, 2022). Personalized health education content can consider language preferences, cultural sensitivities, and specific health challenges faced by different communities. Health information in crisis situations is relevant, accessible, and respectful of the unique needs of individuals.

Community-Based Support Networks

AI applications designed for informal mHealth have the potential to facilitate community-based support networks. In humanitarian contexts, where communities often come together to resolve challenges, AI can enhance knowledge sharing. Community members can share health insights about new improvements, adopt health strategies, and localize information through AI-powered platforms, fostering a sense of solidarity and resilience (Ismail & Kumar, 2021).

Emergency Responses and Resource Optimization

Analysis of real-time data from mHealth records, environmental factors, and population movements can assist AI algorithms in optimizing emergency response efforts (Agbehadji et al., 2020). Streamlining emergency interventions and ensuring rapid aid delivery are enabled by this efficient allocation of healthcare resources.

By marrying AI-driven informal mHealth solutions with the specific needs of people in humanitarian contexts, we create a dynamic and responsive healthcare ecosystem. These solutions not only address the immediate challenges posed by crises but also empower individuals and communities to actively participate in their healthcare, fostering resilience and inclusivity in the face of adversity.

IMPLICATIONS OF THE RESEARCH MODEL

The integration of informal mHealth and AI in the humanitarian context research model carries significant implications, as it can lead to a variety of benefits that collectively enhance the effectiveness and responsiveness of healthcare delivery in crises and can be applied by other groups of individuals whose situation is constrained by circumstantial factors. The collaborative synergy between informal mHealth and AI improves access to healthcare, especially in places with disruptions to formal healthcare infrastructure. As a result of this integration, healthcare service delivery is significantly improved, as individuals can benefit from remote consultations, health monitoring, and real-time dissemination of critical health information, especially in areas where formal health-care infrastructure is lacking. This allows individuals to access timely and essential healthcare support by leveraging the adaptability of mobile technologies powered by AI, transcending geographical boundaries, and facilitating timely healthcare interventions in resource-constrained environments.

However, it leverages informal mHealth practices infused with AI to foster community support and information sharing. Communities can share health-related information, offer peer support, and collectively navigate healthcare challenges through social media, messaging apps, and AI-enabled platforms. In addition to highlighting the adaptability and portability of healthcare solutions, the study also promotes proactive management of health issues through predictive analytics and personalized health insights that enable individuals to predict potential health risks and mitigate them. Informal mHealth, integrated with AI, facilitates the dissemination of basic healthcare queries and first-aid tips. As a result of mobile applications and AI-powered virtual assistants, individuals have instant access to the information they need to address common health issues and administer basic first aid. Informal mHealth combined with AI makes operations more efficient and cost-effective. This research optimizes resource allocation through AI analytics, reduces the need for physical infrastructure, and enhances the efficiency of healthcare delivery, ensuring both cost-effectiveness and efficiency for humanitarian healthcare interventions. Thus, the humanitarian context research model incorporates informal mHealth and AI to address immediate healthcare needs while at the same time establishing a foundation for sustainable, adaptable, and community-centered healthcare solutions in the face of disaster.

CONCLUSION

In conclusion, the study shows the profound impact of informal mHealth practices and AI applications within humanitarian contexts. These practices play a pivotal role in bridging healthcare gaps, strengthening communities with healthcare information, and contributing to resilient healthcare solutions by analyzing their prevalence, adaptability, and transformative potential. It becomes evident as the analysis unfolds that the integration of mobile technologies in humanitarian healthcare is not just a technological advancement; it is a fundamental paradigm shift that places adaptive, community-centric, and responsive healthcare at the heart of crisis response. As a result, informal mHealth practices and AI applications are adaptable and responsive to changing circumstances, which emphasizes their dynamic nature. These practices embody a living, evolving response to the complex challenges presented, whether it is the agility of community-led initiatives responding quickly to emerging health threats or the technological versatility of mobile applications adapting to the changing needs of crisis situations. In the face of adversity, they embrace flexibility and innovation instead of rigid healthcare protocols.

This review has demonstrated that informal mHealth practices and AI applications in humanitarian healthcare go beyond technological advancements. This is a paradigm shift away from conventional models and is based on a more responsive, community-centric approach that is fully aligned with the evolving challenges of crises, among other issues. These practices offer a roadmap for shaping more resilient, inclusive, and effective healthcare responses in the dynamic context of humanitarian crises through adaptability and community engagement. Humanitarian crises provide a dynamic landscape of healthcare delivery that can be shaped to be more resilient, inclusive, and effective within humanitarian contexts. Providing humanitarian healthcare in the future requires not only technological innovation but also the empowerment of communities and healthcare providers working together to build a healthcare ecosystem that thrives in difficult circumstances. This can be achieved with the use of informal mHealth properties such as AI.

REFERENCES

Adeniyi, E. A., Awotunde, J. B., Ogundokun, R. O., Kolawole, P. O., Abiodun, M. K., & Adeniyi, A. A. (2020). Mobile health application and COVID-19: Opportunities and challenges. *Journal of Critical Reviews*, *7*(15), 3481–3488.

Agbehadji, I. E., Awuzie, B. O., Ngowi, A. B., & Millham, R. C. (2020). Review of big data analytics, artificial intelligence and nature-inspired computing models towards accurate detection of COVID-19 pandemic cases and contact tracing. *International Journal of Environmental Research and Public Health*, *17*(15), 5330.

Barbosa, F., Voss, G., & Delerue Matos, A. (2020). Health impact of providing informal care in Portugal. *BMC Geriatrics*, *20*(1), 1–9.

Christie, H. L., Bartels, S. L., Boots, L. M. M., Tange, H. J., Verhey, F. R. J., & de Vugt, M. E. (2018). A systematic review on the implementation of eHealth interventions for informal caregivers of people with dementia. *Internet Interventions*, *13*, 51–59. https://doi.org/10.1016/j.invent.2018.07.002

Churruca-Muguruza, C. (2018). The changing context of humanitarian action: Key challenges and issues. In H-J. Heintze & P. Thielbörger (Eds.), *International Humanitarian Action: NOHA Textbook* (pp. 3–18). Springer, Cham. https://doi.org/10.1007/978-3-319-14454-2_1

Cobham, V. E., & Newnham, E. A. (2018). Trauma and parenting: Considering humanitarian crisis contexts. In M. R. Sanders & A. Morawska (Eds.), *Handbook of Parenting and Child Development across the Lifespan* (pp. 143–169). Cham: Springer International Publishing. https://doi.org/10.1007/978-3-319-94598-9_7

Cross, N. R. (2019). *Overlapping Vulnerabilities: The Impacts of Climate Change on Humanitarian Needs*. Oslo: Norwegian Red Cross. https://www.rodekors.no/globalassets/_english-pages/general-reports/norwegian-redcross_report_overlapping-vulnerabilities.pdf

De Jongh, T., Gurol-Urganci, I., Vodopivec-Jamsek, V., Car, J., & Atun, R. (2012). Mobile phone messaging for facilitating self-management of long-term illnesses. *Cochrane Database of Systematic Reviews*, *12*. https://www.cochranelibrary.com/cdsr/doi/10.1002/14651858.CD007459.pub2/abstract

Dubey, R., Bryde, D. J., Dwivedi, Y. K., Graham, G., & Foropon, C. (2022). Impact of artificial intelligence-driven big data analytics culture on agility and resilience in humanitarian supply chain: A practice-based view. *International Journal of Production Economics*, *250*, 108618.

Efe, A. (2022). A review on risk reduction potentials of artificial intelligence in humanitarian aid sector. İnsan ve Sosyal Bilimler Dergisi, 5(2), 184–205. https://doi.org/10.53048/johass.1189814

European Commission Joint Research Centre. (2020). *Artificial Intelligence in Medicine and Healthcare: Applications, Availability and Societal Impact.* Ispra: Publications Office. https://data.europa.eu/doi/10.2760/047666

Gardner, C. A., Acharya, T., & Yach, D. (2007). Technological and social innovation: A unifying new paradigm for global health. *Health Affairs, 26*(4), 1052–1061. https://doi.org/10.1377/hlthaff.26.4.1052

Glenton, C., Nabukenya, J., Agarwal, S., Meltzer, M., Mukendi, E., Lwanga, I. N., Namitala, J., Reddy, S., Royston, G., & Tamrat, T. (2023a). Using an online community of practice to explore the informal use of mobile phones by health workers. *Oxford Open Digital Health, 1,* oqac003.

Glenton, C., Paulsen, E., Agarwal, S., Gopinathan, U., Johansen, M., Kyaddondo, D., Munabi-Babigumira, S., Nabukenya, J., Nakityo, I., Namitala, J., Neumark, T., Nsangi, A., Pakenham-Walsh, N. M., Rashidian, A., Royston, G., Sewankambo, N., Tamrat, T., & Lewin, S. (2023b). Healthcare workers' informal uses of mobile devices to support their work: A qualitative evidence synthesis. *Cochrane Database of Systematic Reviews, 2023*(7), 18. https://doi.org/10.1002/14651858.CD015705

Goldbach, H., Chang, A. Y., Kyer, A., Ketshogileng, D., Taylor, L., Chandra, A., Dacso, M., Kung, S.-J., Rijken, T., & Fontelo, P. (2014). Evaluation of generic medical information accessed via mobile phones at the point of care in resource-limited settings. *Journal of the American Medical Informatics Association, 21*(1), 37–42.

Hampshire, K., Mwase-Vuma, T., Alemu, K., Abane, A., Munthali, A., Awoke, T., Mariwah, S., Chamdimba, E., Owusu, S. A., & Robson, E. (2021a). Informal mhealth at scale in Africa: Opportunities and challenges. *World Development, 140,* 105257.

Hampshire, K., Mwase-Vuma, T., Alemu, K., Abane, A., Munthali, A., Awoke, T., Mariwah, S., Chamdimba, E., Owusu, S. A., Robson, E., Castelli, M., Shkedy, Z., Shawa, N., Abel, J., & Kasim, A. (2021b). Informal mhealth at scale in Africa: Opportunities and challenges. *World Development, 140,* 105257. https://doi.org/10.1016/j.worlddev.2020.105257

Heymann, D. L., Chen, L., Takemi, K., Fidler, D. P., Tappero, J. W., Thomas, M. J., Kenyon, T. A., Frieden, T. R., Yach, D., & Nishtar, S. (2015). Global health security: The wider lessons from the west African ebola virus disease epidemic. *The Lancet, 385*(9980), 1884–1901.

Hilhorst, D., Mena, R., van Voorst, R., Desportes, I., & Melis, S. (2019). Disaster risk governance and humanitarian aid in different conflict scenarios. *Global Assessment Report on Disaster Risk Reduction (GAR 2019),* 49.

Hunt, M., Chénier, A., Bezanson, K., Nouvet, E., Bernard, C., De Laat, S., Krishnaraj, G., & Schwartz, L. (2018). Moral experiences of humanitarian health professionals caring for patients who are dying or likely to die in a humanitarian crisis. *Journal of International Humanitarian Action, 3*(1), 12. https://doi.org/10.1186/s41018-018-0040-9

Ismail, A., & Kumar, N. (2021). AI in global health: The view from the front lines. In *Proceedings of the 2021 CHI Conference on Human Factors in Computing Systems* (pp. 1–21). New York: ACM. https://doi.org/10.1145/3411764.3445130

Kabra, G., Ramesh, A., Akhtar, P., & Dash, M. K. (2017). Understanding behavioural intention to use information technology: Insights from humanitarian practitioners. *Telematics and Informatics, 34*(7), 1250–1261.

Källander, K., Tibenderana, J. K., Akpogheneta, O. J., Strachan, D. L., Hill, Z., ten Asbroek, A. H., Conteh, L., Kirkwood, B. R., & Meek, S. R. (2013). Mobile health (mHealth) approaches and lessons for increased performance and retention of community health workers in low-and middle-income countries: A review. *Journal of Medical Internet Research, 15*(1), e17.

Kuo, C.-L. (2023). Revolutionizing healthcare paradigms: The integral role of artificial intelligence in advancing diagnostic and treatment modalities. *International Microsurgery Journal (IMJ)*. https://scitemed.com/article/4267/scitemed-imj-2023-00177

Legido-Quigley, H., & Asgari-Jirhandeh, N. (2018). *Resilient and People-Centred Health Systems: Progress, Challenges and Future Directions in Asia*. Geneva: World Health Organization. Regional Office for South-East Asia. https://apps.who.int/iris/handle/10665/276045

Maharazu, M. K., Sabo, S. B., & Utulu, S. C. A. (2022). Community of practice theory approach to understanding factors influencing informal M-health use among janitors in an IT-rich context. In *UK Academy for Information Systems Conference Proceedings*. Oxford. https://aisel.aisnet.org/ukais2022/15/

Mahmood, A., Kim, H., Kedia, S., & Dillon, P. (2022). Wearable activity tracker use and physical activity among informal caregivers in the United States: Quantitative study. *JMIR mHealth and uHealth, 10*(11), e40391.

Mustapha, B. M., Utulu, S. C. A., & Tyndall, J. A. (2024). A smartphone-based surveillance system for acute flaccid paralysis: A technology frames perspective. *The Electronic Journal of Information Systems in Developing Countries, 90*(1), e12295. https://doi.org/10.1002/isd2.12295

Poole, D. N., Escudero, D. J., Gostin, L. O., Leblang, D., & Talbot, E. A. (2020). Responding to the COVID-19 pandemic in complex humanitarian crises. *International Journal for Equity in Health, 19*(1), 41. https://doi.org/10.1186/s12939-020-01162-y

Sagner, M., McNeil, A., Puska, P., Auffray, C., Price, N. D., Hood, L., Lavie, C. J., Han, Z.-G., Chen, Z., & Brahmachari, S. K. (2017). The P4 health spectrum–A predictive, preventive, personalized and participatory continuum for promoting healthspan. *Progress in Cardiovascular Diseases, 59*(5), 506–521.

Sam, S. (2021). Informal mobile phone use by marginalised groups in a plural health system to bridge healthcare gaps in Sierra Leone. *Information Development, 37*(3), 467–482. https://doi.org/10.1177/0266666920932992

Schmidt, M., Schmidt, S. A. J., Adelborg, K., Sundbøll, J., Laugesen, K., Ehrenstein, V., & Sørensen, H. T. (2019). The Danish health care system and epidemiological research: From health care contacts to database records. *Clinical Epidemiology, 11*, 563–591. https://doi.org/10.2147/CLEP.S179083

Sharma, R. (2023). The transformative power of AI as future GPTs in propelling society into a new era of advancement. *IEEE Engineering Management Review*. https://ieeexplore.ieee.org/abstract/document/10250949/

Sudhinaraset, M., Ingram, M., Lofthouse, H. K., & Montagu, D. (2013). What is the role of informal healthcare providers in developing countries? A systematic review. *PloS One, 8*(2), e54978.

Utulu, S. C. A., & Mustapha, B. (2023). Reconceptualizing the indigenous peoples in the era of digital disruption. In W. Leal Filho, I. R. Abubakar, I. Da Silva, R. Pretorius, & K. Tarabieh (Eds.), *SDGs in Africa and the Middle East Region* (pp. 1–24). Cham: Springer International Publishing. https://doi.org/10.1007/978-3-030-91260-4_13-1

Väyrynen, R. (2022). Complex humanitarian emergencies: Concepts and issues. In R. Väyrynen (Ed.), *Raimo Väyrynen: A Pioneer in International Relations, Scholarship and Policy-Making* (Vol. 28, pp. 301–343). Cham: Springer International Publishing. https://doi.org/10.1007/978-3-031-13627-6_12

Whittaker, G., Wood, G. A., Oggero, G., Kett, M., & Lange, K. (2021). Meeting AT needs in humanitarian crises: The current state of provision. *Assistive Technology, 33*(sup1), S3–S16.

World Health Organization. (2010). *How Health Systems Can Address Health Inequities Linked to Migration and Ethnicity*. Geneva: World Health Organization. https://apps.who.int/iris/handle/10665/345463

World Health Organization. (2022). *World Report on the Health of Refugees and Migrants*. Geneva: World Health Organization. https://apps.who.int/iris/bitstream/handle/10665/360404/9789240054462-eng.pdf

Xiao, Z., Liao, Q. V., Zhou, M., Grandison, T., & Li, Y. (2023). Powering an AI chatbot with expert sourcing to support credible health information access. In *Proceedings of the 28th International Conference on Intelligent User Interfaces* (pp. 2–18). Sydney. https://doi.org/10.1145/3581641.3584031

Zhou, B., Yang, G., Shi, Z., & Ma, S. (2022). Natural language processing for smart health-care. *IEEE Reviews in Biomedical Engineering*. https://ieeexplore.ieee.org/abstract/document/9904944/

AI in Healthcare

Social-Legal Impact and Innovations in Digital Hospitals and mHealth

Bhupinder Singh and Christian Kaunert

INTRODUCTION

Artificial intelligence (AI) has the potential to bring in a new era of personalized medicine by creating treatment plans that are unique to each patient based on their genetic composition, medical history, and lifestyle choices. A major shift in the direction of medicine and healthcare is occurring at a time when these two fields are becoming more and more entwined (Bhatt et al., 2022). This section explores the nexus between mobile health (mHealth), AI, and radiography, dissecting the intricacies of these developments through an analysis of their unique traits, historical evolution, and future directions. This chapter offers a comprehensive examination of current conditions and potential future developments, ranging from the democratizing potential of mHealth to the analytical capabilities of AI and the evolutionary transition of medical imaging from analog to digital formats. This might completely change the healthcare industry and do away with the "one size fits all" mentality. AI-powered remote patient monitoring and telemedicine are expanding the scope of healthcare delivery (Singh & Kaunert, 2024). Without leaving their homes, patients can get prescription refills, medical advice, and chronic disease monitoring. This is especially important for people who live in rural areas with little access to medical facilities (Deniz-Garcia et al., 2023).

Maintaining patient trust is crucial when using AI in healthcare because it handles sensitive patient data. Therefore, data privacy and security must be guaranteed. The use of AI in healthcare necessitates a review of existing laws and the draft of new rules and regulations. It investigates the intersection of these domains, illuminating AI's ground-breaking function in enhancing mHealth capabilities via developments in medical imaging. Much of the debate is devoted to a thorough examination of cutting-edge applications and the moral and legal issues that accompany them (Singh & Kaunert, 2024). Subsequently, a prospective analysis is conducted regarding anticipated technological advancements, their possible consequences, and the pivotal role played by politicians and healthcare executives in steering this revolutionary path. To handle the special opportunities and problems presented by AI, such as data ownership and accountability for AI malpractice, legislators must create new laws (Istepanian & AlAnzi, 2020). Therefore, ensuring universal access to AI-powered healthcare is vital, irrespective of an individual's socioeconomic background or geographic location (Sharma et al., 2022). To give their informed permission, patients must be made aware of how AI is being used in their treatment. Sustaining patient autonomy requires openness and education.

Telemedicine enabled by AI has the potential to close healthcare disparities both domestically and internationally. It can improve global health outcomes by making healthcare more accessible in underserved and remote locations. AI can improve and repair the current healthcare infrastructure, relieving pressure on the systems and enhancing patient care. It can boost the effectiveness of healthcare delivery and optimize resource allocation (Sharma & Kshetri, 2020). A fascinating look at the direction that medicine is headed is provided by the combination of AI and healthcare. There is a bright, difficult, and promising future for a better society. The prospects and opportunities AI offers the healthcare industry are highlighted in this paper, ranging from improved patient care to personalized treatment regimens and increased diagnostic accuracy. To highlight the revolutionary potential of this technological trinity, a comprehensive synthesis pulls all the strands from earlier parts together. It is designed to be an interesting investigation, a critical analysis, and a road map for the future as it works together to steer toward a technologically enabled healthcare period (Mbunge et al., 2021). It also looks at how AI may revitalize and mend the healthcare system, as well as the significant effects it will have on social, legal, and ethical facets of healthcare (Singh, 2024).

Background of Study

Healthcare systems are facing problems due to a rise in patient demand, the frequency of chronic illnesses, and resource constraints (Dabla et al., 2021). Simultaneously, there is a profusion of data across all healthcare settings due to the increasing use of digital health technology (Galetsi et al., 2023). If used wisely, this abundance of information may allow medical professionals to concentrate on comprehending the underlying causes of diseases and evaluating the efficacy of therapies and preventative measures. This highlights how crucial it is that lawmakers, politicians, and decision-makers are aware of these developments. There are numerous professionals, such as clinical entrepreneurs and computer and data scientists, who contend that AI, especially machine learning (ML), is essential to the reform of healthcare (Singh, 2023).

Objectives of this chapter

This chapter has the following objectives:

- To examine AI integration in mHealth and digital hospitals.
- To analyze the effects of the usability of AI in healthcare on society and the law.
- To explore the potential and challenges which AI brings for mHealth and develop cutting-edge healthcare systems.

AI IN HEALTHCARE: THE RISE OF AI

AI is the capacity of a computer program to carry out operations related to human intellect, such as learning and reasoning. AI systems learn and adapt through exposure to training data, in contrast to classical computer algorithms that adhere to preset rules. AI has the potential to revolutionize healthcare by providing useful insights from the massive amounts of digital data produced during the provision of healthcare (Istepanian, 2022). In its most basic form, AI refers to a machine's ability to simulate human cognitive processes including understanding, learning, solving problems, and making decisions. The objective of this branch of computer science is to create intelligent machines that can mimic human behavior and carry out a wide range of activities with accuracy and efficiency, from straightforward acts to complex problem-solving.

There are two types of AI: general AI, which can accomplish any intellectual work that a person can, and narrow AI, which is designed for certain tasks like speech recognition. The current period is mostly characterized by narrow AI, which is the use of specialized AI technologies in specific areas, such as image processing, speech recognition in virtual assistants, or customer service utilizing chatbots. The hardware and software are frequently used in healthcare AI solutions. The key component is algorithms, especially those built on artificial neural networks (ANNs). ANNs use weighted communication channels to discover complex correlations in big datasets, imitating the interconnected network of neurons in the human brain. By using training to fix algorithmic flaws, ML increases prediction model accuracy (Seetharam et al., 2019).

Understanding mHealth

mHealth refers to the use of wireless and mobile technology to promote health goals. The definition of electronic health (eHealth), as provided by the Global Observatory for eHealth, is "medical and public health practice supported by mobile devices, such as mobile phones, patient monitoring devices, personal digital assistants, and other wireless devices", which creates new opportunities for receiving healthcare services. Real-time data gathering, location-independent access to healthcare services, prompt healthcare interventions, and improved patient adherence to prescriptions and guidance are among the key characteristics of mHealth. The capacity of mHealth to integrate a wide range of applications, such as wearable technologies, telemedicine, electronic health records (EHRs), healthcare analytics, and Internet of Things (IoT) applications connected to health, is indicative of its versatility.

Combining real-time and longitudinal data, mHealth offers a comprehensive health viewpoint and encourages a personalized and patient-centered approach to healthcare. mHealth lessens the load on healthcare systems by providing remote patient monitoring and diagnostics, which also cuts down on needless hospital visits. By offering customized, predictive, and preventative treatment, mHealth has the potential to completely transform the healthcare industry through the integration of AI and ML algorithms. The use of mHealth confronts obstacles pertaining to privacy, security, interoperability, and regulatory concerns despite its potentially revolutionary potential (Karboub et al., 2019).

Applications of AI in Healthcare

An important area of AI-driven health research is the examination of data from EHRs. If the database and underlying information technology system are unable to stop the spread of inconsistent or poor-quality data, then the usefulness of this type of data may be compromised. However, the incorporation of AI into EHRs presents chances for clinical care optimization, quality improvement, and scientific research (Sharma & Singh, 2022). Instead of following the traditional route of scientific publication, guideline creation, and the development of clinical support tools, appropriately developed and well-trained AI, equipped with sufficient data, can unveil valuable insights into clinical best practices from EHRs. By closely examining patterns in clinical procedures seen in EHRs data, AI may also help develop novel models for healthcare delivery (Gunasekeran et al., 2021).

AI is expected to expedite and simplify the pharmaceutical development process. Robotics and models covering genetic targets, medications, organs, illnesses, progression, pharmacokinetics, safety, and effectiveness are some of the ways AI can change the labor- and resource-intensive nature of drug development. Enhancing efficiency and cost-effectiveness is the goal of using AI in the drug research and development process. The identification of a lead molecule through AI does not ensure the automatic development of a safe and effective therapy, like traditional drug studies. AI has proven useful in the past in identifying potential medicines for diseases like the Ebola virus (Kakhi et al., 2022). An important result of AI in healthcare is that more people can now receive medical treatments, especially those who live in underserved or rural areas where there aren't many medical experts or specialists nearby. Although some of the developments in telemedicine have slowed down, virtual healthcare services are still a vital option for patients who may find it difficult to physically attend appointments. This is evidenced by the recent spike in telemedicine.

PROSPECTS OF AI IN HEALTH

AI's impact on healthcare has grown dramatically influencing the creation of software used by healthcare facilities as well as the use of wearables and sensors in patient care. Recent years have seen more technological advancement than anybody could have predicted, especially in the field of patient-centered healthcare. Technology is extremely important because it helps to improve and streamline human labor, increasing its efficiency. Technology is essential in minimizing errors that are a result of human error, especially in the healthcare industry. For instance, the results of surgical treatments performed by medical personnel may be dangerous and ineffective if technology weren't used. ML is an application of AI that gives systems the capacity to learn from experience and get better on their own without the need for explicit programming. ML is based on the core idea that computers should be able to acquire data and learn on their own. ML is generally divided into three categories: reinforcement learning, where an agent learns decision-making through interactions with its environment, receiving rewards for positive actions, and penalties for negative ones. Supervised learning is where algorithms are trained on labeled data. Unsupervised learning is where algorithms learn from unlabeled data to uncover hidden patterns or intrinsic structures. AI is the computerized imitation of human intellect, designed to mimic human cognitive functions. AI has the potential to improve patient diagnosis, treatment, and prevention, which ultimately leads to improvements in clinical decision-making (Condry & Quan, 2021).

Healthcare workers are finding that they have more time for patient evaluation and sickness and ailment diagnosis as technology takes over more and more critical tasks. AI is accelerating processes and, therefore, saving medical facilities important hours of productivity. Time is money in every sector, and AI can drastically cut important expenditures. The administrative tasks including account filing, review, and resolution account for a large amount of these needless costs. Determining medical necessity is another area that needs improvement (Berrouiguet et al., 2019). To accurately determine medical necessity, traditional approaches involve hours of evaluating patient records and information. The newer technologies that help doctors analyze hospital situations and avoid rejections are natural language processing (NLP) and deep learning (DL) algorithms. By freeing up valuable productivity hours and resources, medical staff members have more time to interact with and support patients.

CHALLENGES OF AI IN HEALTHCARE

The application of AI in healthcare poses questions regarding data security and accuracy, despite the possible advantages (see Figure 7.1). Errors in the high-stakes healthcare industry can have catastrophic repercussions for susceptible patients.

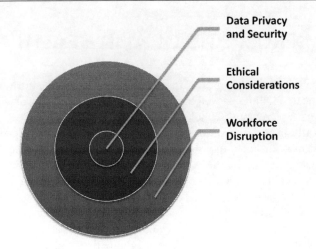

Data Privacy
and Security

Ethical
Considerations

Workforce
Disruption

FIGURE 7.1   Challenges of AI in healthcare delivery.

If handled well, AI and physician collaboration can be quite beneficial. AI has the potential to improve healthcare in several ways, including diagnostics, drug development, epidemiology, tailored treatment, and operational efficiency (Cingolani et al., 2023). It may also serve as a medical decision guide and offer evidence-based management. However to stop the harm caused by unethical action, ethical concerns are essential, and a strong governance structure is required. After being considered a possibility for the future, ML-healthcare applications (ML-HCAs) are now a reality because of the Food and Drug Administration (FDA) clearance of autonomous AI diagnostic systems based on ML. These systems don't require explicit programming; instead, they use algorithms to learn from large datasets and provide predictions (Amjad et al., 2023).

Data Privacy and Security

AI systems are susceptible to sudden and severe malfunctions when conditions or the environment change. AI may quickly move from extremely intelligent to incredibly naïve in a matter of seconds. AI bias cannot be eliminated; all AI systems have intrinsic limits (Chakraborty, 2022). It is imperative that human decision-makers understand these constraints and that the system be built to support their requirements (Denecke et al., 2019). A system that is mostly accurate might cause practitioners in disciplines like medical diagnosis and treatment to become complacent and disregard skill maintenance and work satisfaction (Bhaskar et al., 2020). There's a chance that the outcomes of decision-support systems may be blindly accepted without considering their limits. This has happened in the criminal justice system when decisions have been made based on erroneous risk assessments (Solomon & Rudin, 2020).

Ethical Considerations

Although AI-related actions may not be entirely covered by legal frameworks, people who create and use the technology are ultimately responsible. AI is expected to coexist with or maybe replace current systems despite ethical concerns, bringing in a new age of AI-driven healthcare (Asan et al., 2023). The rights of children are also a concern, since they may be subjected to discrimination based on data gathered during their early years. When people share their data with third parties, they increase the risk of data abuse, such as cyber theft and inadvertent exposure. The data may be used by governments and intelligence services for population tracking, social and political monitoring, security, and social control enhancement. Businesses may use and sell health and other personal data for marketing and other purposes; thus, they have a financial interest in it (Hamberger et al., 2022). Therefore, people's dignity and mental health may be impacted by medical providers' access to and use of patient data by other parties, such as businesses and governmental organizations. So, refusing to accept AI might be seen as immoral and unscientific (Baker & Xiang, 2023).

Human rights can also be violated by the improper or problematic use of personal data, including the right to be free from arbitrary or illegal interference with one's "privacy, family, home, or correspondence". These problems make us wonder who, what, and under what circumstances should be able to use patient and demographic data (Awotunde et al., 2022). The other set of issues is protecting the privacy of medical records and other personal information, as well as the possibility that it may be used for marketing and other reasons other than medicine. Large datasets that contain a variety of information, such as information on illness risks, lifestyle, mental health, family dynamics, sexual orientation, and other sensitive data, are a major component of AI and ML. Real-time data, such as user location and activity information, is generated by the introduction of new mobile devices, tracking applications, wearables, implants, and AI-powered prostheses (Hunt et al., 2020). There are justifiable worries that using this data might lead to privacy infringements and discrimination based on things like a person's health state or potential health problems in the future.

Workforce Disruption

AI may improve the administration of health services, and it is anticipated that AI will soon be included in everyday clinical treatment (Chattu, 2021). In the meantime, concerns have been expressed about the moral and legal ramifications of integrating AI into healthcare (Bhatt & Chakraborty, 2021). These worries include things, like the possibility of bias, the opaqueness of some AI algorithms, privacy issues with the data used to train AI models, and the security and accountability, involved in using AI in healthcare settings. In clinical applications, AI raises ethical questions about privacy, safety, efficacy, information and consent, decision-making autonomy, the "right to try" price, and availability.

The use of robots and AI in healthcare is developing quickly, especially in early diagnosis and detection. With its growing skills, AI can already complete tasks faster and cheaper than humans (Ellahham, 2020). However, there are still dangers and difficulties associated with this advancement, including the possibility of patient injury because of system malfunctions and worries about patient privacy when using AI to gather and analyze data (Babel et al., 2021). AI in preventative care is essential to helping people maintain their health. Applications are made to provide users with more control over their overall health. AI applications for early diagnosis and detection are especially significant for precisely and quickly diagnosing illnesses (Brault & Saxena, 2021).

SOCIAL-LEGAL IMPLICATIONS AND PROSPECTS IN HEALTH

The acquiring of accurate information in a timely manner is essential to diagnosing and treating medical issues. AI improves the efficiency and optimization of critical clinical decision-making by providing healthcare practitioners with instantaneous and accurate data access (Wang et al., 2021). The improved doctor-patient connections can result from the use of real-time analytics (Dahiya et al., 2022). The patients can actively participate in their treatment regimens when vital patient information is made available to them via mobile devices (Iqbal et al., 2023). The cellphone notifications can quickly inform medical professionals, such as physicians and nurses, of crises and urgent changes in patient circumstances (Daley et al., 2022).

AI has had a revolutionary effect on the medical industry, transforming healthcare practices worldwide. These challenges related to control and autonomy become more pronounced with ongoing endeavors to automate the programming of AI technologies, employing computer programs capable of independently developing, deploying, and expanding new AI models and applications. An associated challenge revolves around the reliability and trustworthiness of AI. Errors in algorithms and data, or the use of biased datasets, can result in inaccurate or unfair decisions by AI systems. Such erroneous or biased judgments may impact patient safety and impede the effective implementation of healthcare. The biases in datasets and algorithms can lead to the unfair allocation of resources and discrimination against certain groups, neglecting individuals or groups with limited resources or specific health needs (Xie et al., 2021). The recording of patient histories, clinical information translation, and appointment scheduling automation are only a few examples of innovations (Hackl et al., 2023). AI is essential to the improvement and simplification of many labor-intensive processes that are performed in healthcare facilities. Intelligent radiology equipment, for example, can quickly recognize important visual indicators, saving a great deal of time during a rigorous investigation. Automated systems are in place to handle activities like tracking patients, making suggestions for care, and scheduling appointments.

DIGITAL HOSPITAL AND MOBILE HEALTH (MHEALTH): FUTURISTIC OPPORTUNITIES

Digital technology is driving a transformation in healthcare, from the use of AI and ML to mobile medical applications and software that help doctors with everyday clinical choices. These digital health technologies have the potential to significantly improve our ability to diagnose and treat diseases accurately, which will eventually improve the way that healthcare is provided to individuals. The broad field of digital health includes several subcategories including wearable technologies, telehealth, telemedicine, mHealth, and customized medicine. Global guidelines on the legal ramifications of AI in healthcare vary; the United States and Europe, for example, have different positions on this matter. The European Union (EU) has taken the lead in advancing medical AI innovation and has made it clear that using AI in healthcare presents regulatory issues (Hinton et al., 2019). The AI Act is the first dedicated legal framework for AI and was adopted by the European Commission in order to provide legal clarity and maintain uniformity in liability rules (Chew & Achananuparp, 2022). This approach seeks to both promote technical innovation and the responsible application of AI, especially in high-impact industries like healthcare (Singh & Kaunert, 2024). To provide healthcare and related services, digital health technologies make use of sensors, software, networking, and computer platforms (Singh et al., 2024). These technologies have a wide range of uses, from improving overall health to acting as medical equipment (Dwivedi et al., 2022). They can be made to function as companion diagnostics, as a medical product in and of itself, or as an addition to other medical goods like medications, devices, and biologics. They could also be used in research and development for medical devices.

By enabling access to data, digital technologies are giving healthcare practitioners a more thorough picture of patient health while also giving people greater control over their own health (Rodrigues et al., 2022). Regarding a civil responsibility framework for AI, the European Parliament has made suggestions to the Commission that center on concepts of compensation and accountability. The proposed system specifically denies AI the ability to act freely or take on legal responsibility, arguing that a thorough revision of current liability rules is not now warranted (Araiza-Garaygordobil et al., 2020). Rather, the regime takes a risk-based approach, classifying AI systems as either high risk or low risk, and it depends on accepted legal concepts. There are certain AI systems that are covered by a negligence-based liability scheme, whereas high-risk AI systems are subject to strict responsibility. Medical equipment covered by current EU rules is particularly categorized as high risk, meaning it must adhere to stringent liability requirements. There are genuine prospects to improve efficiency and medical outcomes in the field of digital health. By providing new avenues for promoting prevention, early identification of life-threatening illnesses, and the treatment of chronic ailments outside of traditional healthcare settings, these technologies empower consumers to make better-informed decisions about their health (Al Mamun et al., 2021).

Digital health technologies are utilized by providers and other stakeholders in order to cut down on inefficiencies, improve access, reduce expenses, raise quality, and customize treatment for each patient (Asan & Choudhury, 2021). Digital health technology may be utilized by patients and consumers to efficiently oversee and track their health-related endeavors and general state of health. In addition to revolutionizing communication, the fusion of technologies such as social networks, cell phones, and internet apps is opening new avenues for monitoring health and well-being and expanding information availability. All these developments are coming together to improve healthcare and health outcomes by bringing people, information, technology, and connections together.

CONCLUSION

Healthcare will see a greater presence of AI, which highlights the importance of ethical responsibility. Using unbiased real-time data is essential for preventing data bias in algorithms. It is crucial to create inclusive and diverse programming teams and carry out routine audits of algorithms, including how they are implemented. Healthcare practitioners' ability to make decisions can be improved by AI, even if technology cannot completely replace clinical judgment. AI may be utilized for screening and assessment in scenarios with limited medical competence. Because algorithms are involved, AI decisions are systematic, in contrast to human decision-making. AI technologies can improve patient outcomes and save healthcare costs by quickly and reliably evaluating large amounts of data. The technology provides doctors with individualized therapy suggestions by analyzing large datasets from research papers, medical records, and other sources. In a similar vein, DeepMind Health examines medical photos and recognizes conditions like diabetic retinopathy and breast cancer. These systems have the power to revolutionize the way they provide healthcare, which will eventually help millions of people worldwide.

REFERENCES

Al Mamun, S., Kaiser, M. S., & Mahmud, M. (2021, September). An AI-based approach towards inclusive healthcare provisioning in Society 5.0: A perspective on brain disorder. In *International Conference on Brain Informatics* (pp. 157–169). Cham: Springer International Publishing.

Amjad, A., Kordel, P., & Fernandes, G. (2023). A review on innovation in healthcare sector (telehealth) through AI. *Sustainability*, *15*(8), 66–75.

Araiza-Garaygordobil, D., Jordán-Ríos, A., Sierra-Fernández, C., & Juárez-Orozco, L. E. (2020). On stethoscopes, patient records, AI, and zettabytes: A glimpse into the future of digital medicine in Mexico. *Archivos de Cardiología de México*, *90*(2), 177–182.

Asan, O., & Choudhury, A. (2021). Research trends in AI applications in human factors healthcare: Mapping review. *JMIR Human Factors*, *8*(2), 28–36.

Asan, O., Choi, E., & Wang, X. (2023). AI–based consumer health informatics application: Scoping review. *Journal of Medical Internet Research*, 25(2), 47–60.

Awotunde, J. B., Folorunso, S. O., Ajagbe, S. A., Garg, J., & Ajamu, G. J. (2022). AiIoMT: IoMT-based system-enabled AI for enhanced smart healthcare systems. In Fadi Al-Turjman, & Anand Nayyar (Eds.), *Machine Learning for Critical Internet of Medical Things: Applications and Use Cases* (pp. 229–254). Cham: Springer.

Babel, A., Taneja, R., Mondello Malvestiti, F., Monaco, A., & Donde, S. (2021). AI solutions to increase medication adherence in patients with non-communicable diseases. *Frontiers in Digital Health*, 3(3), 66–79.

Baker, S., & Xiang, W. (2023). AI of Things for smarter healthcare: A survey of advancements, challenges, and opportunities. *IEEE Communications Surveys & Tutorials*, 7(1), 39–47.

Berrouiguet, S., Barrigón, M. L., Castroman, J. L., Courtet, P., Artés-Rodríguez, A., & Baca-García, E. (2019). Combining mobile-health (mHealth) and AI methods to avoid suicide attempts: The Smartcrises study protocol. *BMC Psychiatry*, 19(1), 1–9.

Bhaskar, S., Bradley, S., Sakhamuri, S., Moguilner, S., Chattu, V. K., Pandya, S.,.... & Banach, M. (2020). Designing futuristic telemedicine using AI and robotics in the COVID-19 era. *Frontiers in Public Health*, 70(8), 128–139.

Bhatt, V., & Chakraborty, S. (2021, March). Real-time healthcare monitoring using smart systems: A step towards healthcare service orchestration. In *2021 International Conference on AI and Smart Systems (ICAIS)* (pp. 772–777). Coimbatore: IEEE.

Bhatt, P., Liu, J., Gong, Y., Wang, J., & Guo, Y. (2022). Emerging AI–empowered mHealth: Scoping review. *JMIR mHealth and uHealth*, 10(6), 35–53.

Brault, N., & Saxena, M. (2021). For a critical appraisal of AI in healthcare: The problem of bias in mHealth. *Journal of Evaluation in Clinical Practice*, 27(3), 513–519.

Chakraborty, C. (Ed.). (2022). *Digital Health Transformation with Blockchain and AI*. Boca Raton, FL: CRC Press.

Chattu, V. K. (2021). A review of AI, big data, and blockchain technology applications in medicine and global health. *Big Data and Cognitive Computing*, 5(3), 41.

Chew, H. S. J., & Achananuparp, P. (2022). Perceptions and needs of AI in health care to increase adoption: Scoping review. *Journal of Medical Internet Research*, 24(1), 32–39.

Cingolani, M., Scendoni, R., Fedeli, P., & Cembrani, F. (2023). AI and digital medicine for integrated home care services in Italy: Opportunities and limits. *Frontiers in Public Health*, 10(3), 109–135.

Condry, M. W., & Quan, X. I. (2021). Digital health innovation, informatics opportunity, and challenges. *IEEE Engineering Management Review*, 49(2), 81–88.

Dabla, P. K., Gruson, D., Gouget, B., Bernardini, S., & Homsak, E. (2021). Lessons learned from the COVID-19 pandemic: Emphasizing the emerging role and perspectives from AI, mobile health, and digital laboratory medicine. *Ejifcc*, 32(2), 224–229.

Dahiya, S., Goyal, Y., & Sharma, C. (2022). Designing delivery of healthcare services with health management information system, AI, big data, and innovative digital technologies. *Journal of Young Pharmacists*, 14(4), 78–89.

Denecke, K., Gabarron, E., Grainger, R., Konstantinidis, S. T., Lau, A., Rivera-Romero, O., … & Merolli, M. (2019). AI for participatory health: Applications, impact, and future implications: Contribution of the IMIA Participatory Health and Social Media Working Group. *Yearbook of Medical Informatics*, 28(1), 165–189.

Deniz-Garcia, A., Fabelo, H., Rodriguez-Almeida, A. J., Zamora-Zamorano, G., Castro-Fernandez, M., Alberiche Ruano, M. D. P., … & WARIFA Consortium. (2023). Quality, usability, and effectiveness of mHealth apps and the role of AI: Current scenario and challenges. *Journal of Medical Internet Research*, 25(2), 44–58.

Dwivedi, R., Mehrotra, D., & Chandra, S. (2022). Potential of Internet of Medical Things (IoMT) applications in building a smart healthcare system: A systematic review. *Journal of Oral Biology and Craniofacial Research*, 12(2), 302–318.

Ellahham, S. (2020). AI: The future for diabetes care. *The American Journal of Medicine*, *133*(8), 895–900.

Galetsi, P., Katsaliaki, K., & Kumar, S. (2023). Exploring benefits and ethical challenges in the rise of mHealth (mobile healthcare) technology for the common good: An analysis of mobile applications for health specialists. *Technovation*, *121*(3), 102598.

Gunasekeran, D. V., Tseng, R. M. W. W., Tham, Y. C., & Wong, T. Y. (2021). Applications of digital health for public health responses to COVID-19: A systematic scoping review of AI, telehealth and related technologies. *NPJ Digital Medicine*, *4*(1), 40.

Hackl, W. O., Neururer, S. B., Pfeifer, B., & Section Editors for the IMIA Yearbook Section on Clinical Information Systems. (2023). Transforming clinical information systems: Empowering healthcare through telemedicine, data science, and AI applications. *Yearbook of Medical Informatics*, *32*(1), 127–137.

Hamberger, M., Ikonomi, N., Schwab, J. D., Werle, S. D., Fürstberger, A., Kestler, A. M., ... & Kestler, H. A. (2022). Interaction empowerment in mobile health: Concepts, challenges, and perspectives. *JMIR mHealth and uHealth*, *10*(4), 32–46.

Hinton, G., Obermeyer, Z., Emanuel, E., LeCun, Y., Bengio, Y., Hinton, G., ... & Bekhet, L. (2019). AI in health: State of the art, challenges, and future directions. *Yearbook of Medical Informatics*, *28*(1), 16–26.

Hunt, X., Tomlinson, M., Sikander, S., Skeen, S., Marlow, M., du Toit, S., & Eisner, M. (2020). AI, big data, and mHealth: The frontiers of the prevention of violence against children. *Frontiers in AI*, *3*(1), 543–565.

Iqbal, J., Jaimes, D. C. C., Makineni, P., Subramani, S., Hemaida, S., Thugu, T. R.,... & Hemida, S. (2023). Reimagining healthcare: Unleashing the power of AI in medicine. *Cureus*, *15*(9), 56–74.

Istepanian, R. S. (2022). Mobile health (m-health) in retrospect: The known unknowns. *International Journal of Environmental Research and Public Health*, *19*(7), 3747.

Istepanian, R. S., & AlAnzi, T. (2020). Mobile health (m-health): Evidence-based progress or scientific retrogression. In David Dagan Feng (Ed.), *Biomedical Information Technology* (pp. 717–733). Cambridge, MA: Academic Press.

Kakhi, K., Alizadehsani, R., Kabir, H. D., Khosravi, A., Nahavandi, S., & Acharya, U. R. (2022). The internet of medical things and AI: Trends, challenges, and opportunities. *Biocybernetics and Biomedical Engineering*, *42*(3), 749–771.

Karboub, K., Tabaa, M., Dandache, A., Dellagi, S., & Moutaouakkil, F. (2019). Toward health 4.0: Challenges and opportunities. In *International Conference on Innovation and New Trends in Information Technology* (pp. 20–21). Tangier.

Mbunge, E., Muchemwa, B., & Batani, J. (2021). Sensors and healthcare 5.0: Transformative shift in virtual care through emerging digital health technologies. *Global Health Journal*, *5*(4), 169–177.

Rodrigues, S. M., Kanduri, A., Nyamathi, A., Dutt, N., Khargonekar, P., & Rahmani, A. M. (2022). Digital health–enabled community-centered care: Scalable model to empower future community health workers using human-in-the-loop AI. *JMIR Formative Research*, *6*(4), 29–35.

Seetharam, K., Kagiyama, N., & Sengupta, P. P. (2019). Application of mobile health, telemedicine and AI to echocardiography. *Echo Research & Practice*, *6*(2), R41–R52.

Sharma, R., & Kshetri, N. (2020). Digital healthcare: Historical development, applications, and future research directions. *International Journal of Information Management*, *53*(2), 102–105.

Sharma, A., & Singh, B. (2022). Measuring impact of e-commerce on small scale business: A systematic review. *Journal of Corporate Governance and International Business Law*, *5*(1), 73–87.

Sharma, S. K., Al-Wanain, M. I., Alowaidi, M., & Alsaghier, H. (2022). Mobile healthcare (m-Health) based on AI in healthcare 4.0. *Expert Systems*, *12*(2), 130–145.

Singh, B., & Kaunert, C. (2024). Future of digital marketing: Hyper-personalized customer dynamic experience with AI-based predictive models. In Alex Khang, Pushan Kumar Dutta, Sachin Gupta, Nishu Ayedee, & Sandeep Chatterjee (Eds.), *Revolutionizing the AI-Digital Landscape: A Guide to Sustainable Emerging Technologies for Marketing Professionals* (pp. 189). New York: Taylor & Francis.

Singh, B., Kaunert, C., & Vig, K. (2024). Reinventing influence of AI on digital consumer lensing transforming consumer recommendation model: Exploring stimulus AI on consumer shopping decisions. In T. Musiolik, R. Rodriguez, & H. Kannan (Eds.), *AI Impacts in Digital Consumer Behavior* (pp. 141–169). Hershey, PA: IGI Global.

Solomon, D. H., & Rudin, R. S. (2020). Digital health technologies: Opportunities and challenges in rheumatology. *Nature Reviews Rheumatology, 16*(9), 525–535.

Wang, Q., Su, M., Zhang, M., & Li, R. (2021). Integrating digital technologies and public health to fight COVID-19 pandemic: Key technologies, applications, challenges and outlook of digital healthcare. *International Journal of Environmental Research and Public Health, 18*(11), 60–83.

Xie, Y., Lu, L., Gao, F., He, S. J., Zhao, H. J., Fang, Y.,.... & Dong, Z. (2021). Integration of AI, blockchain, and wearable technology for chronic disease management: A new paradigm in smart healthcare. *Current Medical Science, 41*(2), 1123–1133.

AI Applications in Human Disease Prediction

8

Santhosh Kumar Rajamani
and Radha Srinivasan Iyer

INTRODUCTION

Artificial intelligence (AI) has shown great promise in disease prediction across various domains in healthcare. By leveraging machine learning (ML) and deep learning (DL) algorithms, researchers and clinicians can gain valuable insights from large datasets, enabling early diagnosis, personalized treatment, and improved patient outcomes. AI is a rapidly evolving field that aims to develop intelligent systems capable of performing tasks that typically require human intelligence. AI can be broadly categorized into three types: narrow, general, and super. Each type differs in terms of its capabilities and potential applications. Narrow AI, also known as weak AI or artificial narrow intelligence (ANI), is the most common form of AI currently in existence. Narrow AI is designed to perform specific, predefined tasks with high accuracy and efficiency. It excels at solving well-defined problems within a particular domain, such as image recognition, natural language processing, or playing games like chess. Numerous examples of narrow AI can be found in everyday life, including virtual assistants like Siri and Alexa, recommendation systems on streaming platforms, and facial recognition software used for security purposes (Faggella, 2019).

DOI: 10.1201/9781003479109-8

MACHINE LEARNING (ML)AND DEEP LEARNING (DL): KEY CONCEPTS

ML and DL are subfields of AI that have gained significant attention in recent years due to their ability to solve complex problems and automate decision-making processes. ML algorithms enable computers to learn from data and improve their performance over time, while DL models are a subset of ML that utilize artificial neural networks to process and learn from large amounts of data. ML can be categorized into three main types: supervised, unsupervised, and reinforcement learning. In supervised learning, the algorithm learns from labeled data, where the correct output is provided for each input. This type of learning is commonly used for tasks such as classification and regression. Unsupervised learning, on the other hand, involves finding patterns and relationships within unlabeled data. Clustering and dimensionality reduction are examples of unsupervised learning techniques. Reinforcement learning involves an agent learning through trial and error and receiving rewards or penalties for its actions in a dynamic environment.

DL, a subset of ML, is inspired by the structure and function of the human brain, using artificial neural networks to process and learn from data. DL models consist of multiple layers of interconnected nodes, with each layer transforming the input data and passing it to the next layer. This hierarchical structure allows the model to learn increasingly complex representations of the input data. Convolutional neural networks (CNNs) and recurrent neural networks (RNNs) are two popular types of DL architectures. Several key factors contribute to the success of ML and DL in various applications. First, the availability of large amounts of data has enabled these models to learn more effectively. Second, advances in computing power and hardware, such as graphics processing units (GPUs) and tensor processing units (TPUs), have accelerated the training and inference processes. Finally, the development of novel algorithms and architectures has improved the performance and scalability of ML and DL models.

In recent years, ML and DL have been successfully applied to a wide range of domains, including image and speech recognition, natural language processing, computer vision, healthcare, finance, and autonomous vehicles. As the field continues to evolve, researchers are exploring new techniques and applications, such as generative adversarial networks (GANs) for generating realistic images and text and reinforcement learning for robotics and game-playing agents (e.g., DeepMind's AlphaGo).

ARTIFICIAL INTELLIGENCE (AI) AND HUMANITARIANISM

The intersection between AI and humanitarianism offers promising opportunities for leveraging advanced computational techniques to address complex global challenges. According to Floridi and Cowls (2019), "humanitarian AI" refers to the application of AI technologies to support human welfare, promote social justice, and protect vulnerable populations during crises or disasters. This section highlights some key areas where AI is contributing to humanitarian initiatives, along with relevant research studies.

Disaster Response and Management

AI can assist in disaster preparedness, risk assessment, and management by analyzing vast amounts of data quickly and accurately. Natural language processing (NLP) algorithms, for instance, can extract meaningful insights from social media posts, news articles, and other online content to track disaster events and assess their impacts (Imran et al., 2015; Olteanu et al., 2015). Moreover, computer vision methods can automatically classify satellite imagery to monitor environmental changes and detect damage caused by natural hazards (Zhang et al., 2019). Such approaches enable faster decision-making processes and better resource allocation during emergency situations.

Refugee Support and Integration

ML algorithms can facilitate refugee assistance programs by identifying specific needs, matching individuals with appropriate services, and tracking progress over time (Kim et al., 2019; Martin et al., 2019). Additionally, conversational agents powered by NLP techniques can provide language training, cultural orientation, and mental health support to refugees adjusting to new environments (Cabral et al., 2020).

Global Health Equity

AI has the potential to contribute significantly to achieving global health equity by enhancing diagnosis accuracy, promoting preventive care, and optimizing resource distribution (Luxton, 2016; World Health Organization, 2019). Specifically, ML algorithms can improve medical screening procedures by detecting anomalies in medical images, signals, or electronic health records (EHRs) (Eapen et al., 2020; Rajpurkar et al., 2017). Furthermore, AI-powered chatbots and mobile apps can deliver targeted health education messages based on users' demographic profiles and behavioral patterns (Ventura et al., 2018).

These examples illustrate how AI is increasingly becoming an integral part of humanitarian work, offering innovative solutions to pressing societal problems while adhering to ethical principles such as fairness, accountability, and transparency (Floridi & Cowls, 2019). As such, continued exploration of AI-humanitarian synergies remains crucial for advancing sustainable development goals and fostering inclusive growth worldwide.

APPLICATIONS OF AI IN DISEASE PREDICTION

AI has shown immense potential in the field of healthcare, particularly in disease prediction and early diagnosis. ML and DL algorithms have been employed to analyze large datasets, extract meaningful patterns, and generate predictions about the risk of developing various diseases. One prominent application of AI in disease prediction is the use of ML algorithms for predicting cardiovascular diseases (CVDs). By analyzing patient data, including medical history, lifestyle factors, and biomarkers, ML models can estimate the risk of CVDs with high accuracy. For example, a study by Kwon et al. (2019) demonstrated that a deep neural network (DNN) model outperformed traditional risk prediction models in predicting CVD risk in a large cohort of Korean adults.

In the field of oncology, AI has been used to predict cancer risk and survival outcomes. DL models, such as CNNs, have been employed to analyze medical images, including mammograms and histopathology slides, to detect and classify cancerous lesions. For instance, a study by Bejnordi et al. (2017) showed that a DL model achieved expert-level performance in classifying breast cancer histopathology images. AI has also been applied to predict infectious diseases, such as influenza and COVID-19. ML models have been trained on historical data, including weather patterns, air pollution levels, and search engine query trends, to forecast the spread of these diseases. For example, a study by Wu et al. (2020) demonstrated that a DL model could accurately predict the number of COVID-19 cases in China, based on data from the early stages of the outbreak.

Predicting Disease Outbreaks and Epidemics

The use of AI in predicting disease outbreaks and epidemics has gained significant attention in recent years due to its potential to provide early warnings, improve response time, and reduce the impact of such events on public health. AI-based models can analyze large amounts of data from various sources, including medical records, social media, and environmental factors, to identify patterns and make accurate predictions. One approach to predicting disease outbreaks is the utilization of ML algorithms, such as decision trees, support vector machines (SVMs), and neural networks. These algorithms can be trained on historical data to recognize patterns and relationships between variables that may indicate an impending outbreak (Rajaraman, 2018). For example, a study by Li et al. (2018) used an ML algorithm to predict the outbreak of dengue fever in Guangzhou, China, achieving an accuracy of 88.5%.

Another promising area of research involves the use of DL techniques, such as CNNs and RNNs. These models can process large-scale data, including time-series data, to identify temporal patterns that may signal an upcoming outbreak (Chae et al., 2020). A study by Chae et al. employed a CNN-based model to predict influenza outbreaks in South Korea, resulting in a 77.3% accuracy rate (Xia et al., 2019). In addition to predicting outbreaks, AI can also be used to track the spread of diseases and monitor their impact on the population. This can be achieved through the integration of geographic information systems (GISs) and spatial analysis techniques, allowing for the visualization of disease distribution and the identification of high-risk areas (Wong et al., 2019).

AI-Based Early Detection and Diagnosis of Diseases

Early detection and diagnosis of diseases are critical for effective treatment and improved patient outcomes. With the increasing availability of healthcare data and advancements in AI technology, AI-based early disease detection and diagnosis have gained significant attention in recent years. This review aims to provide an overview of AI-based early disease detection and diagnosis, its applications, and its challenges, as well as its potential impact on healthcare.

Imaging techniques: AI algorithms can be trained to analyze medical images such as X-rays, Computed Tomography (CT) scans, Magnetic Resonance Imaging (MRI) scans, and ultrasounds to detect abnormalities and diagnose diseases at an early stage (Ray et al., 2020). For instance, AI-assisted breast cancer detection from mammography images has shown promising results, with a high accuracy rate of 90% (Kumar et al., 2020).

Clinical decision support systems (CDSSs): AI-powered CDSSs can analyze large amounts of patient data, including medical history, symptoms, and laboratory test results, to provide healthcare professionals with diagnostic suggestions and recommendations (Hanna & Goeree, 2019). CDSSs have been shown to improve diagnostic accuracy and reduce unnecessary tests (Garg et al., 2016).

Wearable devices and remote monitoring: AI-enabled wearable devices and remote monitoring systems can collect vital signs and other health metrics from patients, enabling early detection of anomalies and prompting timely interventions (Mi et al., 2020). For example, AI-powered smartwatches can detect atrial fibrillation with an accuracy rate of 97% (Lau & Fung, 2020).

Predictive Models for Personalized Medicine

Personalized medicine is a growing field that aims to tailor medical treatments to individuals' unique needs and characteristics. One approach to achieving this goal is using predictive models, which can forecast patient outcomes based on various factors such as genetics, medical history, and lifestyle choices. Predictive models can help healthcare providers identify patients who are at risk of developing certain conditions or responding poorly to treatments. For example, a study published in the Journal of the American Medical Association found that an ML algorithm was able to identify patients who were at high risk of developing diabetes with an accuracy rate of 82.2%. This allows healthcare providers to intervene early and potentially prevent the onset of disease or adjust treatment plans accordingly. In addition, predictive models can help streamline clinical trials by identifying the most suitable participants. A study published in the journal Nature Medicine found that an ML algorithm was able to identify patients who were likely to benefit from a new drug for treating cancer with an accuracy rate of 80.6%. By targeting the right patients, researchers can improve the efficiency and effectiveness of clinical trials, ultimately leading to better treatments for patients.

MACHINE LEARNING (ML) APPROACHES FOR DISEASE PREDICTION

ML approaches have shown significant promise in predicting disease outbreaks by analyzing large amounts of data from various sources, including medical records, social media, and environmental factors. These approaches involve training algorithms, such as decision trees, SVMs, and neural networks, on historical data to recognize patterns and relationships between variables that may indicate an impending outbreak. For example, studies have employed ML algorithms to predict dengue fever outbreaks in China and influenza outbreaks in South Korea, with accuracy rates of 88.5% and 77.3%, respectively. By leveraging the power of ML, public health officials can gain valuable insights and implement targeted interventions to mitigate the impact of disease outbreaks on the population.

Supervised Learning: Classification and Regression Techniques

Supervised learning approaches involve training ML models on labeled datasets, where the target variable is a disease label or a continuous measure of disease severity. In this section, we will discuss two common types of supervised learning methods used for disease prediction: classification and regression techniques.

Classification techniques are used when the target variable is categorical or nominal, and the goal is to predict the class or category that a new observation belongs to. Common classification algorithms include logistic regression, decision trees, random forests, and SVMs. Logistic regression is a popular method for binary classification problems, where the goal is to predict the probability of an observation belonging to one of two classes (e.g., diseased or not diseased). Decision trees are another popular classification technique that works by recursively partitioning the feature space into smaller regions based on the values of the input features. Random forests are an ensemble version of decision trees that combine multiple trees to improve the accuracy and robustness of the predictions (Breiman, 2001). SVMs are a type of kernel-based method that can be used for both classification and regression tasks. SVM primarily focuses on finding the best boundary between two distinct classes in each dataset. For example, the best boundary in Figure 8.1 is the tangent to the circles.

Regression techniques are used when the target variable is continuous or ordinal, and the goal is to predict a numerical value. Common regression algorithms include linear

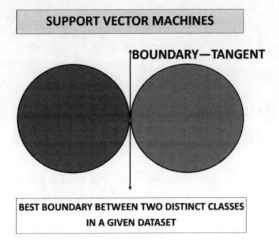

FIGURE 8.1   Illustration of SVMs.

regression, polynomial regression, and neural networks. Linear regression is a simple yet powerful method that models the relationship between the input features and the output variable using a linear function. It is widely used in healthcare research to study the association between risk factors and continuous outcome variables (e.g., blood pressure and cholesterol levels) (Katz & Karat, 2016). Neural networks are a class of ML models inspired by the structure and function of the human brain. They consist of multiple layers of interconnected nodes (neurons) that process the input data and produce an output.

Unsupervised Learning: Clustering and Dimensionality Reduction

The early detection and diagnosis of diseases are crucial for effective treatment and improved patient outcomes. With the increasing availability of healthcare data, ML techniques have gained significant attention in recent years for their potential to revolutionize the field of medicine (Topol, 2019). In this chapter, we will explore the use of AI-based approaches, specifically unsupervised learning techniques such as clustering and dimensionality reduction, for disease prediction. We will also discuss the challenges associated with these methods and their future directions in healthcare research.

The various aspects of supervised learning and unsupervised learning are compared in Table 8.1.

Reinforcement Learning: Optimizing Treatment Strategies

In recent years, the application of Reinforcement Learning (RL) has shown promising results in optimizing treatment strategies for various medical conditions. RL is an ML

TABLE 8.1   Comparison between supervised and unsupervised learning

ASPECT	SUPERVISED LEARNING	UNSUPERVISED LEARNING
Definition	A machine learning (ML) approach where the algorithm learns from labeled training data to map inputs to outputs. The goal is to generalize from past observations to new, unseen data.	An ML approach where the algorithm learns patterns and structures in the input data without any prior labeling or target output. The goal is to discover hidden relationships and dependencies within the data.
Data requirements	Requires labeled data with known input-output pairs for training. This means that each example in the dataset has both an input feature vector and a corresponding output variable (target).	Does not require labeled data; only input features are required. There is no need for a predefined output variable.
Examples	Image classification, spam filtering, speech recognition, fraud detection, and regression analysis.	Clustering, dimensionality reduction, anomaly detection, association rule mining, and density estimation.
Algorithm types	Common algorithms include linear regression, logistic regression, decision trees, random forests, SVMs, neural networks, and k-nearest neighbors.	Common algorithms include k-means clustering, hierarchical clustering, principal component analysis (PCA), independent component analysis (ICA), autoencoders, and t-SNE.
Evaluation metrics	Accuracy, precision, recall, F1 score, ROC curve, confusion matrix, mean squared error, R-squared, etc., depending on the problem type (classification or regression) and specific use case.	Silhouette coefficient, Davies-Bouldin index, Dunn index, Calinski-Harabasz index, elbow method, internal vs external validation metrics, etc.
Advantages	Can produce highly accurate models when trained on large amounts of high-quality labeled data. Provides clear guidance about model performance based on evaluation metrics. Easy to interpret results if using simple models like decision trees or linear regression.	Allows the discovery of unknown patterns and insights in the data without requiring explicit labels. Useful for exploratory data analysis and feature engineering. Scales well to large datasets due to its simplicity.
Disadvantages	Labeled data may be expensive, time-consuming, or difficult to obtain. Overfitting can occur if the model is too complex relative to the size and quality of the training set. Models can become less interpretable as they grow more complex (e.g., deep neural networks).	Results might be harder to interpret than those obtained through supervised methods. It can sometimes be challenging to determine which discovered pattern is meaningful and relevant. Performance evaluation could be subjective and context dependent.

technique that enables an agent to learn and make decisions through interactions with an environment, aiming to maximize a cumulative reward over time. In the context of disease prediction and treatment, RL can be used to develop optimal treatment strategies by balancing the trade-off between the immediate effects of treatment and its long-term impact on the patient's health (Sutton & Barto, 2018). RL has shown promising results in optimizing treatment strategies for various diseases, including diabetes, cancer, and infectious diseases. By learning from interactions with the environment, RL can balance the trade-off between the immediate and long-term effects of treatments, ultimately leading to better patient outcomes. Future research should focus on expanding the applicability of RL to other medical conditions and integrating RL-based treatment strategies into clinical practice (Sutton & Barto, 2018; Zhang et al., 2020; Liu et al., 2019; Komorowski et al., 2018).

Convolutional Neural Networks (CNNs) for Medical Image Analysis

CNNs have gained significant attention in recent years due to their remarkable performance in various computer vision tasks, including medical image analysis. Medical image analysis is a crucial component of modern healthcare, as it enables the detection, classification, and segmentation of diseases and anatomical structures from medical images. CNNs have demonstrated promising results in this domain, outperforming traditional ML methods. In this technical report, we will discuss the fundamentals of CNNs, their architectures, and their applications in medical image analysis. The features of RNNs, long short-term memory (LSTM), and CNNs are compared in Table 8.2.

TABLE 8.2   Comparison between RNNs, LSTMs, and CNNs

MODEL	ARCHITECTURE	INPUT	OUTPUT	PROS	CONS
RNN	Recurrent Neural Network	Sequential data	Sequential data	Can capture long-term dependencies	Slow training, prone to vanishing gradient problem
LSTM	Long Short-Term Memory	Sequential data	Sequential data	Can capture long-term dependencies, mitigates vanishing gradient problem	Complex architecture, slower training
CNN	Convolutional Neural Network	Images	Object detection, image classification	Fast training	Can capture spatial features

TABLE 8.3 Comparison of RNN (LSTM/GRU) vs CNN for healthcare-related tasks

TASK	RNN (LSTM/GRU)	CNN
Speech recognition	Moderate	Excellent
Text sentiment analysis	Good	Moderate
ECG signal analysis	Good	Good
Medical image classification	Poor	Excellent
Disease prediction	Good	Moderate
Time-series data analysis	Good	Moderate

CNNs have shown great potential in medical image analysis, outperforming traditional methods and achieving state-of-the-art results in various tasks. The flexibility and adaptability of CNN architectures allow for the development of customized solutions tailored to specific medical imaging problems. As the field continues to evolve, we can expect further advancements in CNN-based medical image analysis, leading to improved diagnosis, treatment planning, and patient outcomes. As a conclusion, the capabilities of RNNs (LSTMs and Gated Recurrent Units (GRUs)) and CNN in performing healthcare-related tasks, like automated Electro Cardio Gram (ECG), are compared in Table 8.3.

AI IN HEALTHCARE: CHALLENGES AND OPPORTUNITIES

AI has emerged as a promising technology in the field of healthcare, with the potential to revolutionize patient care and improve outcomes. However, the integration of AI in healthcare presents several challenges and opportunities that need to be addressed. One of the major challenges in implementing AI in healthcare is the lack of high-quality, standardized, and interoperable data (Rajkomar et al., 2019). Healthcare data is often scattered across various sources, including EHRs, medical imaging systems, and wearable devices. Moreover, data formats and structures may differ among institutions, making it difficult to integrate and analyze data using AI algorithms. To address this issue, researchers and healthcare providers must collaborate to develop standardized data formats and promote data interoperability (Kim et al., 2020). Another significant challenge is the need for explainability and transparency in AI-based decision-making processes (Holzinger, 2019). Healthcare professionals need to understand how AI algorithms arrive at their conclusions, especially when those conclusions have life-altering consequences for patients. To address this challenge, researchers are developing Explainable Artificial Intelligence (XAI) techniques that provide insights into the decision-making process of AI models (Holzinger, 2019).

FUTURE DIRECTIONS AND OPPORTUNITIES FOR AI IN DISEASE PREDICTION AND HEALTHCARE

AI has significantly transformed the healthcare industry, enabling clinicians to make more accurate diagnoses, predict disease progression, and improve treatment outcomes. As AI technologies continue to evolve, there are three key future directions and opportunities for AI in disease prediction and healthcare.

1. *Enhanced Disease Prediction:* AI algorithms can analyze vast amounts of medical data, including patient demographics, medical histories, genetic information, and environmental factors, to identify patterns and predict disease risks. Integrating AI with EHRs can facilitate the early detection of diseases, allowing for timely intervention and prevention. For example, a recent study by Kermany et al. (2018) demonstrated that DL algorithms can accurately detect diabetic retinopathy from retinal fundus photographs.
2. *Personalized Medicine*: AI can help tailor treatment plans based on individual patient characteristics, improving treatment outcomes and reducing adverse effects. By analyzing patient-specific data, AI can identify the most effective treatments for each patient, considering their unique genetic makeup, lifestyle factors, and medical history. This personalized approach to medicine has the potential to revolutionize healthcare by optimizing treatment effectiveness and minimizing side effects.
3. *Drug Discovery and Development:* AI can accelerate the drug discovery process by identifying potential drug targets, predicting drug efficacy, and optimizing drug design. ML algorithms can analyze large datasets of molecular structures, biological pathways, and clinical trial outcomes to identify promising drug candidates and predict their therapeutic potential. This can significantly reduce the time and cost associated with drug development, ultimately benefiting patients by bringing new treatments to market faster.

AI has the potential to revolutionize disease prediction and healthcare in numerous ways, from enhancing disease prediction and personalized medicine to improving clinical workflows and reducing healthcare costs. As AI technologies continue to evolve, it is crucial for researchers, clinicians, and policymakers to collaborate in harnessing the full potential of AI for the benefit of patients and the healthcare system.

CONCLUSION

In conclusion, the integration of AI in disease prediction and healthcare holds great promise for improving patient outcomes, streamlining clinical workflows, and reducing healthcare costs. AI technologies can enhance disease prediction by analyzing vast amounts of medical data, facilitate personalized medicine by tailoring treatment plans to individual patients, and accelerate drug discovery and development by identifying promising drug candidates. Additionally, AI can improve clinical workflows, enable continuous patient monitoring through wearable devices, and reduce healthcare costs by optimizing resource allocation and reducing unnecessary hospitalizations. However, despite the numerous advantages of AI in healthcare, there are also limitations and challenges that must be addressed. One significant challenge is the lack of high-quality, standardized medical data, which is essential for training accurate AI algorithms. Ensuring patient privacy and data security is another critical concern, as the widespread use of AI in healthcare involves the collection and analysis of sensitive personal information. Moreover, the "black box" nature of some AI algorithms can make it difficult to understand how decisions are made, potentially undermining clinicians' trust in these technologies.

REFERENCES

Bejnordi, B. E., Veta, M., van Diest, P. J., van Ginneken, B., Karssemeijer, N., Litjens, G., & van de Vijver, M. J. (2017). Diagnostic assessment of deep learning algorithms for detection of lymph node metastases in women with breast cancer. *JAMA*, *318*(22), 2201–2209.

Bolukbasi, T., Chang, K-W., Zou, J., Saligrama, V., & Kalai, A. . (2016). Man is to computer programmer as woman is to homemaker? Debiasing word embeddings. *Advances in Neural Information Processing Systems*, 29, 4349–4357.

Breiman, L. (2001). Random forests. *Machine Learning*, *42*(3), 5–32.

Cabral, D. S., Pereira, F. D. O., de Sa, L. G., da Silva, P. M. S., & Rodrigues, M. M. (2020). Chatbot application for Syrian refugees' psychosocial support: Design science research approach. *Information Systems Frontiers*, *22*(2), 249–263. https://doi.org/10.1007/s10796-019-09924-x

Chae, J., Lee, J., Kim, H., & Kang, S. (2020). Predicting influenza outbreaks using deep learning models. *Journal of Medical Internet Research*, *22*(12), e21143.

Chen, Y., Ghassemi, M., & Singh, A. (2019a). Can AI mitigate health disparities? *The Lancet Digital Health*, *1*(1), e13–e14. https://doi.org/10.1016/S2589-7500(19)30012-2

Chen, Y., Zhang, J., Li, J., Zhao, H., & Wang, Y. (2019b). A survey of medical image analysis using deep learning. *IEEE Transactions on Medical Imaging*, *38*(5), 1122–1134.

Eapen, C. A., Carney, P., Burdett, H., Taylor, R., & Steiner, S. (2020). Automated versus manual interpretation of paediatric electrocardiograms: Comparative performance evaluation study. *BMJ Open*, *10*(11), e038667. https://doi.org/10.1136/bmjopen-2020-038667.

Faggella, D. (2019). What Is Narrow AI? [Blog post]. Retrieved from https://Emerj.com/ai-sector-overviews/narrow-artificial-intelligence/

Floridi, L., & Cowls, J. (2019). What is 'human' about humanitarian AI? *Philosophical Transactions of the Royal Society A: Mathematical, Physical and Engineering Sciences*, *377*(2151), 20180399. https://doi.org/10.1098/rsta.2018.0399

Garg, S., Boyd, A. D., & Reis, C. (2016). Machine learning in radiology: Applications, challenges, and future directions. *Radiologic Clinics of North America*, *54*(4), 637–653.

Hanna, G., & Goeree, R. (2019). AI in healthcare: Past, present and future. *Healthcare Management Review*, *44*(3), 257–267.

Holzinger, A. (2019). Current status and future directions of machine learning in healthcare. *Journal of Biomedical Informatics*, 96, 103235. https://doi.org/10.1016/j.jbi.2019.103235

Imran, M., Castillo, C., Diaz, F., & Vieweg, S. (2015). CrisisMMD: Multilingual Twitter message dataset for emergency event analysis. In *Proceedings of the International Conference on Social Media Technologies, Communication Theory and Applications – Volume 2: Communication Theory and Applications* (pp. 134–143). Toronto. https://doi.org/10.5220/0005298701340143

Katz, M. G., & Karat, C. M. (2016). Linear regression and linear mixed effects models. In J. E. B. Myers & K. M. Atkinson (Eds.), *Encyclopedia of Statistics in Behavioral Science* (pp. 517–524). Hoboken, NJ: Wiley.

Kermany, D. S., Goldbaum, M., Clemons, M., Frey, C., Zhang, K., Erickson, B.,... 7 Bernstein, A. (2018). Identifying medical diagnoses and treatable diseases by image-based deep learning. *Cell*, *172*(1), 1122–1131.

Kim, J., Cho, J., Lee, J., Kim, Y., Park, J., Oh, J., & Choi, S. (2019). Smart refugee camp: Utilizing IoT and big data analytics for improving quality of life. *Sustainable Cities and Society*, *47*, 101619. https://doi.org/10.1016/j.scs.2019.101619

Kim, M. S., Kim, J., Park, J. W., & Kim, J. (2020). AI in healthcare: Challenges and future directions. *Healthcare Informatics Research*, *26*(2), 69–78. https://doi.org/10.4258/hir.2020.26.2.69

Krauthammer, M. M., & Boveroux, P. (2020). Collaborative intelligence in healthcare: Why AI needs humans. *NPJ Digital Medicine*, *3*, 1–4.

Kumar, S., Kumar, A., & Kumar, A. (2020). Breast cancer detection using mammographic features and machine learning techniques: A systematic review. *Journal of Medical Systems*, *44*(10), 2105–2123.

Kwon, S. H., Park, S. H., Kim, H. J., Lee, S. W., & Kim, H. J. (2019). Predicting cardiovascular disease risk using deep neural networks: A nationwide cohort study. *PloS One*, *14*(8), 20–36.

Lau, E. T., & Fung, E. (2020). Atrial fibrillation detection using machine learning algorithms and wearable sensors: A systematic review. *Journal of Interactive Cardiac Electrophysiology*, *20*(3), 197–206.

Li, W., Zhou, X., Tang, S., Zhang, Y., & Zhao, Y. (2018). Dengue fever prediction using machine learning in Guangzhou, China. *BMC Infectious Diseases*, *18*(1), 1–9.

Liu, J., Wang, X., & Zhang, Y. (2019). Deep reinforcement learning for personalized chemotherapy scheduling in lung cancer. *Scientific Reports*, *9*(1), 1–11. https://doi.org/10.1038/s41598-019-41634-z.

Luxton, D. D. (2016). mHealth and telemedicine: Advances and challenges. *Current Psychiatry Reports*, *18*(11), 95. https://doi.org/10.1007/s11920-016-0703-y.

Martin, D., Hamadicharef, B., Kabongo, M.-P., Thiam, A., Leclair, F., & Benhlima, M. (2019). Intelligent decision making tools for immigrant services providers. *Expert Systems with Applications*, *127*, 112–124. https://doi.org/10.1016/j.eswa.2019.03.015.

Mi, Q., Tang, J., Li, J., & Chen, Y. (2020). Wearable devices and remote monitoring technologies for health management: A systematic review. *Journal of Healthcare Engineering*, 2020, 1–15.

Olteanu, A., Castillo, C., Diaz, F., & Gomez, A. (2015). How do people use social media during disasters? An overview of empirical studies. *ACM Sigspatial Special*, *4*(1), Article No.: 12. https://doi.org/10.1145/2810150.2810155

Rajaraman, A. (2018). Predicting disease outbreaks using machine learning. *Journal of Biomedical Informatics*, *82*, 94–102.

Rajkomar, A., Oren, E., Chen, K., Dai, A. M., Hajaj, N., Hardt, M., & Kohane, I. S. (2019). Scalable and accurate deep learning with electronic health records. *NPJ Digital Medicine*, *2*(1), 1–9. https://doi.org/10.1038/s41746-018-0100-8

Rajpurkar, P., Irvin, J., Ball, R. L., Hekler, J., Kohane, I. S., & Ng, A. Y. (2017). CheXNet: Radiologist-level pneumonia detection from chest X-rays with deep learning. arXiv preprint arXiv:1711.05225.

Ray, S., Saha, S., & Bandyopadhyay, S. (2020). A comparative study of machine learning techniques for breast cancer diagnosis using mammographic features. *Journal of Medical Systems*, *44*(12), 2415–2427.

Sutton, R. S., & Barto, A. G. (2018). *Reinforcement Learning: An Introduction* (2nd ed.). Cambridge, MA: MIT Press.

Topol, E. J. (2019). High-performance medicine: The convergence of human and AI. *Nature Medicine*, *25*(1), 44–56. https://doi.org/10.1038/s41591-018-0276-1

Ventura, A., Van Gemert, F., van den Broek, P., Schoonderbeek, J., & Meppelink, R. (2018). Mobile apps for self-management of type 2 diabetes mellitus: Scoping review. *JMIR Mhealth Uhealth*, *6*(11), e10484. https://doi.org/10.2196/10484

Wong, W., Chen, S., & Chang, J. (2019). Spatial analysis of disease outbreaks: A review. *Journal of Spatial Science*, *64*(1), 1–18.

World Health Organization. (2019). Digital Health Technical Note Series: Artificial Intelligence. Retrieved January 10, 2023, from https://www.who.int/publications/i/item/digital-health-technical-note-series---artificial-intelligence

Wu, J. T., Leung, K., Leung, G. M., So, R. T. Y., & Tang, J. W. (2020). Nowcasting and forecasting the COVID-19 outbreak in China. *The Lancet*, *395*(10228), 747–750.

Xia, J., Chen, H., Xu, X., & Wang, H. (2019). Deep learning for infectious disease surveillance. *Scientific Reports*, *9*(1), 1–9.

Zhang, L., Tan, P., Shi, X., Du, Y., & Jin, H. (2019). Transferring pretrained CNN features for satellite image change detection. *Remote Sensing*, *11*(11), 1386. https://doi.org/10.3390/rs11111386

Zhang, L., Li, Y., Zhou, J., & Zhang, T. (2020). Deep reinforcement learning for optimal insulin therapy in type 1 diabetes. *IEEE Transactions on Cybernetics*, *50*(9), 4472–4482. https://doi.org/10.1109/TCYB.2019.294012

A Fair Resource-Sharing AI Algorithm for Humanitarian Camps

9

Bamidele Oluwade

INTRODUCTION

Artificial intelligence (AI) is one of the most valuable and revolutionary tools of contemporary times. Its power and effect are glaring in the sciences and technology, as well as in various applied areas of human endeavors. Broadly speaking, the field of AI encompasses machine learning (ML), robotics, knowledge representation, natural language processing, and problem-solving. Others include expert systems, perception, game-playing, programming languages, and hardware (Russell & Norvig, 1995; Oluwade, 2003; Thanaki, 2017). In ML, in particular, the system is trained to learn the patterns of the data it is to recognize. An instance refers to a piece of input data from which an output value is generated. A feature is a vector which describes an instance. This vector characterizes an instance. Given an input value (instance), pattern recognition refers to the assignment of an output value/label to the instance based on a given algorithm. The basic function of the algorithm is to assist in providing realistic answers for all possible inputs and then carry out the matching of inputs based on the principle of fuzzy logic (Bishop, 2006; Koutroumbas & Theodoridis, 2008). In a usual biometric

DOI: 10.1201/9781003479109-9

pattern recognition system, an object is automatically identified or verified from a source, often by comparing selected features of the object with a database. Such features may include the shape of the eyes, fingers, nose, jaw, and cheekbones; skin texture; and relative position.

ML is classified into three namely supervised learning, unsupervised learning, and semi-supervised learning. In supervised learning, a labeled training set/data is provided. This consists of a set of instances which have been properly labeled with the correct output via the hand. An unlabeled set is used in unsupervised learning. Semi-supervised learning uses a combination of both a training set and an unlabeled set. The pattern recognition process of ML includes filtering, feature extraction, and classification. This can be accomplished via two broad procedures, namely, the geometric procedure and the photometric procedure. The former is primarily a non-statistical procedure which considers the distinguishing features of an image. A classic popular example is the nearest neighbor technique (Wakahara & Yamashita, 2014; Zhang et al., 2012). The latter is basically a statistical procedure in which, in a bid to remove variances, an image is reduced into values such that the values are compared with an existing template. The two procedures above are also, for convenience, sometimes classified into four basic approaches, namely, structural approach (use of data structures like graphs to represent classes), statistical approach (use of conditional probability), neural network approach (based on neural network), and syntactic approach (representation of the classes by grammars). In the case of classification, an input value is assigned to one of a given set of classes (Brunelli, 2009; Haykin, 1994; Russell & Norvig, 1995).

This chapter presents an alternative procedure for representing the structures of images of Patent Number 5267332 as lines, nodes, and curves using the qualitative equivalence of autonomous ordinary differential equations. This is a structural approach for the classification stage of a pattern recognition system. Several structural (and non-structural) recognition models have been developed since 1993, including the use of principles like the decision tree, Bayesian statistics, fractional calculus, and edge detection (e.g. Quinlan, 1983, 1986; Farid et al., 2014; Di Nunzio, 2014; Pestov, 2013; Chen et al., 2023; Hassan et al., 2022; Huang et al., 2023; Joshi et al., 2023; Karim et al., 2022; Khan et al., 2024; Lavin-Delgado et al., 2024; Appati et al., 2022; Asokan & Anitha, 2019; Balochian & Baloochian, 2022; Burger & Burge, 2022). However, none of them used the novel and elegant qualitative equivalence procedure that is presented. The procedure involves the use of the geometrical representation (called phase portraits) of the first-order autonomous ordinary differential equation with a polynomial nonlinear part given by

$$x' = f(x) = \Sigma a_i x^i \tag{9.1}$$

where $i = 1, 2, \ldots, n$, such that $a_n \neq 0$. This is based on the critical points of the equation, where n is a member of the set N (set of natural numbers). The relevant qualitative properties are the existence and uniqueness of solutions. The basic similarity between the method introduced in this chapter and many methods in the literature is that the classes are represented as data structures such as arrays, graphs, trees, and matrices. However, the qualitative equivalence approach does not use a distance metric but rather converts images to equivalent geometric structures of a differential equation, called phase portraits. The images are then grouped into distinct classes based on images which have the same phase portraits.

An autonomous differential equation or system such as Equation (9.1) is one which doesn't depend explicitly on the independent variable t. On the other hand, a non-autonomous system is of the form

$$x' = f(x,t) \tag{9.2}$$

and depends on the independent variable (Oluwade, 1999; Arrowsmith & Place, 1982). In general, autonomous mechanical systems exhibit a high degree of independence and can perceive, learn, and respond intelligently to unexpected environmental changes. An example of such a system is an autonomous vehicle. In addition, batteries, especially in solar engineering systems, are designed to have some degree of autonomy to guarantee the performance of such systems. In general, two trajectories of Equation (9.1) are said to be qualitatively equivalent if they have the same number of critical points of the same nature and are arranged in the same order along the fixed line, i.e. the trajectories are similar in shape. Qualitative equivalence leads to the generation of qualitative classes. This chapter thus presents a new procedure for the classification stage of the ML algorithm. Two of the most popular AI learning algorithms are the nearest neighbor classifier algorithm and the backpropagation algorithm. Some common general recognition algorithms include principal component analysis with eigenface, which is a statistics-based algorithm (Jolliffe & Cadima, 2016), linear discriminate analysis, which is a statistics-based algorithm (Gorban et al., 2018), hidden Markov model (HMM), which is a statistics-based algorithm (Gagniuc, 2017), elastic bunch graph matching fisherface, which is essentially a geometric-based algorithm (Gunther, 2009), and neuronally motivated dynamic link matching, which is essentially a geometric-based algorithm (Wurtz et al., 1999).

The implication of the research work reported in this chapter is that a machine is trained to perform its task using the number of nodes and the number of links in an alphabet. This provides guidance in recognizing the equivalence class of an alphabet and, subsequently, the alphabet. That is, the machine is initially just fed with the number of nodes and a number of links, and then it is allowed to carry out the identification/recognition. The research has potential applications for the unique identification of persons in emergency humanitarian situations such as refugee camps. In general, classification algorithms assist in the effective processing of large data sets stored in databases, which, in modern times, reach up to terabytes.

LITERATURE REVIEW

In Walch and Pawlicki (1993), the authors presented a class of recognition systems in which images are characterized and compared based on internal structure, which is independent of image size and image orientation. In the system, a library of reference images is first generated and stored, and then each input image (i.e. test image) is compared to the images stored in the library until a match is found. The images are represented in memory as nodes, lines, and curves. For instance, the letter "H" has an internal structure of six (6) nodes, such that four (4) nodes have one (1) link each, while the remaining two (2) nodes have three (3) links each. Some works on general pattern recognition include Bishop (2006) and Koutroumbas and Theodoridis (2008). In Omolu and Oluwade (2017), the authors used a geometric-based k-nearest neighbor supervised ML classification algorithm to train and test the English alphabet. The work of Dasarathy (1991) is also geometrically based, and it is premised on the principle that classification of unknown instances can be accomplished by relating the unknown to the known using distance/similarity function. Essentially, the work emphasizes that, given an instant space and a suitable distance function, two instances which are close in the instant space are more likely to be in the same class than those which are far apart. Joachims (2002) used an implicit distance/similarity measure by implicitly mapping the data into a higher dimensional space. The classification algorithms are based on kernel functions (support vector machine). Liu and Ozsu (2009) presented an algorithm which is based on Bayesian statistics. It involves the use of frequencies of instances to classes, and of classes, in the training set. The research paper by Ralescu et al. (2015) dwelt on both geometric and statistical methods. The authors presented a classification algorithm based on distance frequency. The algorithm combines both the explicit geometric and statistical characteristics of data into a class representation. By using two well-known data sets with and without noise, the authors showed that the algorithm is less sensitive to the training data set than other classifiers.

The HMM is a statistical technique in which a sequence is modeled as the output of a discrete stochastic process. This is facilitated via a series of states which are somehow hidden from the observer (i.e. latent). A Markov model is a model in which the future states of a pseudo-randomly changing system depend solely on the current state and not on the events which precede this state. This property is known as the Markov property. Thus, HMM is the Markov model in which the observations are dependent on a hidden Markov process. In a typical HMM, there is the Markov process X. There is also an observable process Y such that its outcome is a function of X in a known way. Since X cannot be measured directly, the goal is to learn about the state of X through the observation of Y. As the name implies, this model is used when the system is controlled but the system state is partially observable (Azeraf et al., 2023; Chatzis & Demiris, 2012; Gassiat et al., 2016; Kundu et al., 1989; Sipos, 2016; Chatzis & Kosmopoulos, 2011). Apart from AI, HMM has been applied to many areas of study including bioinformatics (Shah et al., 2019a, b; Pratas et al., 2017), finance (Petropoulos et al., 2016; Sipos et al., 2016), information theory (Abraham et al., 2023), solar energy utilization (Munkhammar & Widen, 2018a, b), electrical power forecasting (Carpinone et al., 2015), etc.

Oluwade et al. (2020) presented a general model for studying human languages via the structure of computer languages using the concept of equivalence classes. The work of Agbogun et al. (2018) was on the application of an ML algorithm for pattern recognition of unstructured web data. On the other hand, Agbogun et al. (2019) focused on the application of ML algorithms to the information extraction of structured academic data from unstructured web documents. Some works on face recognition algorithms and applications include O'Toole et al. (2007), Aro et al. (2017), Akpan et al. (2017), Schwarzer and Massaro (2001), and Yacoob and Davis (2002). In Akpan and Osakwe (2009), the authors used principal component analysis and eigenfaces algorithms to subject 480 human faces to experimental analysis such that 360 faces served as the training set and 120 faces as the test set. Some related works on the qualitative theory of differential equations include Belattar et al. (2023), which is on the qualitative theory of differential systems with respect to the study of limit cycles. Jin et al. (2023) discussed the AI of a special type of neural network systems (Poisson neural networks) as they relate to autonomous differential systems. In Anastassiou et al. (2012), Bujac and Vulpe (2015), as well as Jiang and Llibre (2005), the authors presented the qualitative classification of certain dynamical systems. General principles of the qualitative equivalence of autonomous ordinary differential equations were highlighted in Oluwade (1999), and the cases when $n=1$ and $n=2$ in Equation (9.1) were used as case studies. Oluwade (2004) studied many binary systems of computer and communication codes, which can be viewed as special cases of the quartic code arising from the phase portraits of (1.1) when $n=1$.

METHODOLOGY AND RESULTS

The methodology used in this book chapter is based on the qualitative equivalence of autonomous ordinary differential equations, as derived from the qualitative theory of differential equations. Given a family of trajectories in Equation (9.1) which are related by translations, the qualitative behavior of an individual member of the family determines that of the whole family. This behavior is determined by the function f. By defining an equivalence relation on Equation (9.1), it follows that two or more equations which are qualitatively equivalent belong to the same equivalence class, called the qualitative class. Generally, two families of trajectories of Equation (9.1) are said to be qualitatively equivalent if they are similar in shape, i.e. if they have the same number of critical points of the same nature and are arranged in the same order along the fixed line. Thus, the phase portrait (i.e. geometrical representation) of Equation (9.1) is completely determined by the nature of its critical points. It follows that all equations in the same qualitative class exhibit the same qualitative behavior which describes the qualitative characteristics or properties of the solutions. The relevant qualitative properties are the existence and uniqueness of solutions. In the case in which $n=1$, Equation (9.1) becomes an equation on the line. The phase portrait of Equation (9.1) on line, H, when there is a unique critical point, is given by

$H \in \sigma = \{$Attractor (A), Repellor (R), Positive Shunt (P), Negative Shunt $(N)\}$, where $\in$ is the set symbol for "element of".

Definition

Let $g_i \in \sigma$ and suppose $\Theta = g_1 g_2 \ldots g_n$, an n-wise combination of elements g_i of σ. Then g_i is said to be a generation of σ. It follows that the phase portrait of Equation (9.1) is a generation of σ.

Theorem (Oluwade, 2005)

Let H_r is the universal set of the phase portraits of Equation (9.1) when all the critical points have real values, H_{rc} the universal set of the phase portraits of Equation (9.1) when the critical points are both real and complex, while H_c is the universal set of the phase portraits of the equation when all the critical points are complex conjugates. Then the total number of qualitative classes of Equation (9.1) is given by $K = o(H_r) + o(H_{rc}) + o(H_c)$.

Proof

Since $H_r \cap H_{rc} \cap H_c = \emptyset$, the result follows from the fundamental principle of set theory, with respect to the order of a union of sets.

To describe the phase portraits of Equation (9.1) in space, it is necessary to establish a basis for comparing a real-valued critical point and a complex-valued critical point, as well as comparing two complex-valued critical points of Equation (9.1). By applying the well-ordering principle, a natural order can be provided for a subset of the set of complex numbers (C) (an unordered field), to which all the critical points of Equation (9.1) belong. Suppose $u_1 = (r_1, s_1) = r_1 + is_1$ and $u_2 = (r_2, s_2) = r_2 + is_2$ are two critical points of Equation (9.1), where $r_1, r_2, s_1, s_2 \in \mathbf{R}$ (the set of complex numbers). If $r_1 = r_2$, consider $u_1 \leq u_2$ if $s_1 \leq s_2$, where $\leq$ has the usual meaning of 'less than or equal to'. Is $s_1 = 0$, consider $u_1 \leq 0 (> 0)$ if $r_1 < 0 (> 0)$. If $r_1 \neq r_2$, consider $u_1 \leq u_2$ if $r_1 \leq r_2$.

Theorem

Let $\Theta = \{\Theta_i : I = 1, 2, ..., 26\}$ be the set of uppercase English alphabets. Define a relation on Θ such that $\Theta_i \tilde{} \Theta_j$ iff Θ_i and Θ_j have exactly the same number of nodes and same number of links. Then $\tilde{}$ is an equivalence relation.

Proof

It shall be shown that $\tilde{}$ satisfies reflexivity, symmetry and transitivity properties. Let α_{1i} be the number of nodes of Θ_i, and α_{2i} the number of links of Θ_i given by the pair $(\alpha_{1i}, \alpha_{2i})$. Since $(\alpha_{1i}, \alpha_{2i}) = (\alpha_{1i}, \alpha_{2i})$, then $\tilde{}$ is reflexive. Now, $(\alpha_{1i}, \alpha_{2i}) = (\alpha_{1j}, \alpha_{2j})$ implies that $(\alpha_{1j}, \alpha_{2j}) = (\alpha_{1i}, \alpha_{2i})$ and so $\tilde{}$ is symmetric. Finally, if $(\alpha_{1i}, \alpha_{2i}) = (\alpha_{1j}, \alpha_{2j})$ and $(\alpha_{1j}, \alpha_{2j}) = (\alpha_{1k}, \alpha_{2k})$ implies $(\alpha_{1i}, \alpha_{2i}) = (\alpha_{1k}, \alpha_{2k})$. That is, $\tilde{}$ satisfies the transitivity property. Hence $\tilde{}$ is an equivalence relation. It follows that $\tilde{}$ has distinct equivalence classes which happen to be ten in number, as shown in Table 9.2. Table 9.1 shows the number of nodes and the number of links for the 26 English alphabets.

TABLE 9.1 Number of nodes and number of links for the 26 English alphabets

S/N	CHARACTER/ ALPHABET	(TOTAL) NUMBER OF NODES	(TOTAL) NUMBER OF LINKS	PAIR OF NUMBER OF NODES AND NUMBER OF LINKS
1	A	5	10	(5,10)
2	B	3	4	(3,4)
3	C	2	2	(2,2)
4	D	4	4	(4,4)
5	E	6	10	(6,10)
6	F	5	8	(5,8)
7	G	3	4	(3,4)

(Continued)

TABLE 9.1 (*Continued*)   Number of nodes and number of links for the 26 English alphabets

S/N	CHARACTER/ ALPHABET	(TOTAL) NUMBER OF NODES	(TOTAL) NUMBER OF LINKS	PAIR OF NUMBER OF NODES AND NUMBER OF LINKS
8	H	6	10	(6,10)
9	I	6	10	(6,10)
10	J	4	6	(4,6)
11	K	5	8	(5,8)
12	L	3	4	(3,4)
13	M	5	7	(5,7)
14	N	4	6	(4,6)
15	O	1	0	(1,0)
16	P	3	4	(3,4)
17	Q	3	4	(3,4)
18	R	5	10	(5,10)
19	S	2	2	(2,2)
20	T	4	5	(4,5)
21	U	2	2	(2,2)
22	V	3	4	(3,4)
23	W	5	8	(5,8)
24	X	5	8	(5,8)
25	Y	4	6	(4,6)
26	Z	4	6	(4,6)

TABLE 9.2   Equivalence classes of the set of uppercase English alphabets

$(\alpha_{1i}, \alpha_{2i})$	ALPHABETS SATISFYING $(\alpha_{1i}, \alpha_{2i})$	NUMBER OF ALPHABETS SATISFYING $(\alpha_{1i}, \alpha_{2i})$
(1,0)	O	1
(2,2)	C, S, U	3
(3,4)	B, G, L, P, Q, V	6
(4,4)	D	1
(4,5)	T	1
(4,6)	J, N, Y, Z	4
(5,7)	M	1
(5,8)	F, K, W, X	4
(5,10)	A, R	2
(6,10)	E, H, I	3
	Total number of alphabets	26

where $\alpha_{1i}, \alpha_{2i} \in N$ (the set of natural numbers)

APPLICATION TO HUMANITARIAN CAMPS

A humanitarian or refugee camp is considered a typical application. Let each letter of the English alphabet represent a unique person/identity in a humanitarian camp. Suppose the nodes and links of the alphabet represent the prior determined characteristics of a person, each of which is weighted equally. That is, every node or link represents a particular generic characteristic. Refugees can then be grouped together according to the stated criteria, depending on the circumstances. For instance, these criteria may include:

- Same number of nodes.
- Same number of links.
- Same total number of nodes and links.
- Least number of nodes and/or links.
- Highest number of nodes and/or links.

Suppose further that, due to management policy, refugees with similar affinities are to be grouped together, say, for the purpose of sharing limited resources/palliatives. Table 9.3 shows a typical list of 11 refugees in a humanitarian camp. The table shows that both Desibi Deinke (S/N 2) and Zaynab Fitira (S/N 3) have the highest number of nodes by surname, while Quenette Ross (S/N 10) has the least number of nodes by surname. On the other hand, Lina Abdulmalik (S/N 6) has the highest number of nodes by link, Zaynab Fitira has the second highest number of links by surname, and Anne Coin (S/N 11) has the least number of links by surname. However, it is Lina Abdulmalik

TABLE 9.3   Computation of the total number of nodes and links for a typical list of persons in a humanitarian camp

S/N	NAME	NUMBER OF NODES BY SURNAME	NUMBER OF LINKS BY SURNAME	TOTAL NUMBER OF NODES AND COLUMNS BY SURNAME
1	Aleb Van	12	20	32
2	Desibi Deinke	31	48	79
3	Zaynab Fitira	31	53	84
4	Cosmas Nwobi	19	28	47
5	Adelewa Kayode	25	38	63
6	Lina Abdulmalik	41	63	104
7	Amitabh Susan	15	22	37
8	Chun Chan	17	28	45
9	Bruconni Wendy	23	34	57
10	Quenette Ross	10	24	34
11	Anne Coin	13	18	31

who has the highest total number of nodes and links, while Anne Coin has the lowest total number of nodes and links. Thus, the resources may be distributed according to a pre-determined protocol based on the number of nodes and/or links. For instance, it may be decided that Lina Abdulmalik will be served first for having the highest total count of nodes and links. In another sense, both Desibi Deinke and Zaynab Fitira may be put in the same group because they have the same number of nodes.

In a real case scenario, there may be hundreds or thousands of such refugees. In the table, the total number of nodes and the total number of links per surname are indicated. When two or more persons have the same surname, then a shift is made to the alphabet of the first name, starting with the first alphabet, then the second alphabet, and so on. If the surnames and first names are the same, then there will be a further shift to the middle names, etc.

Several traditional and technical pre-determined protocols have been used with respect to the order to follow in sharing resources with a group of persons from time immemorial. These include sharing based on surname, needs, contribution, geographical location, religious affiliation/belief, age, seniority in rank, first come, first serve, etc. Sometimes, an arbitrary protocol may be used. Many of the above protocols are popular and may be easily predicted, guessed, or predicted to favor some persons in a group. Generally, the modus operandi of sharing resources may be fair or unfair. The focus of this chapter is on the fair sharing of scarce or abundant resources. The humanitarian principle which this chapter aligns with relates to the famous (fair) cake-cutting problem (Procaccia, 2016; Steinhaus, 1949; Segal-Halevi et al., 2017; Balkanski et al., 2014; Nyman et al., 2020; Segal-Halevi, 2021; Bel et al., 2022). This is a problem which considers how to find the best or optimal way in which a cake (i.e. resource) can be shared among a set of people so that all are happy with their share. In the classic case, this problem involves cutting arbitrarily small pieces of a heterogeneous resource and sharing the pieces fairly among persons who have different preferences. This is in direct contrast to Pareto efficiency, which is also known as Pareto optimality. Pareto optimality is an economic state or system in which it is impossible to improve the welfare of one person in a group without causing harm or damage to the welfare of another person in the same group. Thus, this chapter is not in line with Pareto optimality. The basic assumption is that no one person (or refugee) in the humanitarian camp has a prior advantage over another.

CONCLUSION

This chapter presents a novel pattern recognition classifier algorithm based on the qualitative equivalence of autonomous ordinary differential equations. The focus is on the 26 uppercase English alphabets. Similar applications may be carried out on the lowercase English alphabets and the digits. The principle upon which the qualitative theory is based is that equations are not solved explicitly. However, differential equations which have similar solution curves are put in the same class. It is an effective method in the sense that if two differential equations A and B have the same solution curves and the properties of A are well known, these properties may simply be extended to B without any investigation of the properties of B. The present chapter relates only to the properties of existence and the uniqueness of solutions. The technique described in this chapter may be integrated into other AI systems by using the qualitative equivalence of differential equations as the classifier.

ACKNOWLEDGMENT

The work in this chapter was supported by a generous research grant by a group of foreign-based Nigerians. The author would like to thank the group for their support.

REFERENCES

Abraham, K., Gassiat, E., & Naulet, Z. (2023). Fundamental limits for learning hidden Markov model parameters, *IEEE Transactions on Information Theory*, 69(3), 1777–1794.

Agbogun, J. B., Akpan, V. A., Oluwade, B., & Yemi-Peters, V. I. (2019). A prototype machine learning algorithm and it's possible application to information extraction of structured academic data from unstructured web documents. *African Journal of Management Information System*, 1(2), 30–43.

Agbogun, J. B., Akpan, V. A., Yemi-Peters, V. I., Oluwade, B. A., & Bakpo, F. S. (2018). Dynamic modeling based on machine learning approach for unstructured web data pattern recognition and predictions. *American Journal of Computer Science and Engineering*. https://www. openscienceonline.com/journal/ajcse.

Akpan, V. A., & Osakwe, R. A. O. (2009). Face image processing, analysis and recognition algorithms for enhanced optimal face recognition systems design: A comparative study. *African Journal of Computing & ICT*, 2(2), 21–40.

Akpan, V. A., Agbogun, J. B., Babalola, M. T., & Oluwade, B. A. (2017). Radial basis function neuroscaling algorithms for efficient facial image recognition. *Machine Learning Research*, 2(4), 152–168.

Anastassiou, S., Pnevmatikos, S., & Bountis, T. (2012). Classification of dynamical systems based on a decomposition of their vector fields. *Journal of Differential Equations*, 253(7), 2252–2262.

Appati, J. K., Owusu, E, Soli, M. A. T., & Adu-Manu, K. S. (2022). A novel convolutional Atangana-Baleanu fractional derivative mask for medical image edge analysis. *Journal of Experimental & Theoretical Artificial Intelligence*. https://doi.org/10.1080/09528 13X.2022.2108147

Aro, T. O., Oluwade, B., Abikoye, O., & Bajeh, A. (2017). A 2-dimensional Gabor-filters for face recognition system: A survey. *Annals, Computer Science Series Journal Romania Tome* 15(Fasc 1), 104–112.

Arrowsmith, D. K., & Place, C. M. (1982). *Ordinary Differential Equations: A Qualitative Approach with Applications*. London: Chapman and Hall.

Asokan, A., & Anitha, J. (2019). Edge preserved satellite image denoising using median and bilateral filtering. In K. C. Santosh & R. S. Hegad (Eds.), *Recent Trends in Image Processing and Pattern Recognition* (pp. 688–699). Singapore: Springer. https://doi.org/10.1007/978-981-13-9181-1-59

Azeraf, E., Monfrini, E., & Pieczynski, W. (2023). Equivalence between LC-CRF and HMM, and discriminative computing of HMM-based MPM and MAP. *Algorithms*, *16*(3), 173.

Balkanski, E., Branzel, S., Kurokawa, D., & Procaccia, A. (2014). Simultaneous cake cutting. *Proceedings of the 28th AAAI Conference on Artificial Intelligence (AAAI)* (pp. 566–572). Québec City.

Balochian, S., & Baloochian, H. (2022). Edge detection on noisy images using Prewitt operator and fractional order differentiation. *Multimedia Tools and Application*, *81*(7), 9759–9770. https://doi.org/10.1007/s11042-022-12011-1

Bel, X., Lu, X., & Suksompong, W. (2022). Truthful cake sharing. *Proceedings of the AAAI Conference on Artificial Intelligence*, *36*(5), 4809–4817.

Belattar, M., Cheurfa, R., & Bendjeddou, A. (2023). Cubic planar differential systems with non-algebraic limit cycles enclosing a focus. *International Journal of Dynamical Systems and Differential Equations*, *3*, 197–208.

Bishop, C. (2006). *Pattern Recognition and Machine Learning*. New York: Springer.

Brunelli, R. (2009). *Template Matching Techniques in Computer Vision: Theory and Practice*. New York: Wiley.

Bujac, C., & Vulpe, N. (2015). Classification of cubic differential systems with invariant straight lines of total multiplicity eight and two distinct infinite singularities. *Electronic Journal of the Qualitative Theory of Differential Equations*, *74*, 1–38.

Burger, W., & Burge, M. J. (2022). *Digital Image Processing: An Algorithmic Introduction*. Cham: Springer. https://doi.org/10.1007/978-1-4471-6684-9

Carpinone, A., Giorgio, M., Langello, R., & Testa, A. (2015). Markov chain modelling for very short term wind power forecasting. *Electrical Power Systems Research*, *122*, 152–158.

Chatzis, S., & Demiris, Y. (2012). A reservoir-driven non-stationary hidden Markov model. *Pattern Recognition*, *45*(11), 3985–3996.

Chatzis, S., & Kosmopoulos, D. (2011). A variational Bayesian methodology for hidden Markov models utilizing Student's-t mixtures. *Pattern Recognition*, *44*(2), 295–306.

Chen, L., Gao, J., Lopes, A. M., Zhang, Z., Chu, Z., & Wu, R. (2023). Adaptive factional-order genetic-particle swarm optimization Otsu algorithm for image segmentation. *Applied Intelligence*, *53*(22), 26949–26966. https://doi.org/10.1007/s10489-023-04969-8

Dasarathy, B. V. (1991). *Nearest Neighbor (NN) Norms: NN Pattern Classification Techniques*. Los Alamitos, CA: IEEE Computer Society Press.

Di Nunzio, G. M. (2014). A new decision to take for cost-sensitive naïve-Bayes classifiers. *Information Process Management*, *50*(5), 653–674.

Farid, D. M., Chang, L., Rahman, C. M., Hossain, M. A., Strachan, R. (2014). Hybrid decision tree and naïve Bayes classifiers for multi-class classification tasks. *Expert System and Application*, *41*(4, Part 2), 1937–1946.

Gagniuc, P. A. (2017). *Markov Chains: From Theory to Implementation and Experimentation*. John Wiley & Sons, Amsterdam.

Gassiat, E., Cleynen, A., & Robin, S. (2016). Inference in finite state space non parametric Hidden Markov models. *Statistics and Computing*, *26*(1), 61–71.

Gorban, A. N., Mirkes, E. M., & Tyukin, I. Y. (2018). Corrections of AI systems by linear discriminants: Probabilistic foundations. *Information Sciences*, *466*, 303–322.

Gunther, M. (2009). Face detection and recognition using maximum likelihood classifiers on Gabor graphs. *International Journal of Pattern Recognition and Artificial Intelligence*, *23*, 433–461.

Hassan, N. M., Hamad, S., & Mahar, K. (2022). Mammogram breast cancer cad systems for mass detection and classification: A review. *Multimedia Tools and Application*, *81*(14), 20043–20075. https://doi.org/10.1007/s11042-022-12332-1

Haykin, S. (1994). *Neural Networks, a Comprehensive Foundation*. New York: Macmillan College Publishing Company Inc.

Huang, T., Wang, X., Wang, C., Liu, X., Yu, Y., & Qiu, W. (2023). Super-resolution reconstruction algorithm for depth image based on fractional calculus. In *35th Chinese Control and Decision Conference (CCDC)* (pp. 389–396). Yichang: IEEE. https://doi.org/10/1109/CCDC58219.2023.10326972.

Jiang, Q., & Llibre, J. (2005). Qualitative classification of singular points. *Qualitative Theory of Dynamical Systems*, 6(1), 87–167.

Jin, P., Zhang, Z., Kevrekidis, L. G., & Karniadakis, G. E. (2023). Learning Poisson systems and trajectories of autonomous systems via Poisson neural networks. *IEEE Transactions on Neural Networks and Learning Systems*, 34(11), 8271–8283.

Joachims, T. (2002). *Learning to Classify Text Using Support Vector Machines – Methods, Theory and Algorithms*. New York: Kluwer/Springer.

Jolliffe, I. T., & Cadima, J. (2016). Principal component analysis: A review and recent developments. *Philosophical Transactions of the Royal Society A: Mathematical, Physical and Engineering Sciences*, 374, 20150202.

Joshi, M., Bhosale, S., & Vyawahare, V. A. (2023). Survey of fractional calculus applications in artificial neural networks. *Artificial Intelligence Review*, 56(11), 13897–13950. https://doi.org/10.1007/s10462-023-10474-8

Karim, F. K., Jalab, H. A., Ibrahim, R. W., & Alaa, R. (2022). Mathematical model based on fractional trace operator for COVID-19 image enhancement. *Journal of the King Saud University – Science*, 34(7), 102254.

Khan, M. A., Ullah, A., Fu, Z. J., Khan, S., & Khan, S. (2024). Image restoration via combining a fractional order variational filter and a TGV penalty. In *Multimedia Tools and Application*. https://doi.org/10.1007/s11042-023-17774-17779

Koutroumbas, K., & Theodoridis, S. (2008). *Pattern Recognition*. Boston, MA: Academic Press.

Kundu, A., He, Y., & Bahl, P. (1989). Recognition of handwritten word: First and second order hidden Markov model based approach. *Pattern Recognition*, 22(3), 283–297.

Lavin-Delgado, J. E., Solis-Perez, J. E., Gomez-Aguila, J. F., Razo-Hernandez, J. R., Etemad, S., & Rezapour, S. (2024). An improved object detection algorithm based on the Hessian matrix and conformable derivative. In *Circuits, Systems, and Signal Processing*. Berlin: Springer Nature. https://doi.org/10.1007/s00034-024-02669-3

Liu, L., & Ozsu, M. T. (Eds.). (2009). *Encyclopedia of Database Systems*. Boston, MA: Springer.

Munkhammar, J., & Widen, J. (2018a). An n-state Markov chain mixture distribution model of the clear-sky index. *Solar Energy*, 173, 487–495.

Munkhammar, J., & Widen, J. (2018b). A Markov-chain probability distribution mixture approach to the clear-sky index. *Solar Energy*, 170, 174–183.

Nyman, K., Su, F. E., & Zerbibi, S. (2020). Fair division with multiple pieces. *Discrete Applied Mathematics*, 283, 115–122.

Oluwade, B. (1999). *Qualitative equivalence of autonomous ordinary differential equations* (unpublished Master of Science thesis). Obafemi Awolowo Universlty, Ile-Ife, Nigeria.

Oluwade, B. (2003). *An Introductory Course on Computer Science (with Exercises)*. Ibadan, Nigeria: Peerless Grace Prints & Publishing.

Oluwade, B. (2004). *Design and analysis of computer-coded character sets* (doctoral thesis). University of Ibadan, Ibadan, Nigeria.

Oluwade, B. (2005). Modelling fractal patterns via the qualitative equivalence of a nonlinear ODE. *Nonlinear Analysis*, 63, e2409–e2414.

Oluwade, B., Osofisan, A., Ilori, S. A., Shola, P. B., & Akin-Ojo, R. (2020). A computational model for studying the characteristics of languages using coded character sets. *University of Ibadan Journal of Science and Logics in ICT Research*, 4(1), 85–95.

Omolu, B., & Oluwade, B. (2017). On the application of the nearest neighbour classifier algorithm to character pattern recognition. *African Journal of Computing & ICT*, 10(1 & 2), 1–17.

O'Toole, A. J., Phillips, P. J., Jiang, F., Ayyad, J., Penard, N., & Abdi, H. (2007). Face recognition algorithms surpass humans matching faces over changes in illumination. *IEEE Transactions on Pattern Analysis and Machine Intelligence*, *29*(9), 1642–1646.

Pestov, V. (2013). Is the k-NN classifier in high dimensions affected by the curse of dimensionality. *Computer and Mathematics with Application*, *65*(10), 1421–1437.

Petropoulos, A., Chatzis, S. P., & Xanthopoulos, S. (2016). A novel corporate credit rating system based on Student'st-hidden Markov models. *Expert Systems with Applications*, *53*, 87–105.

Pratas, D., Hosseini, M., & Pinho, A. J. (2017). Substitutional tolerant Markov models for relative compression of DNA sequences. In *PACBB 2017-11th International Conference on Practical Applications of Computational Biology & Bioinformatics* (pp. 265–272). Cham: Switzerland.

Procaccia, A. (2016). Cake Cutting Algorithms. In F. Brandt, V. Conitzer, U. Endriss & J. Lang (Eds.), *Handbook of Computational Social Choice* (pp. 311–330). Cambridge: Cambridge University Press.

Quinlan, J. R. (1983). Learning efficient classification procedures and their application to chess end games. In R. S. Michalski, J. G. Carbonell & T. M. Mitchell (Eds.), *Machine Learning, an Artificial Intelligence Approach* (pp. 463–482). Berlin, Heidelberg: Springer.

Quinlan, J. R. (1986). Induction of decision trees. *Machine Learning*, *1*(1), 81–106.

Ralescu, A., Diaz, I., & Rodriguez-Muniz, L. J. (2015). A classification algorithm based on geometric and statistical information. *Journal of Computational and Applied Mathematics*, *275*, 335–344.

Russell, S. J., & Norvig, P. (1995). *Artificial Intelligence: A Modern Approach*. Upper Saddle River, NJ: Prentice-Hall.

Schwarzer, G., & Massaro, D. W. (2001). Modelling face identification processing in children and adults, *Journal of Experimental Child Psychology*, *79*, 139–161.

Segal-Halevi, E. (2021). Fair muti-cake cutting. *Discrete Applied Mathematics*, *291*, 15–35.

Segal-Halevi, E., Nitzan, S., & Aumann, Y. (2017). Fair and square: Cake cutting in two dimensions. *Journal of Mathematical Economics*, *70*, 1–28.

Shah, S., Dubey, A. K., & Reif, J. (2019a). Programming temporal DNA barcodes for single molecule fingerprinting. *Nano Letters*, *19*(4), 2668–2673.

Shah, S., Dubey, A. K., & Reif, J. (2019b). Improved optical multiplexing with temporal DNA bar odes. *ACS Synthetic Biology*, *8*(5), 1100–1111.

Sipos, I. R. (2016). Parallel stratified MCMC sampling of AR-HMMs for stochastic time series prediction. In *Proceedings, 4th Stochastic Modeling Techniques and Data Analysis International Conference with Demographics Workshop (SMIDA2016)* (pp. 295–306). Valletta.

Sipos, I. R., Ceffer, A., & Levendovszky, J. (2016). Parallel optimization of sparse portfolios with AR-HMMs. *Computational Economics*, *49*(4), 563–578.

Steinhaus, H. (1949). The problem of fair division. *Econometrica*, *17*, 315–319.

Thanaki, J. (2017). *Python Natural Language Processing*. Birmingham: Packt.

Wakahara, T., & Yamashita, Y. (2014). K-NN classification of handwritten characters via accelerated {GAT} correlation. *Pattern Recognition*, *47*(3), 994–1001.

Walch, M. A., & Pawlicki, J. A. (1993). Image recognition system (United States Patent No. 5267332), United States Patent and Trademark Office. https://patft.uspto.gov/netacgi/nph-Parser?patent number=5267332

Wurtz, R. P., Konen, W., & Behrmann, K.-O. (1999). On the performance of neuronal matching algorithms. *Neural Networks*, *12*(1), 127–134.

Yacoob, Y., & Davis, L. (2002). Smiling faces are better for face recognition. In *Proceedings of the Fifth IEEE International Conference on Automatic Face and Gesture Recognition* (pp. 59–64), 20–21 May. *IEEE*, Washington DC.

Zhang, N., Yang, J., & Qian, J. J. (2012). Component-based global k-NN classifier for small sample size problems. *Pattern Recognition Letters*, *33*(13), 1689–1694.

Exploring Humanitarian Applications of Artificial Intelligence in Cardiovascular Disease Diagnosis

10

Tarcízio Ferrão and Adeyemi Abel Ajibesin

INTRODUCTION

Currently, new techniques for detecting cardiovascular diseases (CVDs) are being developed through the application of artificial intelligence (AI), which has shown promising results compared to traditional methods. As in other scientific areas, challenges are being faced for an efficient implementation of AI algorithms while respecting human principles. First, it is necessary to understand some essential concepts that connect these two areas of great interest.

CVD encompasses a set of very dangerous diseases that affect the heart, blood vessels, arteries, and veins, resulting in processes that compromise the structure and functioning of the cardiovascular system. They are the leading cause of death worldwide (Vellasamy et al., 2021). CVD is a chronic syndrome that leads to heart failure, dysfunction of blood

119

vessels, and coronary artery infarction (Baghdadi et al., 2023). Harmful alcohol consumption, unhealthy eating, and physical inactivity form a set of behavioral risk factors (WHO, 2024). Additionally, age is an independent risk factor as the elderly are more prone to developing heart diseases and pathologies such as diabetes and hypertension (Ciumărnean et al., 2022). It is important to underline that healthy eating habits, adequate sleep, and cessation of excessive smoking already yield acceptable results in combating CVD and promoting cardiorespiratory fitness (Kaminsky et al., 2022).

Various diagnostic techniques for CVD are being explored. Biosensors and nanotechnology devices are current strategies for reducing the detection time of these diseases (Wu et al., 2021). The most common techniques employed to diagnose cardiovascular diseases include magnetic resonance imaging, computed tomography, electrocardiography, and echocardiography (Shi et al., 2020). Magnetic resonance imaging uses radio waves to produce a three-dimensional representation of the heart, often employed in the detection of stroke and atherosclerosis. Computed tomography, on the other hand, utilizes X-ray beams to generate high-resolution images of tissues, enhancing contrast. Electrocardiography records the electrical activity of the heart and is beneficial in assessing symptoms such as chest pain in instances of angina, heart attack, and arrhythmia. Lastly, echocardiography employs sound waves to produce a visual depiction of the heart, facilitating the detection of potential cardiac disorders (Picard et al., 2019; Sabir et al., 2021).

Currently, there is no conventional method for the diagnosis of CVD. This challenge is due to the nature of the disease being silent until significant complications occur. The predominant diagnosis can be carried out through expensive imaging techniques or high-risk invasive procedures. Advanced imaging methods, such as magnetic resonance imaging or high-speed computed tomography, require sophisticated equipment and highly specialized professionals. Similarly, invasive procedures, including cardiac or cerebrovascular surgeries, are recognized for their associated risks, making them impractical for large-scale screening (Mamun & Elfouly, 2023; Oliveira et al., 2023). Figure 10.1 describes some diagnostic techniques for CVD.

As can be observed, there is still a need to develop new techniques for the detection of CVD. In addition to nanosystems, DL algorithms have shown better results in this task. DL techniques use a complex combination of feature encoding techniques to learn from old data and make accurate future predictions (Ahmad et al., 2021). The availability of CVD datasets in hospital databases provides enormous potential for training advanced DL algorithms for early detection and diagnosis of these diseases to contribute to early treatment (Baghdadi et al., 2023). DL utilizes a multilayered structure of algorithms called artificial neural networks (ANNs), inspired by human neural networks, to perform automated feature learning (Lee et al., 2022). Although few studies still explore the application of DL for disease prediction, these algorithms are effective and have demonstrated efficacy in the early detection of CVD (Lee et al., 2022; Quer et al., 2021).

The remainder of this chapter presents the application of deep learning (DL) for cardiovascular disease diagnosis, followed by a discussion of the proposed DL-based method for predicting cardiovascular disease and an analysis of the results. Additionally, this chapter explores future trends in AI applications in healthcare, including humanitarian perspectives and ethical issues. This chapter concludes with a summary of key points.

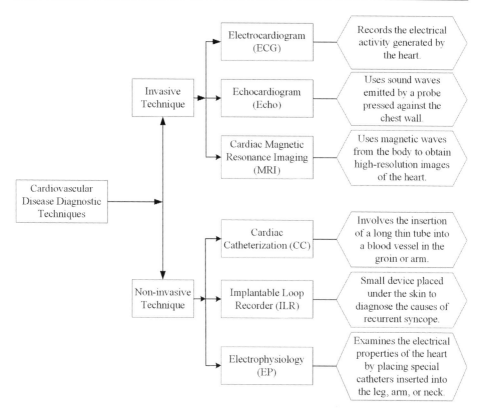

FIGURE 10.1   Examples of some common CVD diagnostic techniques.

APPLICATION OF DEEP LEARNING FOR CARDIOVASCULAR DISEASE DIAGNOSIS

Several DL algorithms have been used for CVD diagnoses. Traditional machine learning (ML) algorithms have a low level of accuracy in predictions and may not take into account differences in data (Hussain et al., 2021; Saheed, Longe, Baba, Rakshit, & Vajjhala, 2021; Subramani et al., 2023). However, some ML techniques are still very useful for CVD prediction, such as decision tree (DT), random forest (RF), support vector machine (SVM), and naive Bayes (NB) (Gavande & Chawan, 2021; Rakshit, Clement, & Vajjhala, 2022).

DL algorithms can be combined with other methods to offer promising results. A different approach to diagnosing CVD uses deep neural network (DNN) and statistical model to improve prediction patterns (Ramprakash et al., 2020). Meanwhile, SVM and ANN were analyzed to form two methods for heart disease diagnosis (Faieq & Mijwil, 2022). In this study, the authors concluded that SVM provides high-precision prediction results compared to DL-based mechanisms. Thus, it can be observed that, despite DL algorithms having advantages in more advanced aspects, ML remains an effective and reliable method for CVD detection. However, the major limitation of ML is its inability to handle large-scale datasets due to the lack of an intelligent framework that can utilize different data sources for disease prediction (Ali et al., 2020). In summary, algorithms such as CNN, SVM, ANN, RNN, and KNN have demonstrated better results for predicting CVD, with the former algorithms being the most used for different types of datasets (Alkayyali et al., 2023; Borah et al., 2022a).

All the research demonstrated the strong capabilities of DL in predicting CVD, but none of them addressed ethical aspects for implementation in real-world contexts. This fact underscores the need for studies to assess the applicability and predictive accuracy of DL techniques in real-world settings (Hu et al., 2023).

PROPOSED DL-BASED METHOD FOR PREDICTING CARDIOVASCULAR DISEASE

Most of the research implements DL algorithms such as CNN, DNN, or RNN for modeling new techniques for preventive diagnosis of CVD, in addition to ML algorithms such as SVM, KNN, and NB, which have also shown promising results (Ramprakash et al., 2020; Alkayyali et al., 2023; Borah et al., 2022b). Thus, this chapter tests the application of the recurrent convolutional neural network (RCNN) for CVD prediction as an acceptable alternative since it combines two models (CNN and RNN). The methodological procedures are summarized in the diagram in Figure 10.2.

Data Preparation

One of the essential steps in modeling DL algorithms is selecting the appropriate dataset as it affects the quality of the final model (Gong et al., 2023). For modeling the RCNN, the Cleveland dataset (*Heart Disease*) from the University of California, Irvine, was used, containing about 76 instances of which 14 are consistently used (Lin et al., 2022). This dataset has been widely used in recent works to assess the effectiveness of new models (Musa & Muhammad, 2022; Sarra et al., 2022). Selecting this dataset will facilitate the comparison of results obtained, as most recent models have also used this dataset. The Cleveland dataset consists of a total of 303 records, including attributes such as patient identification numbers, ages, social security numbers, type of chest pain, blood pressure, cholesterol levels, and blood sugar readings, among other health data. Of these data, 54.37% of people have a heart disease, and 45.63% do not have any heart disease (Sarra et al., 2022; Vijayashree & Sultana, 2020), as described in Figure 10.3.

Figure 10.4 depicts the correlation of the top 14 attributes present in the Cleveland dataset. Each attribute is explained in Table 10.1.

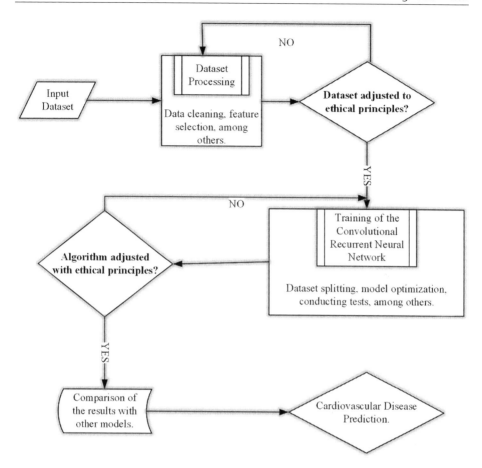

FIGURE 10.2 Methodological procedure diagram for recurrent convolutional neural network (RCNN).

Recurrent Convolutional Neural Network

As it is known, RCNN is a combination of CNN and RNN for application in sequential data and time series analysis in images. An RCNN consists of a CNN containing a recurrent convolutional layer (RCL) with recurrent connections from the generic RNN model with feed-forward input $s(t)$ and internal state $y(t)$ (Wang & Hu, 2017) given by

$$y(t) = H[s(t), y(t-1), \phi].$$ (10.1)

In this case, H represents the nonlinearity of the RNN and ϕ is its respective parameter. Meanwhile, the internal state of the RCL evolves in discrete time steps (Liang & Hu, 2015), that is,

$$y_{\mathrm{RCL}}(t) = \left(w_k^f\right)^T s^{(i,j)}(t) + \left(w_k^r\right)^T y^{(i,j)}(t-1) + \phi_k$$ (10.2)

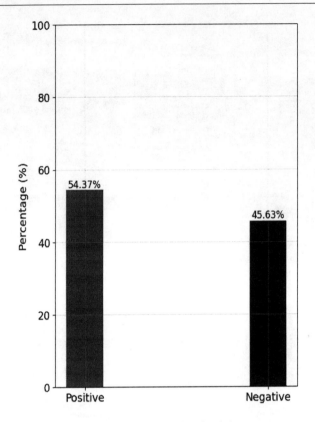

FIGURE 10.3   Class distribution for CVD in the Cleveland dataset.

where

(i, j) is the attribute unit at position k;
w_k^f and w_k^r are the vectorized feed-forward and recurrent weights, respectively.

The basic diagram of an RCNN is presented in Figure 10.5.

Evaluation Metrics of the Model

Table 10.2 describes a confusion matrix for binary classification, which indicates the errors and successes of a model compared to the expected results (Kulkarni et al., 2020). It is a very popular metric for evaluating ML and DL models that can be used for both binary classification problems and multiclass classification. From the confusion matrix, one can observe the following.

- *True Positive (TP)*: the accuracy rate for classifying the positive class.
- *True Negative (TN)*: the accuracy rate for classifying the negative class.

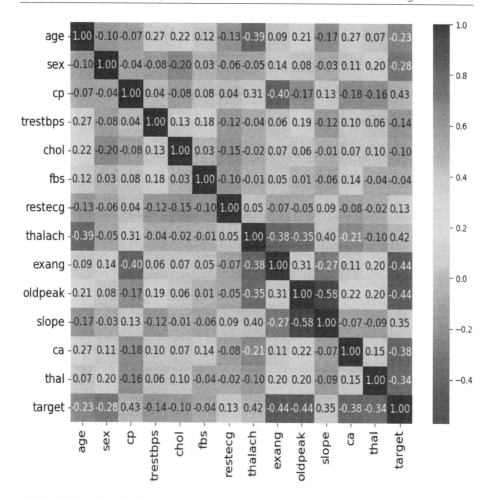

FIGURE 10.4   Correlation map of attributes in the Cleveland dataset.

- *False Positive (FP)*: also known as Type I error, occurs when the model predicts the positive class while it should predict the negative class.
- *False Negative (FN)*: also known as Type II error, occurs when the model predicts the negative class while it should predict the positive class.

Thus, the main evaluation metrics for ML and DL models have been outlined below.

- *Accuracy (A)*: it is a general performance metric of the model overall correctly classified attributes, given by

$$A = \frac{TN + TP}{TN + FP + FN + TP}.$$

(10.3)

TABLE 10.1   Description of attributes in the Cleveland dataset

ATTRIBUTE	DESCRIPTION	TYPE
age	Age in years between 29-77	Numeric
sex	Male (1) or Female (0)	Nominal
Cp	Type of chest pain: Typical angina (1); Atypical angina (2); Non-anginal pain (3); Asymptomatic (4);	Nominal
trestbps	Resting blood pressure in mmHg ranging from 94-200.	Numeric
chol	Serum cholesterol ranges from 126-564 mg/dL.	Numeric
fbs	It compares the fasting blood glucose level of an individual with 120mg/dl: False (0); True (1).	Numeric
restecg	Resting electrocardiographic results: Normal (0); ST-T wave abnormality (1); Left ventricular hypertrophy (2).	Nominal
thalach	Maximum heart rate achieved by an individual: 71-202 bpm.	Numeric
exang	Exercise-induced angina: No (0); Yes (1).	Nominal
oldpeak	Exercise-induced segment (ST) depression compared to rest: 0-6.20.	Numeric
slope	Peak exercise ST segment: Upsloping (1); Flat (2); Down sloping (3).	Nominal
ca	Number of major vessels colored by fluoroscopy: 0-3.	Nominal
thal	Thalassemia: Normal (3) Fixed defect (6) Reversible defect (7).	Nominal
target	Predicted values: CVD Negative (0); CVD Positive (1-4).	Nominal

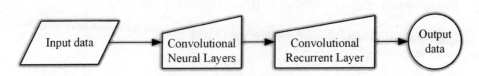

FIGURE 10.5   Diagram of the basic structure of the RCNN.

TABLE 10.2 Confusion matrix for binary classification

	PREDICTED VALUES	
Actual values	TP (True Positives)	FP (False Positives)
	FN (False Negatives)	TN (True Negatives)

- *Precision (P)*: measures the rate of correct classification for the entire positive class, including FP, given by

$$P = \frac{TP}{TP + FP}. \tag{10.4}$$

- *Recall (R)*: measures the rate of correct classification for the entire positive class, including FN, given by

$$R = \frac{TP}{TP + FN}. \tag{10.5}$$

- *F1-score (F1)*: it is the harmonic mean between precision and recall. This metric is used to evaluate models with balanced data where the model needs to balance predictions. It is given by

$$F_1 = 2\frac{P \times R}{P + R}. \tag{10.6}$$

Accuracy is useful when all classes are balanced or have similar distributions. Precision can be used when the focus is on minimizing FP, meaning when incorrectly classifying an instance as positive is undesirable because it has a high cost, such as in fraud detection. On the other hand, recall is ideal when the focus is on minimizing FN, meaning it is crucial to correctly identify all positive instances. For example, in disease detection problems, where missing a positive case classified by the model as negative (FN) can have serious consequences. Finally, F1-score can be used when both precision and recall are important, such as in information retrieval problems, where one desires the return of as many relevant results as possible (high recall), which are also truly relevant (high precision).

Therefore, for model evaluation, the following metrics from Equations (10.3) and (10.5) will be used as they are appropriate for the task of this model. Precision is included since it helps balance the recall metric.

ANALYSIS OF RESULTS

In general, the first evaluation metric of a model has been accuracy, which demonstrates overall performance. However, higher accuracy does not necessarily mean that the model will perform better in executing the assigned task, as this metric is appropriate for a specific characteristic of the dataset, namely, in situations where the classes in the dataset have approximately identical samples, as discussed earlier.

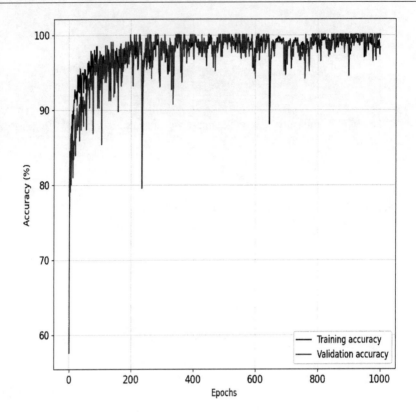

FIGURE 10.6   Validation and training accuracy.

Regarding accuracy, the RCNN algorithm demonstrated learning the data by achieving a value of 98.29%, which most algorithms have not easily reached. This is because the model is a combination of CNN and an RCL, making it an appropriate algorithm to achieve maximum values in metrics. However, it is important to note that other factors influence the performance of the models, including dataset quality and the requisite preprocessing procedures to expedite and ensure the fidelity of data assimilation.

As can be observed in Figure 10.6, the RCNN easily learned the samples from the Cleveland dataset, whereas, from epoch 600, the training and validation accuracies significantly improved. This means that this algorithm can also demonstrate promising results in other types of datasets for cardiovascular disease prognosis.

As is known, RCNN is designed in this work for medical applications. Thus, the evaluation metrics should be chosen according to the final objectives. Precision would not be very necessary to assess this model, as a high number of this metric indicates the possibility of the model admitting false negatives, which would lead to a situation where a set of positive patients would go untreated and without the necessary medical attention due to model errors. Therefore, recall is considered, as it tends to admit false positives, meaning that the higher the recall number, the model will guarantee the diagnosis of all cases of CVD, but it tends to include negative cases that are classified as positive.

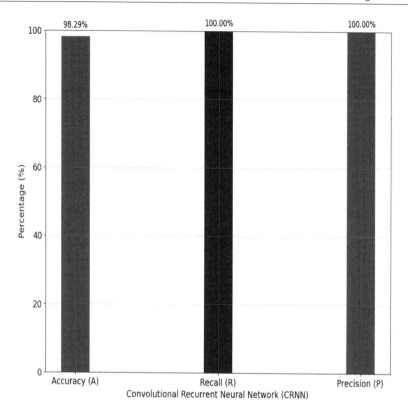

FIGURE 10.7   Comparison of validation metrics.

It should be noted that precision is not merely of low importance, as it balances the value of recall, and significantly reduces the number of false positives, which would save time in patient care and medical resources. Therefore, both metrics are important, but for disease prediction algorithms, the preferred condition is $R \geq P$.

Figure 10.7 demonstrates that the RCNN ensures accurate prediction of samples in the Cleveland dataset, meeting the necessary conditions as well as the ability to avoid false positives. Additionally, the recall and precision metrics are essential in these cases where the dataset is unbalanced, as discussed in previous sections. The combination of CNN and RCL demonstrates great potential by tending to balance the two metrics P and R in unbalanced datasets, which are typical in healthcare contexts.

From Figure 10.8, it is possible to observe that the model gradually reduces learning errors. After epoch 800, a reduction in errors is noticeable, ranging between 0 to 0.1, which is acceptable, given that errors for disease detection models should always be close to zero or very close to ensure real results. The loss values were obtained using the binary cross-entropy function H_P or logarithmic loss, given by

$$H_P(i) = -\frac{1}{K}\sum_{i=1}^{K} y_i \log[p(y_i)] + (1 - y_i)\log[1 - p(y_i)]. \tag{10.7}$$

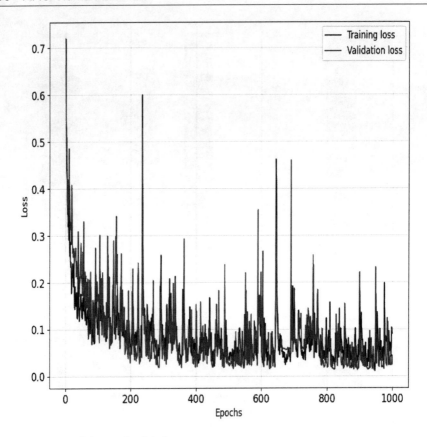

FIGURE 10.8   Training and validation errors.

And

> y_i is the actual result for prediction;
> $p(y_i)$ is the probability of the result y_i being positive, or $1-p(y_i)$ being negative for the entire dataset K.

Table 10.3 illustrates how the RCNN can be the best option compared to common ML and DL algorithms in recent literature for CVD prediction. To make a fair comparison, most of the selected models were trained using the same dataset presented in this chapter. Therefore, this algorithm can be explored with other datasets and has enormous potential to achieve acceptable results for CVD prediction, as it adapts and learns effortlessly from unbalanced data without requiring deep and complex data treatment. Additionally, it can be observed that the majority of the research (Vincent Paul et al., 2022) adopted accuracy as the primary evaluation metric, which would not be consistent for ML or DL models for disease diagnosis. This means that model evaluation metrics should be selected according to the objectives of the model application. For example,

TABLE 10.3 Comparison of RCNN with other common models

METHOD	REFERENCE	EVALUATION METRIC (%)		
		RECALL	PRECISION	ACCURACY
Machine learning	SVM (Sarra et al., 2022)	67.45%	85.71%	84.21%
	Chi-Squared and sequential minimal optimization (SMO) (Reddy et al., 2021)	86.50	86.50	86.47
	RF	99.63	99.02	98.44
	NB (Nashif et al., 2018)	86.40	86.40	86.40
	SVM (Nagavelli et al., 2022)	81.30	66.10	89.40
	KNN (Ogunpola et al., 2024)	97.44	96.50	96.50
	Logistic Regression (LR) (Srivenkatesh, 2020)	74	81	77.06
	Learning vector quantization (Srinivasan et al., 2023)	95.31	98.07	98.78
Deep learning	Backpropagation neural network (BP-NN) (Vincent Paul et al., 2022)	94.58	97.68	98.75
	Deep trained neocognitron neural network (DTNNN) (Vijayashree & Sultana, 2020)	95.31	98.07	98.78
	CardioHelp (Mehmood et al., 2021) with CNN	96.35	97.06	97
	DNN (Lee et al., 2022)	87.90	93.90	91.10
	CNN (Hussain et al., 2021)	100	94.73	96.77
	MLP (Ali et al., 2020)	82.50	84.50	83.50
	CNN with bidirectional long short-term memory (BiLSTM) (Ahmad et al., 2023)	93	94	94.07
	CNN with long short-term memory (LSTM) (Hossain et al., 2023b)	72.04	81.82	74.15
	Proposed RCNN	**100**	**100**	**98.29**

a model with accuracy A=100% and recall R=80% would not be preferable to a model with the opposite values, that is, A=80% and R=100%, despite the need to balance the latter parameter with precision P.

TRENDS IN FUTURE APPLICATIONS OF ARTIFICIAL INTELLIGENCE IN HEALTHCARE

AI is revolutionizing the healthcare sector, and its impact is only poised to grow in the coming years. Several promising trends are already in development or in the early stages of implementation, with the potential to completely transform the way healthcare is delivered. One of the trends in AI application in healthcare is the creation of person-alized treatment and prevention plans for each patient, considering their genetic data, health history, lifestyle, and other relevant factors, which may also include the patient's living environment. This technology will lead to more accurate diagnoses, more effec-tive treatments, and better outcomes for patients. Additionally, AI can automate many administrative and repetitive tasks currently performed by healthcare professionals, freeing up their time to focus on more complex activities that require more human inter-action, such as direct patient care.

Another future trend would be to improve assistance to physicians in the analy-sis of medical images, such as X-rays and computed tomography (CT) scans, to iden-tify anomalies and aid in disease diagnosis. The aim of this trend is to provide faster and more accurate diagnoses and reduce the need for invasive and unnecessary tests. Analogously, AI can evolve to accelerate the process of developing new drugs and therapies by analyzing large datasets and identifying new therapeutic targets, thereby improving treatments for severe and chronic diseases.

A recent area harnessing the potential of AI is 3D printing. AI can be used to create 3D models of organs and tissues, which can be utilized in custom implants and prosthetics to revolutionize regenerative medicine and enable the development of new treatments for chronic diseases. The application of AI in surgical procedures may increase, providing greater precision and control during operations. Similarly, AI can be used to expedite the vaccine development process by analyzing genomic data and identifying new vaccine targets (Biba & Vajjhala, 2022a; Biba & Vajjhala, 2022b). Improving telemedicine is also a focus of AI to enable physicians to conduct virtual consultations with patients and provide diagnoses and treatments remotely, thereby increasing access to healthcare for people in remote areas or with difficulty accessing a medical office.

A HUMANITARIAN PERSPECTIVE ON AI APPLICATIONS IN HEALTHCARE

The future of healthcare is intertwined with the rapid advancement of AI. Beginning with personalized medicine to early disease detection, AI promises to revolutionize how health is viewed and approached (J. Biomed. Inform., 2020). This technology has the potential to bridge the gap in healthcare access, particularly in underserved communi-ties and developing countries, by providing remote diagnosis, personalized treatment plans, and affordable healthcare solutions.

AI's impact extends beyond accessibility. It can optimize resource allocation, streamline processes, and improve efficiency, leading to cost savings in healthcare delivery. This makes healthcare more affordable and accessible to a wider population, ultimately improving health outcomes for individuals worldwide. Furthermore, AI can empower healthcare professionals by providing data-driven insights, automating tasks, and supporting decision-making (IEEE J. Biomed. Health Inform., 2019), allowing them to focus on patient care and complex cases.

The humanitarian potential of AI in healthcare is immense. It can help address global health challenges, such as chronic diseases, infectious outbreaks, and maternal mortality, by providing innovative solutions and improving access to care for those who need it most. AI-enabled tools can be used to develop new vaccines, track disease outbreaks, and provide remote healthcare services to remote areas, ultimately contributing to a healthier and more equitable world.

However, the ethical considerations surrounding AI in healthcare cannot be ignored. Ensuring data privacy and security is paramount, as is mitigating bias in algorithms to prevent discriminatory outcomes. Additionally, the potential for job displacement in the healthcare sector requires careful consideration and strategies to support healthcare professionals through this transition (J. Med. Ethics, 2020).

HUMANITARIAN AND ETHICAL ISSUES IN AI HEALTHCARE

Integrating AI into humanitarian efforts comes with significant challenges. Key ethical concerns include potential biases, privacy issues, and the necessity for transparency and accountability. It is crucial to develop and implement AI technologies responsibly, ensuring that they uphold human dignity and protect fundamental rights. Therefore, algorithms of AI should be implemented while observing ethical principles applied in the healthcare sector. Currently, there are no well-defined regulations to address the legal and ethical issues that may arise due to the use of AI in healthcare settings (Naik et al., 2022). Concerns exist regarding the application of AI not only in healthcare but also in everyday human life, such as cybersecurity, data privacy, transparency, cultural respect, and ensuring anti-racist policies.

ML and DL techniques must be reliable for both physicians and patients. Furthermore, the results predicted by the models should be clear, interpretable, and ensure a positive impact to preserve the dignity and well-being of the patient, as a fundamental ethical requirement (Rasheed et al., 2022). Figure 10.9 presents some ethical concerns regarding the application of AI in humanity.

Regarding the issue of who is responsible for ethical principles, it can be said that current medical AI is merely an auxiliary tool used in healthcare to diagnose and treat diseases, not qualified to be a responsible subject (Zhang & Zhang, 2023). This means that medical AI must adhere to a series of principles grouped into structural categories (privacy and security, mitigation of bias, transparency, accountability, governance, and inclusiveness), professional (explainability, fairness and justice, safety and reliability, decision-making and collegiality), and patient (autonomy, human values, equity and equality, non-maleficence, and beneficence) (Currie et al., 2020).

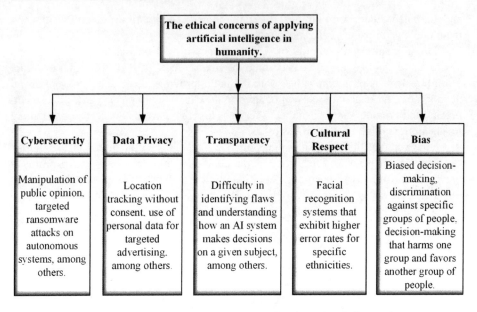

FIGURE 10.9   Some ethical concerns about the application of AI in humanity.

CONCLUSION

This chapter presents the main DL algorithms used for predicting CVD. Most of the research implements DL algorithms such as CNN, DNN, or RNN for the development of new CVD diagnostic techniques, in addition to ML algorithms such as SVM, KNN, and NB, which have also demonstrated better results. Thus, this chapter explored the application of RCNN as an alternative method to the most used models. The results were surprising, as RCNN was able to easily learn from the sample data, outperforming several techniques with an accuracy of 98.29% and a recall of 100%. This data shows that this model can predict CVD with greater precision, avoiding false negatives. Additionally, ethical principles of AI application in healthcare were analyzed, and it was found that all of humanity is susceptible to ethical violations when implementing AI algorithms. Thus, by knowing most of the ethical concerns, it is possible to minimize the risks of violation through the assumption of responsibility by developers, who should clarify how they addressed issues of possible violation of the ethical principles of the models they developed. This clarification can be achieved through the objective documentation suggested in this chapter. For future research, the RCNN could be tested on other, more recent datasets to assess its consistency in learning, as well as its balance in important metrics. Additionally, there is a need for the development of new datasets for CVD that are more recent and that consider ethical principles in AI.

Furthermore, responsibly developed and deployed, AI can greatly advance humanitarian goals and foster a more equitable world. To achieve this, AI initiatives should prioritize protecting vulnerable populations and promoting social equity. This chapter serves as a call to action, urging all stakeholders to embrace the opportunities and address the challenges presented by AI in humanitarian work.

REFERENCES

Ahmad, H., Asghar, M. U., Asghar, M. Z., Khan, A., & Mosavi, A. H. (2021). A hybrid deep learning technique for personality trait classification from text. *IEEE Access*, *1*(9), 146214–146232. https://doi.org/10.1109/ACCESS.2021.3121791

Ahmad, S., Asghar, M. Z., Alotaibi, F. M., & Alotaibi, Y. D. (2023). Diagnosis of cardiovascular disease using deep learning technique. *Soft Computing*, *27*(13), 8971–8990. https://doi.org/10.1007/s00500-022-07788-0

Ali, F., El-Sappagh, S., Islam, S. M. R., Kwak, D., Ali, A., Imran, M., & Kwak, K.-S. (2020). A smart healthcare monitoring system for heart disease prediction based on ensemble deep learning and feature fusion. *Information Fusion*, *1*(63), 208–222. https://doi.org/10.1016/j.inffus.2020.06.008

Alkayyali, Z. K. D., Idris, S. A. B., & Abu-Naser, S. S. (2023). A systematic literature review of deep and machine learning algorithms in cardiovascular diseases diagnosis. *Journal of Theoretical and Applied Information Technology*, *101*(4), 1353–1365, https://www.jatit.org/volumes/Vol101No4/16Vol101No4.pdf.

Baghdadi, N. A., Farghaly Abdelaliem, S. M., Malki, A., Gad, I., Ewis, A., & Atlam, E. (2023). Advanced machine learning techniques for cardiovascular disease early detection and diagnosis. *Journal of Big Data*, *10*(1), 1–11. https://doi.org/10.1186/s40537-023-00817-1

Biba, M., & Vajjhala, N. R. (2022a). Machine learning for metabolic networks modelling: a state-of-the-art survey. In Sanjiban Sekhar Roy, & Y.-H. Taguchi (Eds.), *Handbook of Machine Learning Applications for Genomics* (pp. 145–153). Singapore: Springer.

Biba, M., & Vajjhala, N. R. (2022b). Statistical relational learning for genomics applications: a state-of-the-art review. In Sanjiban Sekhar Roy, & Y.-H. Taguchi (Eds.), *Handbook of Machine Learning Applications for Genomics* (pp. 31–42). Singapore: Springer Nature.

Borah, S., Aliliele, K. C., Rakshit, S., & Vajjhala, N. R. (2022a). Applications of artificial intelligence in software testing. In Pradeep Kumar Mallick, Akash Kumar Bhoi, Paolo Barsocchi, & Victor Hugo C. de Albuquerque (Eds.), *Cognitive Informatics and Soft Computing: Proceeding of CISC 2021* (pp. 727–736). Singapore: Springer Nature.

Borah, S., Kama, C., Rakshit, S., & Vajjhala, N. R. (2022b). Applications of artificial intelligence in small-and medium-sized enterprises (SMEs). In Pradeep Kumar Mallick, Akash Kumar Bhoi, Paolo Barsocchi, & Victor Hugo C. de Albuquerque (Eds.), *Cognitive Informatics and Soft Computing: Proceeding of CISC 2021* (pp. 717–726). Singapore: Springer Nature.

Ciumărnean, L., Milaciu, M. V., Negrean, V., Orăşan, O. H., Vesa, S. C., Sălăgean, O., Iluţ, S., & Vlaicu, S. I. (2022). Cardiovascular risk factors and physical activity for the prevention of cardiovascular diseases in the elderly. *International Journal of Environmental Research and Public Health*, *19*(1), 1–16. https://doi.org/10.3390/ijerph19010207

Currie, G., Hawk, K. E., & Rohren, E. M. (2020). Ethical principles for the application of artificial intelligence (AI) in nuclear medicine. *European Journal of Nuclear Medicine and Molecular Imaging*, *47*(4), 748–752. https://doi.org/10.1007/s00259-020-04678-1

D'Antonoli, T. A. (2020). Ethical considerations for the use of artificial intelligence in healthcare. *Journal of Medical Ethics*, *46*, 549–554.

Gavande, S. B., & Chawan, P. M. (2021). Heart disease prediction using deep learning techniques. *Multimedia Tools and Applications*, *8*(11), 31759–31773. https://doi.org/10.1007/s11042-023-14817-z

Gong, Y., Liu, G., Xue, Y., Li, R., & Meng, L. (2023). A survey on dataset quality in machine learning. *Information and Software Technology*, *162*(1), 107268–107290. https://doi.org/10.1016/j.infsof.2023.107268

Hossain, M. M., Ali, M. S., Ahmed, M. M., Rakib, M. R. H., Kona, M. A., Afrin, S., Islam, M. K., Ahsan, M. M., Raj, S. M. R. H., & Rahman, M. H. (2023a). Cardiovascular disease identification using a hybrid CNN-LSTM model with explainable AI. *Informatics in Medicine Unlocked*, *42*(1), 101370–101393. https://doi.org/10.1016/j.imu.2023.101370

Hossain, M. I., Maruf, M. H., Khan, Md. A. R., Prity, F. S., Fatema, S., Ejaz, M. S., & Khan, M. A. S. (2023b). Heart disease prediction using distinct artificial intelligence techniques: Performance analysis and comparison. *Iran Journal of Computer Science*, *1*(1), 1–21. https://doi.org/10.1007/s42044-023-00148-7

Hu, W., Yii, F. S. L., Chen, R., Zhang, X., Shang, X., Kiburg, K., Woods, E., Vingrys, A., Zhang, L., Zhu, Z., & He, M. (2023). A systematic review and meta-analysis of applying deep learning in the prediction of the risk of cardiovascular diseases from retinal images. *Translational Vision Science & Technology*, *12*(7), 14–43. https://doi.org/10.1167/tvst.12.7.14

Hussain, S., Nanda, S. K., Barigidad, S., Akhtar, S., Suaib, M., & Ray, N. K. (2021). Novel deep learning architecture for predicting heart disease using CNN. *Conference on Information Technology (OCIT)*, *2021*(1), 353–357. https://doi.org/10.1109/OCIT53463.2021.00076

Faieq, A. K., & Mijwil, M. (2022). Prediction of of heart diseases utilising support vector machine and artificial neural network. *Indonesian Journal of Electrical Engineering and Computer Science*, *26*(1), 374–380. https://doi.org/10.11591/ijeecs.v26.i1

Kaminsky, L. A., German, C., Imboden, M., Ozemek, C., Peterman, J. E., & Brubaker, P. H. (2022). The importance of healthy lifestyle behaviors in the prevention of cardiovascular disease. *Progress in Cardiovascular Diseases*, *70*(1), 8–15. https://doi.org/10.1016/j.pcad.2021.12.001

Khan Mamun, M. M. R., & Elfouly, T. (2023). Detection of cardiovascular disease from clinical parameters using a one-dimensional convolutional neural network. *Bioengineering*, *10*(7), 796–814. https://doi.org/10.3390/bioengineering10070796

Kulkarni, A., Chong, D., & Batarseh, F. A. (2020). Foundations of data imbalance and solutions for a data democracy. *Data Democracy*, *1*(1), 83–106. https://doi.org/10.1016/B978-0-12-818366-3.00005-8

Lee, S.-J., Lee, S.-H., Choi, H.-I., Lee, J.-Y., Jeong, Y.-W., Kang, D.-R., & Sung, K.-C. (2022). Deep learning improves prediction of cardiovascular disease-related mortality and admission in patients with hypertension: Analysis of the Korean national health information database. *Journal of Clinical Medicine*, *11*(22), 22–47. https://doi.org/10.3390/jcm11226677

Liang, M., & Hu, X. (2015). Recurrent convolutional neural network for object recognition. *2015 IEEE Conference on Computer Vision and Pattern Recognition (CVPR)*, *1*(1), 3367–3375. https://doi.org/10.1109/CVPR.2015.7298958

Lin, Y.-S., Lin, L.-S., & Chen, C.-C. (2022). An integrated framework based on GAN and RBI for learning with insufficient datasets. *Symmetry*, *14*(2), 339–364. https://doi.org/10.3390/sym14020339

Mehmood, A., Iqbal, M., Mehmood, Z., Irtaza, A., Nawaz, M., Nazir, T., & Masood, M. (2021). Prediction of heart disease using deep convolutional neural networks. *Arabian Journal for Science and Engineering*, *46*(4), 3409–3422. https://doi.org/10.1007/s13369-020-05105-1

Musa, U. A., & Muhammad, S. A. (2022). Enhancing the performance of heart disease prediction from collecting cleveland heart dataset using bayesian network. *Journal of Applied Sciences and Environmental Management*, *26*(6), 1093–1098. https://doi.org/10.4314/jasem.v26i6.15

Nagavelli, U., Samanta, D., & Chakraborty, P. (2022). Machine learning technology-based heart disease detection models. *Journal of Healthcare Engineering, 2022*(1), 7351061–7351084. https://doi.org/10.1155/2022/7351061

Naik, N., Hameed, B. M. Z., Shetty, D. K., Swain, D., Shah, M., Paul, R., Aggarwal, K., Ibrahim, S., Patil, V., Smriti, K., Shetty, S., Rai, B. P., Chlosta, P., & Somani, B. K. (2022). Legal and ethical consideration in artificial intelligence in healthcare: Who takes responsibility? *Frontiers in Surgery, 9*(4), 862322–862361. https://doi.org/10.3389/fsurg.2022.862322

Nashif, S., Raihan, M. R., Islam, M. R., & Imam, M. H. (2018). heart disease detection by using machine learning algorithms and a real-time cardiovascular health monitoring system. *World Journal of Engineering and Technology, 6*(4), 4–19. https://doi.org/10.4236/wjet.2018.64057

Ogunpola, A., Saeed, F., Basurra, S., Albarrak, A. M., & Qasem, S. N. (2024). Machine learning-based predictive models for detection of cardiovascular diseases. *Diagnostics, 14*(2), 144–188. https://doi.org/10.3390/diagnostics14020144

Oliveira, M., Correia, V. M., Herling, L. L., Soares, P. R., & Scudeler, T. L. (2023). Evolving diagnostic and management advances in coronary heart disease. *Life, 13*(4), 951–979. https://doi.org/10.3390/life13040951

Panayides, A. S., Amini, A., Filipovic, N. D., Sharma, A., Tsaftaris, S. A., Young, A., Foran, D., Do, N., Golemati, S., Kurc, T., Huang, K., Nikita, K. S., Veasey, B. P., Zervakis, M., Saltz, J. H., & Pattichis, C. S. (2019). Artificial intelligence in medical imaging: A review of applications and challenges. *IEEE Journal of Biomedical and Health Informatics, 23*, 1051–1064.

Picard, F., Sayah, N., Spagnoli, V., Adjedj, J., & Varenne, O. (2019). Vasospastic angina: A literature review of current evidence. *Archives of Cardiovascular Diseases, 112*(1), 44–55. https://doi.org/10.1016/j.acvd.2018.08.002

Quer, G., Arnaout, R., Henne, M., & Arnaout, R. (2021). Machine learning and the future of cardiovascular care: jacc state-of-the-art review. *Journal of the American College of Cardiology, 77*(3), 300–313. https://doi.org/10.1016/j.jacc.2020.11.030

Rakshit, S., Clement, N., & Vajjhala, N. R. (2022). Exploratory review of applications of machine learning in finance sector. In *Advances in Data Science and Management: Proceedings of ICDSM 2021* (pp. 119–125). Singapore: Springer Nature.

Ramprakash, P., Sarumathi, R., Mowriya, R., & Nithyavishnupriya, S. (2020). Heart disease prediction using deep neural network. *2020 International Conference on Inventive Computation Technologies (ICICT), 1*(1), 666–670. https://doi.org/10.1109/ICICT48043.2020.9112443

Rasheed, K., Qayyum, A., Ghaly, M., Al-Fuqaha, A., Razi, A., & Qadir, J. (2022). Explainable, trustworthy, and ethical machine learning for healthcare: A survey. *Computers in Biology and Medicine, 149*(1), 106043–106073. https://doi.org/10.1016/j.compbiomed.2022.106043

Reddy, K. V. V., Elamvazuthi, I., Aziz, A. A., Paramasivam, S., Chua, H. N., & Pranavanand, S. (2021). Heart disease risk prediction using machine learning classifiers with attribute evaluators. *Applied Sciences, 11*(18), 8352–8377. https://doi.org/10.3390/app11188352

Sabir, F., Barani, M., Mukhtar, M., Rahdar, A., Cucchiarini, M., Zafar, M. N., Behl, T., & Bungau, S. (2021). Nanodiagnosis and nanotreatment of cardiovascular diseases: an overview. *Chemosensors, 9*(4), 67–94. https://doi.org/10.3390/chemosensors9040067

Saheed, Y. K., Longe, O., Baba, U. A., Rakshit, S., & Vajjhala, N. R. (2021). An ensemble learning approach for software defect prediction in developing quality software product. In *Advances in Computing and Data Sciences: 5th International Conference, ICACDS 2021*, Nashik, India, April 23–24, 2021, Revised selected papers, part I 5 (pp. 317–326). Springer International Publishing.

Sarra, R. R., Dinar, A. M., Mohammed, M. A., & Abdulkareem, K. H. (2022). Enhanced heart disease prediction based on machine learning and $\chi 2$ statistical optimal feature selection model. *Designs, 6*(5), 87–109. https://doi.org/10.3390/designs6050087

Shi, C., Xie, H., Ma, Y., Yang, Z., & Zhang, J. (2020). Nanoscale technologies in highly sensitive diagnosis of cardiovascular diseases. *Frontiers in Bioengineering and Biotechnology*, *8*(2), 531–550. https://doi.org/10.3389/fbioe.2020.00531

Siddiqui, S. S., Loganathan, S.,. Elangovan, V. R., & Yusuf Ali, M. (2020). Artificial intelligence in precision medicine: A review of applications and challenges. *Journal of Biomedical Informatics*, *97*, 103368.

Srinivasan, S., Gunasekaran, S., Mathivanan, S. K., Benjula Anbu Malar, M. B., Jayagopal, P., & Dalu, G. T. (2023). An active learning machine technique based prediction of cardiovascular heart disease from UCI-repository database. *Scientific Reports*, *13*(1), 13588–13612. https://doi.org/10.1038/s41598-023-40717-1

Srivenkatesh, M. (2020). Prediction of cardiovascular disease using machine learning algorithms. *International Journal of Engineering and Advanced Technology*, *9*(3), 2404–2414. https://doi.org/10.35940/ijeat.B3986.029320

Subramani, S., Varshney, N., Anand, M. V., Soudagar, M. E. M., Al-keridis, L. A., Upadhyay, T. K., Alshammari, N., Saeed, M., Subramanian, K., Anbarasu, K., & Rohini, K. (2023). Cardiovascular diseases prediction by machine learning incorporation with deep learning. *Frontiers in Medicine*, *10*(2), 1150933–1150968. https://doi.org/10.3389/fmed.2023.1150933

Vellasamy, S., Murugan, D., Abas, R., Alias, A., Seng, W. Y., & Woon, C. K. (2021). Biological activities of paeonol in cardiovascular diseases: A review. *Molecules*, *26*(16), 16–38. https://doi.org/10.3390/molecules26164976

Vijayashree, J., & Parveen Sultana, H. (2020). Heart disease classification using hybridized Ruzzo-Tompa memetic based deep trained neocognitron neural network. *Health and Technology*, *10*(1), 207–216. https://doi.org/10.1007/s12553-018-00292-2

Vincent Paul, S. M., Balasubramaniam, S., Panchatcharam, P., Malarvizhi Kumar, P., & Mubarakali, A. (2022). Intelligent framework for prediction of heart disease using deep learning. *Arabian Journal for Science and Engineering*, *47*(2), 2159–2169. https://doi.org/10.1007/s13369-021-06058-9

Wang, J., & Hu, X. (2017). Gated recurrent convolution neural network for OCR. *31st Conference on Neural Information Processing Systems (NIPS 2017)*, *1*(1), 334–343. https://dl.acm.org/doi/abs/10.5555/3294771.3294803

WHO. (2024). Ethics and Governance of Artificial Intelligence for Health. Guidance on Large Multi-Modal Models. World Health Organization, Geneva. https://www.who.int/publications-detail-redirect/9789240084759

Wu, Y., Vazquez-Prada, K. X., Liu, Y., Whittaker, A. K., Zhang, R., & Ta, H. T. (2021). Recent advances in the development of theranostic nanoparticles for cardiovascular diseases. *Nanotheranostics*, *5*(4), 499–514. https://doi.org/10.7150/ntno.62730

Zhang, J., & Zhang, Z. (2023). Ethics and governance of trustworthy medical artificial intelligence. *BMC Medical Informatics and Decision Making*, *23*(1), 7–23. https://doi.org/10.1186/s12911-023-02103-9

Advancing Humanitarian Efforts in Alzheimer's Diagnosis Using AI and MRI Technology

11

Pooja Sharma, Ayush Verma, and Manju Khari

INTRODUCTION

AD is a very serious type of dementia. It is the term used to describe memory loss and other cognitive impairments that have a significant impact on human life. Sixty to eighty percent of dementia cases are caused by this degenerative disease. AD is not typically a symptom of healthy aging. Aging is the most well-known threat, and AD is most common in people 65 years of age and older. AD is not regarded as an adult disease. As anticipated, approximately 7% of adults aged 65 and older and about 17% of those aged 80 and above are affected by AD and various forms of dementia. But early-onset AD, which affects people between the ages of 40 and 65 in about 1 in 20 cases, is known. Although AD is still incurable, present treatment methods have the potential to temporarily improve patients' quality of life and slow the progression of the disease's

DOI: 10.1201/9781003479109-11

symptoms. The development and spread of AD are currently being treated more effectively across the board. This chapter's goal is to provide an overview of AD classification using AI for humanitarian and medical development. Dementia with AD is further classified into four categories.

1. Very mild dementia: As people age, they begin to lose their memories.
2. Mild dementia: This condition has symptoms such as memory loss, behavioral changes, and difficulty carrying out daily tasks.
3. Moderate dementia: People with moderate dementia experience a complex daily existence and need additional care and support.
4. Severe dementia: Patients in this stage may not be able to speak clearly and need medical attention. Physical control could be lost.

Humanitarian Efforts in Medical Diagnosis Using AI

AI research has proven to be highly applicable in the healthcare domain. It plays a transformative role in medical diagnosis, offering significant benefits in the humanitarian context and promoting the principles of humanitarianism. AI can process large volumes of medical data quickly, making it possible to serve more patients efficiently and cost-effectively, thereby expanding access to healthcare and supporting humanitarianism by reducing disparities in healthcare access. By automating the diagnostic process, AI can reduce the need for expensive diagnostic tests and procedures. This is particularly beneficial in low-resource settings where humanitarian organizations operate, and healthcare budgets are limited. AI can streamline clinical workflows, reducing the time and resources needed for diagnosis and allowing healthcare providers to focus more on patient care, enhancing humanitarian efforts by optimizing resource utilization.

Our approach to healthcare is evolving due to the power of AI and DL. It is like an extremely intelligent physician assistant. This aligns with humanitarian efforts to bring quality healthcare to vulnerable populations. For example, it performs exceptionally well when analyzing medical images such as MRIs and X-rays, assisting physicians in identifying problems early on. Additionally, it analyses vast volumes of data to forecast illnesses and develop personalized therapies based on everyone's distinct profile. It speeds up finding possible new medications through drug discovery. Consider it to be a language expert as well. It makes it simpler for doctors to obtain the information they require by @@analyzing and understanding the disorganized notes in your electronic health records. It even assists in forecasting the course of diseases and provides remote patient monitoring, which is useful, particularly for long-term ailments. It provides a level of precision to surgeries, improving safety and accuracy. Additionally, this technology is frequently used by healthcare chatbots to facilitate appointments and provide health advice. To put it briefly, DL is like having an intelligent doctor's assistant that helps with diagnosis, treatment planning, and overall more effective medical humanitarianism.

AI and DL are shaping our society in impactful ways. In healthcare, it is helping doctors catch diseases early by analyzing medical images, improving patient outcomes and reducing healthcare costs for humanity. In education, AI and DL personalize learning experiences, making education more accessible and inclusive for students with diverse needs. Communication has become more seamless with the rise of voice assistants and language translation services, making technology user-friendly and breaking down language barriers. However, the automation brought about by AI and DL raises questions about job displacement and the need for workforce reskilling. It is also influencing urban living through smart city initiatives, optimizing transportation and urban planning. Yet, concerns about privacy, especially in surveillance and facial recognition, highlight the need for balancing security measures with protecting individual freedoms.

LITERATURE REVIEW

Early detection and diagnosis of AD have been discussed in extensive research, and even today, significant amounts of AI research are being conducted within this area because of its value in medical and humanitarian context. This section provides a deep insight into the previous works related to AD detection and discusses their performance under various evaluation metrics.

Sharma et al. (2021) performed an analysis of eight transfer learning models to categorize AD into four different classes: MildDemented, ModerateDemented, NonDemented, and VeryMildDemented. The authors compared the results on models of Inception ResNet-V2, DenseNet-169, ResNet-101, MobileNet-V2, Inception-V3, VGG-19, ResNet-50, and VGG-16 using transfer learning. The evaluation results for medical imaging issues were provided by the transfer learning model that received the best marks, which had 98.0% and 98.01% accuracy and precision, respectively. Nawaz et al. (2020) explored the use of pre-trained layers from an AlexNet model to extract profound characteristics from the CNN. They utilize established ML algorithms like support vector machine (SVM), K-nearest neighbor (KNN), and random forest (RF) for categorizing the extracted deep features. Their results demonstrate that a model incorporating deep features surpassed with an accuracy of 99.21%. Moreover, the suggested model surpasses the latest cutting-edge techniques.

Another method for AD detection, which uses transfer learning to categorize AD into four different classes, was performed (Ghazal et al., 2022). For the multi-stage detection of AD, they developed a system based on a transfer learning classification model. Their algorithm reports a validation accuracy of 91.7%. A related study (Zhu et al., 2021) proposed a dual-attention multi-instance DL (DA-MIDL) network for aiding in computer-assisted AD diagnosis. The evaluation encompassed 1689 participants from two distinct datasets, ADNI and AIBL, wherein the DA-MIDL method underwent assessment across various AD-related diagnostic tasks. The results of these assessments showcase the superiority of their approach over several state-of-the-art techniques in terms of diagnostic accuracy, along with its capability to pinpoint specific pathological regions in MRI scans.

Ding et al. (2019) developed and validated a DL algorithm applying fluorine 18 (18F) fluorodeoxyglucose (FDG) PET brain imaging to predict the ultimate diagnosis of AD. Its efficacy was compared to that of radiologists. A retrospective independent test set comprising 40 imaging studies from 2006 to 2016 (40 patients) and prospective 18F-FDG PET brain images from the ADNI dataset spanning 2109 imaging studies from 2005 to 2017 (1002 patients) were collected. The CNN architecture InceptionV3 was trained on 90% of the ADNI dataset and assessed on the existing 10% as well as an independent test set. The DL algorithm, designed for early AD prediction, achieved a specificity of 82% at 100% sensitivity using 18F-FDG PET brain imaging, on average 75.8 months prior to the final diagnosis.

A DL model that can distinguish between individuals who are healthy and those who are at risk of AD is developed (Borkar et al., 2023). MRI scans were used to extract different brain characteristics. Then, the collected data were used to train the model. The results of the study suggest that this model can be used to screen for AD in people with normal cognitive functioning. It was also better than the existing diagnostic techniques. With its combination of CNN and LSTM models and Adam optimization, this approach may provide a non-invasive, more affordable option to current methods while also improving accuracy. The accuracy that can be attained by the suggested model is 99.7%. An overview of the various approaches to AD using DL and conventional learning frameworks, as well as a detailed analysis of prior research in this area, is done (Goenka & Tiwari, 2021). DL frameworks that work for multi-modality biomarkers and manifest multi-class classification of AD are receiving more attention these days.

Four different optimization algorithms, including genetic algorithm (GA), particle swarm optimization (PSO), grey wolf optimization (GWO), and cuckoo search (CS), were carried out (Chitradevi & Sundaravadivel, 2020) to diagnose AD by considering brain subregions. A DL classifier was used to classify the segmented regions, and the results were confirmed using images from ground truth (GT). Based on a 98% similarity between the segmented region and GT, the results demonstrate that GWO can accurately segment brain subregions. After that, a DL classifier is used to classify the segmented regions, and the outcomes demonstrate a high accuracy of 95%.

A similar method, proposed by Murugan et al. (2021), uses high-resolution disease probability maps from local brain structures to create detailed visualizations of individual AD risk across four dementia stages. This approach relies on a multi-layer perceptron and provides precise and interpretable results. To implement this, a novel approach called DEMentia NETwork (DEMNET) was developed to identify different dementia stages from MRI scans. Notably, DEMNET outperforms previous methods, achieving an impressive accuracy of 95.23%, an area under curve (AUC) of 97%, and a Cohen's Kappa value of 0.93 when tested on the Kaggle dataset.

Vashishtha et al. (2023) developed a hybrid model for detecting AD, utilizing DL techniques. To address the issue of imbalanced classes, the SMOTE method was employed to ensure an equal distribution. Their hybrid model integrates Inception V3 and Resnet50, utilizing MRI to recognize AD traits. The final classification stage involves a dense layer within a CNN. Compared with the previous work, the hybrid method achieves a remarkable 99% accuracy in the classification of MRI datasets. Evaluation based on criteria such as accuracy, specificity, sensitivity, and other metrics underscores the superior effectiveness of this approach compared to existing methodologies, marking a significant advancement in AD detection.

Agarwal et al. (2024) aimed to develop an extensive portal employing ML for the prediction and early identification of diseases like heart disease, diabetes, and breast cancer, with a specific focus on naive Bayes, SVM, and logistic regression algorithms. The study contributes to the field by showcasing the potential of ML in multi-disease prediction, enabling early disease identification and accurate diagnosis, which can be crucial for tailoring personalized treatment plans for patients. By utilizing machine learning algorithms like SVM, DT, and LR, the research highlights the performance of these methods in predicting diseases like heart disease, diabetes, and cancer. Naive Bayes (NB) algorithm achieved an accuracy of 85% in predicting heart disease, showcasing a sharp degree of reliability and effectiveness in disease prediction. The SVM algorithm attained a commendable accuracy of 75% in predicting diabetes, contributing to the robustness of the platform for disease identification. LR model stood out by gaining an outstanding accuracy of 98% in detecting cancer, highlighting the methodology's ability for accurate disease diagnosis.

These studies collectively underscore the promising advancements in AD detection and diagnosis facilitated by DL and AI which are crucial in humanitarian contexts where preventative care can reduce the burden on strained healthcare systems. Furthermore, the application of DL techniques extends beyond AD to revolutionize smart healthcare for diseases such as multiple sclerosis (Afzal et al., 2022).

RESEARCH METHODOLOGY

This work proposes a comprehensive framework of AD recognition using CNN. The proposed framework is compared to standard benchmark architectures like GoogLeNet, AlexNet, VGG-16, and ResNet to provide a comparative analysis of these architectures with the proposed framework for AD detection. This section provides a deep insight of the systematic and structured approach used by researchers to conduct this study, which is divided into four sub-sections: pre-processing, data description, proposed framework, and model training.

Pre-Processing

Data pre-processing is a data mining method employed to convert raw data into a more efficient and usable format. Prior to data analysis, data cleaning is required so that you can identify patterns in the data.

- *Data cleaning*: In the initial dataset, there can be issues like missing data, inaccuracies, or noise. Data cleaning is the process of addressing these concerns, which involves handling inaccurate data, noisy data, and other related issues to ensure data quality.
  a. *Missing data*: Information absent or incomplete in a dataset.
  b. *Noisy data*: Data with errors, outliers, or inaccuracies.

- *Data transformation*: This step entails converting data into an alternative format or structure, altering its values, units, or scales while preserving the meaningful information.
- *Data reduction*: This aims to reduce the volume or complexity of the dataset by summarizing, selecting, or transforming features, resulting in a more manageable yet representative data set for analysis or modeling. These processes are crucial for efficient data handling and meaningful insights extraction.
- *Normalization/standardization*: Scaling numerical features to a standard range, making it easier for models to learn and improving convergence.
- *Feature engineering*: Creating new features or modifying existing ones to enhance the model's ability to capture patterns in the data.
- *Dealing with outliers*: Identifying and handling outliers to prevent them from disproportionately influencing the model.
- *Handling imbalanced data*: Addressing class imbalances in classification problems to ensure that the model is not biased toward the majority class.
- *Data splitting*: Dividing the dataset into training, validation, and test sets for model training, tuning, and evaluation.

Image data augmentation is a method for generating new images from old ones. This can be achieved by making a few minor adjustments to images, such as altering its brightness, rotating it, or moving the subject horizontally or vertically. Using image augmentation techniques, it is possible to artificially expand the size of the training dataset and give the model much more data to work with. As a result, the model will better recognize the novel variations of your training data, increasing its accuracy. The following are the augmentation techniques which are applied to the *MRI images*: rotation, brightness adjustment, zoom in/out, vertical shift, horizontal shift, vertical flip, and horizontal flip.

- *Zoom:* This parameter is applied to zoom the brain MRI images. The zoom range is set to [0.99, 1.01], which means the images were zoomed in or out by a factor between 0.99 and 1.01.
- *Brightness range:* This parameter was applied to the brain MRI images. The brightness range was set to [0.8, 1.2], which means the brightness of the brain MRI images be adjusted between 80% and 120% of the original brightness.
- *Horizontal flip:* This parameter was applied to the brain MRI images horizontally flip the images. In this case, it is set to true, which means the images can be flipped horizontally.
- *Fill mode:* This parameter was applied to fill the pixels that may be created during brain MRI image transformations. In this case, the fill mode was set to "constant," which means the new pixels will be filled with a constant value.
- *Data format:* The data format parameter specified the ordering of the dimensions in the brain MRI image data. In this case, it is set to "channels last," which means the image data is represented in the format (height, width, channels).

Data Description

The Alzheimer's disease neuroimaging initiative (ADNI) dataset is employed in this work. The ADNI dataset is a well-known, licensed, and widely used resource in the field of AD research. It was launched in 2004 as a public-private partnership to advance understanding, diagnosis, and treatment of AD. The dataset includes various types of data collected from participants, such as the following.

- *Clinical data*: Information about cognitive assessments, demographic details, and medical history.
- *Imaging data*: Structural and functional brain imaging data, including MRI scans.
- *Genetic data*: Genetic information from participants.

ADNI is a longitudinal study, meaning data is collected from participants over an extended period, allowing researchers to track changes in cognitive function and brain structure over time. The dataset has been valuable for developing and testing ML algorithms to predict and diagnose. This dataset is acquired from Kaggle (Alzheimer's dataset (4 Class of Images), 2019) and consists of data in the form of images. The dataset is split into two parts: testing and training both containing a total of 6400 images. There are 5121 sample images for training, which is categorized into four different classes, and 1279 samples for testing also categorized into four different classes.

Training and testing consist of these classes.

1. *MildDemented:* In total, there are 896 sample images, with 717 allocated for training and 179 for testing.
2. *ModerateDemented:* In total, there are 64 sample images, with 52 allocated for training and 12 for testing.
3. *NonDemented:* In total, there are 3200 sample images, with 2560 allocated for training and 640 for testing.
4. *VeryMildDemented:* In total, there are 2240 sample images, with 1792 allocated for training and 448 for testing.

Proposed Framework

CNN is a class of DL algorithms that have demonstrated remarkable effectiveness in various tasks involving visual data, such as image recognition, object detection, image segmentation, and more. They are specifically designed to process grid-like data, like images, by taking advantage of the spatial relationships between neighboring pixels. This section explains the proposed framework in a structured plan outlining the methods, algorithms, and tools employed for addressing AD. The flowchart represented in Figure 11.1 serves as a roadmap, guiding the project's implementation by detailing the steps and processes needed to attain the desired outcomes effectively and efficiently.

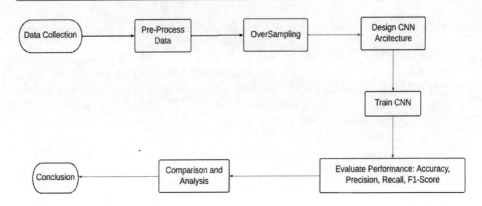

FIGURE 11.1   Workflow diagram.

The proposed CNN model is a sequential model from the Keras library. In this study, the ADNI dataset was used, which includes MRI images with both AD and non-AD samples. The collected data was pre-processed, including zooming, brightness, flip and fill of the MRI images. To address any potential class inequality, oversampling techniques like synthetic minority oversampling technique (SMOTE) were applied. Typically, datasets for AD's prediction might have fewer instances of patients with the disease compared to those without. This imbalance can skew ML models. SMOTE comes into play by generating synthetic data points for individuals with Alzheimer's, creating artificial but realistic instances based on the existing patient data. By doing this, SMOTE helps ensure that the model learns from a more balanced representation of both AD and non-AD cases. This improves the model's ability to make accurate predictions, particularly for the minority class of AD cases. The proposed method is CNN architecture, as shown in Figure 11.2. The provided CNN architecture is designed for predicting AD. It follows a sequential model structure with various layers to extract and learn hierarchical features from input data which are images of dimensions 176×176. The architecture starts with convolutional 2D layers (Conv2D) and convolutional 2D_1 layer, which are designed to capture spatial patterns in the input data. The same padding is used for convolutional layers to maintain feature maps having equal size as that of the original image. Subsequently, Max Pooling2D layers are employed to down sample the spatial dimensions, reducing computational complexity while retaining important features.

The model incorporates dropout layers, sequential_3, and dropout_1, to prevent overfitting by randomly switching off a fraction of neural units during training. The flatten layer is then used to convert the 2D feature maps into a vector, facilitating the transition from convolutional layers to densely connected layers. Following this, dense layers (dense_3) are utilized for the final classification, where the output represents the likelihood of AD. Additionally, the specifics of data pre-processing, training parameters, and evaluation metrics are vital considerations for the overall model performance. The CNN model was initialized with appropriate weights, either random or pre-trained on a substantial dataset.

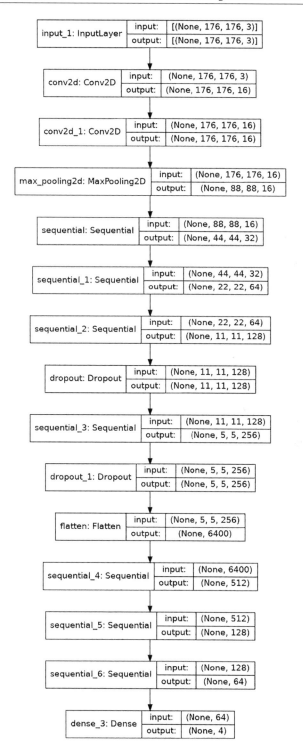

FIGURE 11.2   CNN architecture representation.

Model Training

This section emphasizes the model training procedure carried out for this study. The suggested CNN architecture is educated on 5121 training MRI pictures. Training phase is where an ML or profound learning model acquires knowledge from data. It resembles instructing the model to identify patterns and formulate forecasts by modifying its configurations based on the given instances. The aim is to enhance the model's efficiency, rendering it adept at managing novel, undisclosed data accurately. The CNN architecture was educated up to 100 training cycles. Cycles portray the frequency at which the model is exposed to the entire training dataset throughout the training procedure. Every cycle enables the model to revise its internal parameters based on the training data, progressively refining its efficiency. The optimization approach utilized is Adam. Eighty percent of the dataset is allocated for training, whereas the remaining 20% is reserved for testing.

RESULTS AND DISCUSSION

Model training was performed using 100 epochs. The model achieves 95.16% testing accuracy and 99.68% training accuracy. Accuracy (ACC), AUC, and loss are calculated for each epoch to check whether the model is correctly separating positive (+ve) and negative (−ve) categories.

Evaluation Metrics

1. *The Confusion Matrix*: This is a matrix that displays details regarding the correct positives, correct negatives, incorrect positives, and incorrect negatives in the forecasts of a classification model, as illustrated in Figure 11.3.

    A classifier's predicted and actual values can be combined in one of four ways.
    - *Positive correct*: This depicts the number of affirmative cases that have been accurately anticipated as affirmative.
    - *Negative correct*: This indicates the number of pessimistic cases that have been accurately anticipated as pessimistic.
    - *Incorrect positive*: This relates to the number of pessimistic cases that have been inaccurately anticipated as affirmative.
    - *Incorrect negative*: This denotes the number of affirmative cases that have been inaccurately anticipated as pessimistic.
2. *Accuracy*: Accuracy is a metric employed to assess the overall performance of a classification model. It is calculated by dividing the number of correct predictions (true positives and true negatives) by the total number of predictions.

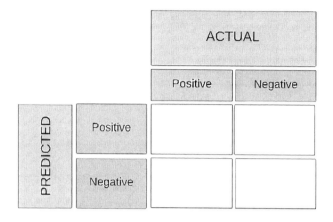

FIGURE 11.3 Confusion matrix for a binary class dataset.

It provides an indication of how well the model is able to correctly classify instances.

$$Accuracy = \frac{TP + TN}{TP + TN + FP + FN}.$$

3. *Precision*: Precision quantifies the number of correctly predicted positive samples out of all samples predicted as positive. It serves as a metric for assessing the model's capacity to minimize false positives.

$$Precision = \frac{TP}{TP + FP}.$$

4. *Recall*: Recall tells us how good the model is at finding everything it is supposed to find. Another way to say this is "sensitivity" or "true positive rate." A high recall means that the model rarely misses important positive cases

$$Recall = \frac{TP}{TP + FN}.$$

5. *F1-score*: The F1-score combines two other measures, precision and recall, into a single score. This is useful when both precision and recall are important, or when the data has unequal numbers of positive and negative examples. The F1-score helps to find a middle ground between a model that makes mostly correct positive predictions but misses some important ones, and a model that finds many positive cases but also makes a lot of mistakes

$$F1\text{-}Score = \frac{2 * Precision * Recall}{Precision + Recall}.$$

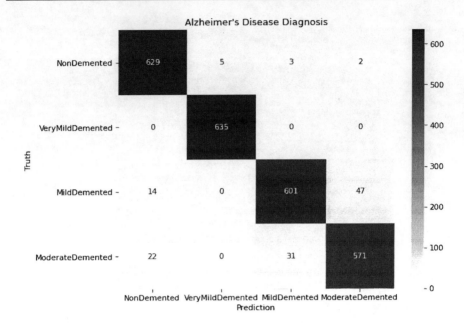

FIGURE 11.4   Confusion matrix for each class.

TABLE 11.1   Evaluation metrics of each class

	PRECISION	*RECALL*	*F1-SCORE*	*SUPPORT*
NonDemented	0.95	0.98	0.96	639
VeryMildDemented	0.99	1.00	1.00	635
MildDemented	0.95	0.91	0.93	662
ModerateDemented	0.92	0.92	0.92	624
Micro avg	0.95	0.95	0.95	2560
Macro avg	0.95	0.95	0.95	2560
Weighted avg	0.95	0.95	0.95	2560
Samples avg	0.95	0.95	0.95	2560

The calculation of each class metric is done using the confusion matrix represented in Figure 11.4. The evaluation metric results corresponding to the confusion matrix are displayed in Table 11.1.

The proposed model attains a validation accuracy of 95.16%, as represented in training-validation accuracy plot in Figure 11.5. The proposed model achieves AUC score of 96%, as represented in Figure 11.6. The training-validation loss plot is

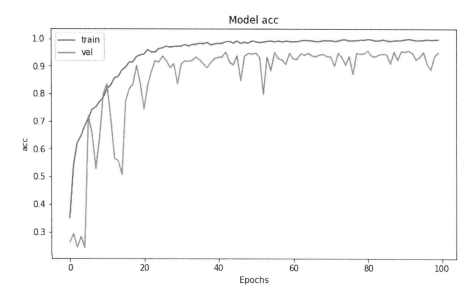

FIGURE 11.5   Training-validation accuracy plot.

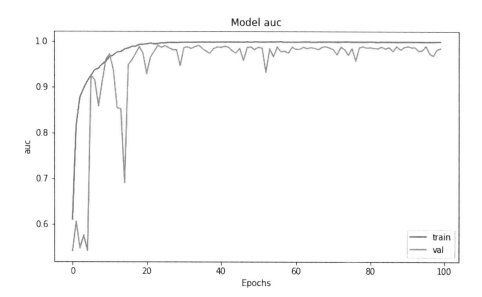

FIGURE 11.6   Training-validation AUC plot.

represented in Figure 11.7. Compared with previous works, they achieved an accuracy of 98.25% (Prakash et al., 2019), but in this proposed model achieved an accuracy of 95.16%, as given in Table 11.2.

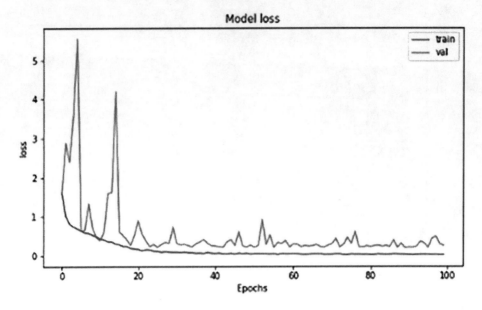

FIGURE 11.7   Training-validation loss plot.

TABLE 11.2   Comparison of various models

MODEL	TRAINING ACCURACY (%)	TESTING ACCURACY (%)
Proposed model	99.68	95.16
VGG-16	98.37	88.66
AlexNet	99.18	93.97
GoogLeNet	99.84	98.25
ResNet-18	99.02	96.8

CONCLUSION

In summary, AI has the potential to revolutionize medical diagnosis by making it more accurate, accessible, and cost-effective, thereby enhancing healthcare delivery and outcomes. By integrating AI into healthcare, we can support humanitarian efforts and uphold the principles of humanitarianism, ensuring that quality healthcare is available to all, especially the most vulnerable populations. In this paper, a CNN model is proposed to identify the type of AD from the given classified images. The proposed model achieved a 95.16% accuracy when tested using testing data from four classes. As a result, we examine and contrast the accuracy of four models, namely AlexNet, GoogLeNet, VGG-16, and ResNet-18 with accuracy rates of 99.84% and 98.25% for training and testing, respectively. The GoogLeNet model provided the best results.

As a result, the GoogLeNet model is absolutely an effective method for classifying MRI images. Even though DL techniques have achieved significant performance in detection of AD, more robust methodologies are needed to address some key limitations like availability of datasets and advanced training methods. In future, these issues will be addressed. Also, the performance of traditional CNN models can be compared, such as LeNet-5, with more advanced architectures, including VGGNet, GoogLeNet, and ResNet. These CNN models will be trained on large datasets of brain MRI scans, consisting of both AD patients and healthy individuals which may provide more relevant information. AI can inform public health policies by providing insights into health trends and disparities, guiding efforts to improve health equity and access, which are central to humanitarianism.

REFERENCES

Afzal, H., Luo, S., Ramadan, S., Khari, M., Chaudhary, G., & Lechner-Scott, J. (2022). Prediction of conversion from CIS to clinically definite multiple sclerosis using convolutional neural networks. *Computational and Mathematical Methods in Medicine*, *20*(2), 1–8. https://doi.org/10.1155/2022/5154896

Agarwal, A., Verma, A. K., & Khari, M. (2024). Comparative assessment of machine learning methods for early prediction of diseases using health indicators. In Srikanta Patnaik and Priti Das (eds), *Advances in Medical Technologies and Clinical Practice Book Series* (pp. 160–186). Hershey, PA: IGI Global. https://doi.org/10.4018/979-8-3693-2238-3.ch007

Alzheimer's Dataset (4 Class of Images). (2019). https://www.kaggle.com/datasets/tourist55/alzheimers-dataset-4-class-of-images

Borkar, P., Ashok, W. V., Mane, D., Limkar, S., Ramesh, J. V. N., & Ajani, S. N. (2023). Deep learning and image processing-based early detection of Alzheimer disease in cognitively normal individuals. *Soft Computing, 11*(1), 39–56. https://doi.org/10.1007/s00500-023-08615-w

Chitradevi, D., & Sundaravadivel, P. (2020). Analysis of brain sub regions using optimization techniques and deep learning method in Alzheimer disease. *Applied Soft Computing, 86*(1), 105–127. https://doi.org/10.1016/j.asoc.2019.105857

Ding, Y., Sohn, J. H., Kawczynski, M., Trivedi, H., Harnish, R., Jenkins, N. W., Lituiev, D., Copeland, T. E., Aboian, M., Aparici, C. M., Behr, S. C., Flavell, R. R., Huang, S., Zalocusky, K. A., Nardo, L., Seo, Y., Hawkins, R. A., Pampaloni, M. H., Hadley, D., & Franc, B. L. (2019). A deep learning model to predict a diagnosis of Alzheimer disease by using 18F-FDG PET of the brain. *Radiology*, *290*(2), 456–464. https://doi.org/10.1148/radiol.2018180958

Ghazal, T. M., Abbas, S., Munir, S., Khan, M. A., Ahmad, M., Issa, G. F., Zahra, S. B., Khan, M. A., & Hasan, M. K. (2022). Alzheimer disease detection empowered with transfer learning. *Computers, Materials & Continua/Computers, Materials & Continua (Print)*, *70*(3), 5005–5019. https://doi.org/10.32604/cmc.2022.020866

Goenka, N., & Tiwari, S. (2021). Deep learning for Alzheimer prediction using brain biomarkers. *Artificial Intelligence Review*, *54*(7), 4827–4871. https://doi.org/10.1007/s10462-021-10016-0

Murugan, S., Venkatesan, C., Sumithra, M. G., Gao, X., Balan, E., Akila, M., & Manoharan, S. (2021). DEMNET: A deep learning model for early diagnosis of Alzheimer diseases and dementia from MR images. *IEEE Access*, *9*(2), 90319–90329. https://doi.org/10.1109/access.2021.3090474

Nawaz, H., Maqsood, M., Afzal, S., Aadil, F., Mehmood, I., & Rho, S. (2020). A deep feature-based real-time system for Alzheimer disease stage detection. *Multimedia Tools and Applications*, *80*(2), 35789–35807. https://doi.org/10.1007/s11042-020-09087-y

Prakash, D., Madusanka, N., Bhattacharjee, S., Park, H., Kim, C., & Choi, H. (2019). A comparative study of Alzheimer's disease classification using multiple transfer learning models. *Journal of Multimedia Information System*, *6*(4), 209–216. https://doi.org/10.33851/jmis.2019.6.4.209

Sharma, G., Vijayvargiya, A., & Kumar, R. (2021). Comparative assessment among different convolutional neural network architectures for Alzheimer's disease detection. In *2021 IEEE 8th Uttar Pradesh Section International Conference on Electrical, Electronics and Computer Engineering (UPCON)*. Dehradun: IEEE. https://doi.org/10.1109/upcon52273.2021.9667607

Vashishtha, A., Acharya, A. K., & Swain, S. (2023). Hybrid model: Deep learning method for early detection of Alzheimer's disease from MRI images. *Biomedical and Pharmacology Journal/Biomedical & Pharmacology Journal*, *16*(3), 1617–1630. https://doi.org/10.13005/bpj/2739

Zhu, W., Sun, L., Huang, J., Han, L., & Zhang, D. (2021). Dual attention multi-instance deep learning for Alzheimer's disease diagnosis with structural MRI. *IEEE Transactions on Medical Imaging*, *40*(9), 2354–2366. https://doi.org/10.1109/tmi.2021.3077079

Ethical AI in Humanitarian Contexts

12

Challenges, Transparency, and Safety

Neelatphal Chanda and Ishayu Gupta

INTRODUCTION

Organizations that deal with humanitarian services can very likely use AI (artificial intelligence) to catalyze their services like data collection and disaster response which they provide in relief operations. On the contrary, this prospective path might also lead to ethical issues. The purpose of this study is to identify those ethical concerns that accompany the application of AI in humanitarian services and operations with a special emphasis on routing guidelines for AI implementation. The background of this study is to investigate and suggest a set of moral guidelines for the application of AI to humanitarian initiatives. The reason why it becomes essential to understand well on ethics as regards this class of studies is that, during this period whereby there is an increased use of AI, it calls for adherence to basic ethics that incorporate humanitarianism, respect for human beings' dignity, and the safety of potential victims. AI is playing an increasingly important role in humanitarian work over the past decade. The rationale of AI technologies integration into humanitarian endeavors is to improve the efficacy, effectiveness, and scale of aid interventions. The aspects of AI like data analysis, pattern recognition,

DOI: 10.1201/9781003479109-12

and decision-making create opportunities to address complex issues faced by humanitarian organizations in delivering prompt assistance that is specifically directed at vulnerable populations.

AI technologies could help humanitarian intervention in many areas, such as disaster response allocation of resources, healthcare, and socioeconomic development. For instance, predictive analytics and machine learning algorithms make it possible to predict natural disasters so that, in advance, proactive measures can be implemented or timely evacuation plans put into action. Using an AI-driven data analysis, it is easy to spread resources and aid so that help gets on time. Besides, there are some AI applications that can help with diagnostics and disease monitoring, as well as developing good health strategies in resource-poor settings of the healthcare industry. Highlighting the reasons for the inclusion of AI in humanitarian work is relevant to establishing ethical considerations. This section paves the way for the ethical endeavor that follows, highlighting the need to consider how AI technologies can be deployed in environments characterized by instability and often crises.

REVIEW OF LITERATURE

AI and the need for ethical concepts is a buzzing concept in recent times, and there have been various studies which were held to understand the dimensions of artificial intelligence and its impact. Cath (2018) emphasizes the growing spread of AI technologies and their benefits, including increasing economic welfare, social wellbeing, as well as human rights practice. There are potential hazards of AI, such as misuse or unintended behavior, particularly in areas with high risks (Anderson et al., 2018). Cath (2018) also engaged with fundamental questions regarding how AI should be managed to ensure accountability, fairness, and transparency. Cath (2018) presented several key issues, including ethical governance, explainability and interpretability issues, as well as AI system-ethical auditing. These issues indicated the interdisciplinary character of the multi-dimensional AI governance debate, where experts from various fields are involved, including but not limited to computer science, data sciences, engineering, ethics, law, policy, robotics, and social sciences (Resnik, 2011).

Pizzi, Romanoff, and Engelhardt (2020) explore how AI holds transformative prospects for humanitarianism, given that it presents unique challenges to matters related with rights. Pizzi et al. (2020) state that only a governance framework based on international human rights law and complemented by ethical aspects can ensure the right implementation and meeting human interests. Pizzi et al. (2020) base their findings on research, expert consultations, and extant frameworks in determining areas of consensus on guaranteeing that AI advances humanitarian endeavors without jeopardizing human rights. They stress the importance of an anchoring framework informed by international human rights law that acts as a foundation for embedding humanity's core ideas within AI systems. Moreover, they stress the role of ethics in supplementing legal arrangements and lifting standards over minimal provisions. Pizzi et al. (2020)

analyze the benefits of this architecture and pinpoint particular instruments and finest practices for applying human rights principles in AI development, as well as its use. They recognize the evolving role of AI in crisis responses around the world, particularly during global pandemics like COVID-19, and promote action to ensure measures that encourage proactive formulation of policies regarding creation as well as accountability mechanisms on human rights.

Ethical Principles – Human-Centric Approach

AI technology holds great potential to advance humanitarian work; however, its deployment in such a context should be processed respecting ethical principles to create transparency, safety, and effectiveness. This chapter examines ethics frameworks aimed at guiding the deployment of AI in humanitarian settings focusing on challenges and stressing transparency and safety.

Beneficence – the duty of humanitarian actors to maximize benefits and minimize harm – underlies the concerns about ethics. The humanitarian AI initiatives ought to focus on the welfare of the vulnerable segments, plan to reduce suffering, and improve the effectiveness of the delivery of aid. Similarly, the principle of nonmaleficence underpins the obligation to prevent harm or worsen the existing weaknesses because of the application of AI technologies (Resnik, 2011). Effective risk assessment and mitigation methods must be considered to implement people-first and do-no-harm principles and avoid unwanted consequences. In the end, adherence to ethical principles is critical to the responsible and ethical deployment of AI in humanitarian settings stakeholders can guarantee that AI technologies are serving the greatest interests of the affected populations, minimizing risks and safeguarding human rights by practicing beneficence, respect for human dignity and autonomy, justice and equity, transparency and accountability, privacy and data protection, and cultural sensitivity.

Respect for Human Dignity

Human dignity comprises the natural esteem and worth of every person whatever their situation or condition (Donnelly, 2013). It values the dignity, independence, and freedom of individuals to live lives of dignity and satisfaction. For the humanitarian AI sector, human dignity provides directional value in terms of how technology is deployed such that the humanity of the people affected by the crisis is safeguarded. Protecting the privacy and individual dignity is core to safeguarding human worth in humanitarian AI projects (Nissenbaum, 2011). Humanitarian actors should prioritize the confidentiality and integrity of individuals' personal data such that AI systems comply with stringent data protection norms. Respect for privacy helps individuals to have ownership of their personal data thus upholding their dignity in the information age.

Equity and inclusivity creation is imperative in ensuring human dignity in humanitarian AI initiatives (Anderson et al., 2018). It calls for tackling systemic injustices through AI interventions that do not reinforce or exacerbate the status quo disparities.

Humanitarian actors should give priority to the needs of marginalized and underprivileged individuals, adopting inclusive methods which allow equal access to information and resources. Reducing risks and harms is paramount in the protection of human dignity in the use of AI technologies (Confludi & Sanders, 2004). Humanitarian organizational actors should conduct thorough risk assessments and measures of predictive power to preclude the prospective hazards of AI, for example, bias, discrimination, or casualties. All interventions of AI should be transparent, accountable, and be governed by oversight mechanisms to ensure that they put first the wellbeing and dignity of the affected populations.

In essence, human dignity is the ethical foundation for the utilization of AI in humanitarian settings. Through respect to autonomy and agency, privacy and personal integrity protection, promotion of equity and inclusivity, cultural sensitivity and diversity appreciation, and risks and harms minimization, humanitarian actors can guarantee that AI technologies preserve the inherent worth and value of individuals affected by the conflicts.

Inclusivity and Diversity

Diversity and inclusivity involve the different groups of people and groups who work to balance power and increase the recognition and celebration of differences among people and communities, including but not limited to factors such as race, ethnicity, gender, age, and religion, since such factors vary among individuals and communities. With respect to humanitarian AI, inclusivity and diversity focus on the participation of and responding to the needs of different groups who are impacted by crises (Sen, 2006).

Cultural sensitivity is crucial because AI interventions are concerned carefully with cultural values, norms, and practices of the involved communities (Floridi & Sanders, 2004). Humanitarian actors need to consider and understand the cultural variety of the populations, being free of ethnocentrism and adopting a culturally humble approach. Through community engagement and cross-cultural awareness raising, AI projects can enhance their attractiveness to culturally diverse groups. Inclusiveness necessitates ethical representation and bias mitigation during the development and use of AI systems (Mittelstadt et al., 2016). Humanitarian actors should work on eliminating biases and stereotypes in AI systems making sure that they do not reinforce or exacerbate alienations. This translates into various representations in data collection, algorithm design, and decision-making processes, as well as continuous monitoring and evaluation to detect and address biases.

Criteria for Measuring the Impact of Ethical AI Implementations in Humanitarian Settings

Going further, with the growing use of AI in the aid circumstances, it is important to establish its impact on beneficiary populations and to confirm that ethical principles turn into real good news. In this part, the methods and indicators of measuring the influence of AI ethical implementations are recommended in the context of the humanitarian field. This creates a communication bridge between theories and practice-oriented performance.

- *Benefit assessment:* One of the ways to gauge the contribution of ethical AI practices to humanitarian activities is to have an assessment of the benefits that highlight the positive effects and improvements brought by AI technologies. This evaluation may be by metrics, including how fast the aid is delivered, how appropriate resources are allocated, and how good the services are provided. The concerned humanitarian organization will be able to set specific objectives to be achieved by their AI interventions through the quantification of the benefits possessed by the targeted communities at the end of the intervention (Bourguignon et al., 2019).
- *Harm reduction analysis:* However, it is not enough to measure the benefits; the degree also needs to be assessed at which ethical AI-based implementations reduce harm in humanitarian settings. This review entails completion, noting down, and forestalling possible poor outcomes that could be brought about by AI technologies like biases, discrimination, and invasion of privacy. By assessing the responsiveness of vulnerable groups to AI interventions and mitigating their disadvantageous effects, humanitarian agencies will guarantee that professional principles are respected at every stage of the deployment process (Veale & Binns, 2017).
- *Stakeholder engagement and feedback:* Feedback mechanisms and stakeholder engagement also represent vital instruments for tracking AI systems' performance by their ethical usage. It is a process during which the communities affected, local populations, and key stakeholders are taken through the entire AI intervention cycle, including design, implementation, and assessment. Humanitarian organizations get a chance to receive feedback, issues, and suggestions from those who directly experience the implementation of AI technologies. This, in turn, allows us to assess the efficiency and relevance of the applied methods, considering possible unanticipated outcomes or ethical obstacles (Haklay et al., 2020).

METHODOLOGIES FOR INVOLVING DIVERSE GROUPS IN DEVELOPING AND OVERSEEING AI TECHNOLOGIES

Community-Based Participatory Research (CBPR): CBPR in AI technology development will require engaging with the community members and stamping down on risky populations through meetings that will be facilitated in an open platform where there will be discussions about AI intervention and the issues it creates. The fact that these innovative techniques are people-centric implies that AI technologies are crafted according to the wants of the community people and their thinking, which are driven by their own experiences (Israel et al., 2018).

Co-Design Workshops and Hackathons: AI workshops and hackathons will provide a range of activities including stakeholder involvement (e.g., community members and technologists), humanitarian practitioners, and leveraging of co-designing and proto-type (prototype) methodology. Those dynamic workshops do not just provide a room where participants chat out their different views and are able to benefit from each other's knowledge and talents; instead, they provide an environment where everyone works as a team. The inclusion of a variety of actors in the co-design process would result in customizing AI appliances for the cultural, linguistic, and environment-specific particu-larities of the communities served (Haklay et al., 2020).

Participatory design and user-centered approaches: User-participatory design rather than using solely the expert-driven planner methods involves all the communities con-cerned as the groups affected and health workers who are on the forefront. It is a sequen-tial process that first focuses on users' concerns, second on their rates, and third on their preferences that users have and this, in turn, guarantees that AI products are natural, easy to use, and user-oriented. Developing along with the participation of a diversity of stakeholders, humanitarian organizations can remain away from the creation of AI technologies that are obviously to be either not taken by, not accepted by, or applied in such circumstances (Schuler & Namioka, 1993).

CHALLENGES IN ETHICAL IMPLEMENTATION

Limited resources and infrastructure: The resource and infrastructure limitations are the main challenges regarding the ethical implementation of AI in humanitarian cases. This chapter examines the consequences of the scarcity of resources and infrastructure for the ethical use of AI in humanitarian operations. Many humanitarian organizations work in resource-constrained settings where they deal with scarcity of technology, bud-get, and skilled personnel (Vinck et al., 2014). Facilitated by digital divide, disparities in access to AI technologies will be amplified, leaving the disadvantaged demanding access to AI technologies more. Limited resources constitute huge barriers for humani-tarian practitioners' keen on deploying the right and appropriate AI effectively.

Inadequately established infrastructure constitutes a substantial obstacle for the integration and upkeep of AI technologies in humanitarian situations (Gillespie et al., 2016). Unstable power supply, poor internet connectivity, and lack of technical support can undermine the usability and stability of AI systems. In addition, reliance on external infrastructure providers and technology partners can create weaknesses and imposi-tions that can undermine the ethical integrity of humanitarian AI.

Cultural sensitivity and local contexts: In the application of AI in humanitarian aspects, the ethical implementation challenge is placing importance on cultural sensitiv-ity and understanding of local contexts as a crucial factor. This chapter focuses on the question of cultural sensitivity and local contexts in relation to the ethical implementation of AI in humanitarian projects. Linguistic and communicative barriers create problems for the implementation of AI technologies in humanitarian programs (Floridi & Sanders, 2004). Lack of adaptation to local languages/dialects of AI systems causes communication issues, which may lead to low uptake and acceptance of technology. Humanitarian actors must consider linguistic diversity among communities and guarantee that AI solutions are available and understandable among such diverse linguistic communities. Local contexts are formed by persistent historical, sociopolitical, and economic factors that affect community mechanisms and perception of humanitarian interventions (Vinck et al., 2014). Historical injustices, conflicts, and power dynamics could shape people's attitudes toward external actors, as well as influence the perception of AI technologies. Sensitivity to culture and understanding of local contexts are mandatory for the ethical deployment of AI in humanitarian situations. By acknowledging and accommodating cultural diversities, values, and practices, humanitarian actors can develop and implement AI technologies that are responsive to the needs and preferences of affected populations. By means of meaningful interaction, collaboration, and development, AI initiatives can have a positive social impact while maintaining ethical values and the concept of cultural diversity.

Potential criticisms of ethical frameworks proposed: However, the ethical frameworks of AI deployment in humanitarian issues are noble and supposed to help deal with complex issues, but critics argue that they may not be without any shortcomings. These criticisms arise from various aspects including capability, cultural accuracy, inclusivity, and accountability. The implementation of comprehensive ethical frameworks may require a lot of time and money, expertise, and may not be available immediately during crisis situations (Anderson et al.,2018). Furthermore, the swift development of AI technologies creates obstacles in terms of keeping ethical rules updated and adjusting to new conditions as necessary.

One more criticism is the lack of cultural sensitivity and the adaptability of the proposed models. While the frameworks stress the urgency of cultural sensitivity and the community connection in principle, the existent cultural variety, values, and contexts might be poorly integrated into the humanitarian settings in practice (Sen, 2006). Any practices that are considered ethically acceptable or even appropriate in one cultural setting may not necessarily be the same in another context, so communication can entail confusion or even conflict. An absence of consideration of cultural requirements generally could weaken the efficiency and credibility of AI interventions among affected communities.

Collaboration and coordination among stakeholders: The humanitarian sector comprises a wide range of actors such as governments, non-governmental organizations (NGOs), academia, the private sector, and affected communities (Anderson et al., 2018). Every stakeholder is characterized by his expertise, resources, and perspectives, and thus collaboration and coordination are the only remedy to be able to develop collective efforts and ensure maximum positive impact. Nevertheless, steering successfully through the intricate stakeholder maze is difficult when it comes to ensuring the commonality of objectives, priorities, and approaches. Power dynamics and various interests among stakeholders may entail problems for effective collaboration and coordination in humanitarian AI initiatives (Sen, 2006). Variables like organizational mandates, sources of funding, and political goals may result in tensions and conflicts that hinder cooperation. Humanitarian actors should address these concerns carefully and transparently while promoting trust and mutual respect among actors to overcome the difficulties in collaboration.

Multi-stakeholder and stakeholder organizations need to work in a space that is open and trustworthy when it comes to the sharing of information and regulation of data (Floridi & Sanders, 2004). Humanitarian orgs need to create policies that will facilitate data, knowledge, and resource sharing which will go together with privacy, confidentiality, and security protection. Industry specific standards and regulations should be established so that data ownership, access, and use rules ensure that ethical principles and legal requirements are met by AI initiatives. The trust and accountability matter very much in building effective collaboration of the stakeholders (Vinck et al., 2014). Transparency, honesty, and integrity are core values that form the foundation of ethical engagement and partnership. Humanitarian actors have to exhibit an accountability to the set of mechanisms such as regular reporting, monitoring, and evaluation of AI interventions. By using trust and accountability, stakeholders can work more efficiently together to deal with humanitarian problems and ensure the ethical use of AI.

ENSURING TRANSPARENCY

Open-source initiatives: Open-source initiatives are important means through which transparency is affected via facilitation of access to AI algorithms, data, and tools that people can explore, collaborate, and innovate with (Geiger & Piller, 2016). These measures are aimed at equal access to AI resources for researchers, developers, and humanitarian practitioners to study, rework, and develop better AI technologies (Dabbish et al., 2012). Through facilitating the creation of an open and collaborative atmosphere, open-source initiates play a major role in the ethical progress of AI in humanitarian settings.

Open-source initiatives have the potential to give wider access to AI resources by making software code, datasets, and models available in the public domain (Geiger and Piller, 2016). With transparency, stakeholders can grasp the internal mechanisms of the AI systems that are driving up their trustworthiness and reliability. Furthermore, open-source venues promote peer review and the validation of AI algorithms and models so that researchers and practitioners may openly share their work, benefit from others' feedback, and rely on collaborative efforts for verification purposes (Jupyter Development Team, 2016). The peer review procedure increases the trustworthiness and permanence of AI technologies thus eliminating risks of bias, mistakes, and other undesirable effects.

Open-source initiatives in AI research and development support reproducible and replicable outcomes. Offering the code and data for experiments, researchers can do the job twice and check the results, therefore assuring AI quality and reliability. Reproducible research practices help ensure transparency and trustworthiness and allow stakeholders to decide whether the proposed AI solution could be applied in a specific humanitarian context. Additionally, open-source communities promote community engagement and feedback, hence making AI technologies (Lakhani & Von Hippel, 2003) development and deployment more enriching. The diversity of perspectives brings together contributors, who exchange views, express ideas, and work toward a mutually beneficial solution.

Auditing and certification processes: In trust building and accountability implementation of AI ethically in the humanitarian domain, transparency is a must. The auditing and certification processes have an indispensable role in establishing transparency through independent investigation of the design, development, and deployment of AI (Floridi & Taddeo, 2016). These procedures are undertaken to ensure the meeting of ethics, law, and human rights standards by AI technologies, thereby increasing their trustworthiness and reliability.

Communication plan for stakeholders: Transparent and straightforward communication makes AI creators, users, and others concerned with the effects of these technologies are aware of their purpose, design, development, and implications, hence strengthening trust and accountability (Turilli & Floridi, 2009). Communication plans geared toward stakeholders are crucial and should be devised to assure transparency and facilitate more informed decision-making in the implementation of AI systems. Effective communication strategies involve a stakeholder dialogue approach to involving stakeholders using dialogue and consultation processes (Borenstein et al., 2021). AI developers and implementers proactively look for suggestions and opinions of the users, civil society, regulatory authorities, and others who may directly or indirectly be affected by artificial intelligence-based solutions. Dialogue sessions, public town halls, focus groups, and online forums provide opportunities for stakeholders to express their concerns, state their opinions, and contribute to the responsible use of AI.

STRATEGIES TO MITIGATE BIAS IN AI ALGORITHMS

A core tactic for stopping the biased training of AI algorithms is to guarantee that the training data used to create these algorithms is diversified and representative of the population it serves. From the humanitarian relief point of view, data coming from different sources need to be collected and should be demonstrated that it represents the diversity in terms of demographic, socioeconomic, and cultural groups in the affected communities. Through the introduction of multi-faceted data, AI algorithms become less susceptible to the propagation of stereotypes or marginalization of specific groups (Gebru et al., 2018).

Determining mechanisms of detecting and assessing bias in AI algorithms is essential for revealing and rectifying the possible spots of bias. Such studies entail undertaking extensive audits on AI systems and examination of their outcomes in terms of the different socioeconomic groups to find out if there is any disparity or bias. Constant bias monitoring by humanitarian organizations can lead to identification and correction of the issues before their effect on the harmful consequences arises (Obermeyer et al., 2019). The extent to which AI algorithms are susceptible to conflicts of interest and transparency in their decision-making processes is important to know the underlying mechanisms and their shortcomings. By enabling stakeholders to see the inner workings of AI systems, transparency allows them to verify the ethical and accuracy of such systems. In addition, explainable AI methods including model interpretability and feature importance analysis can reveal the causes that led to the conclusions of the algorithm, as well as determine any hidden prejudice it may carry (Rudin, 2019).

FUTURE RESEARCH DIRECTIONS

The relationship between AI evolution and humanitarian causes is firmly linked to technological advancements of which both promising opportunities and intricate ethical dilemmas are borne. As AI technologies keep refining and growing, it is vital to deliberate about the ethics of these technologies to ensure that these are developed and used in a responsible manner to reach the goals of humanitarian efforts, i.e., saving lives and alleviating human suffering. In this chapter, we probe into the possible directions for the future AI technologies and the ethical issues this raises, thereby putting an emphasis on the need for strong ethical frameworks to be developed.

The role of AI in humanitarian affairs grows more and more, and now the call for laws and regulations that are suitable is louder than ever. This chapter focuses on the regulatory regime governing AI technology in humanitarian activities, which explores the relevance of AI for these events as well as posing challenges and opportunities while promoting transparency, accountability, and safety. The introduction of AI to humanitarian scenarios appears to be changing the ways how the future may be guided in terms of AI rulemaking. It is this book section that touches on the collaborative multi-sectoral approach of AI ethics enhancement for humanitarian affairs focusing particularly on the partnership of various stakeholders that would help to resolve the problems and maintain transparency and safety.

CONCLUSION

Considering the applications of AI in the humanitarian areas of interest are developing with every passing moment, the outcomes on the future projects in this area deserve the attention of every stakeholder. The ethical principles that underpin AI for humanitarian tasks serve as building blocks, providing guidelines for the creation and deployment of AI in a way that puts the responsibility of the end-user first, as well as fairness, transparency, and safety. A detailed analysis of the issues and points of view presented in this paper points out some leading implications for the future of humanitarian AI projects. Moral precepts enunciated within the frameworks highlight the supreme role of maintaining humanistic values in all conservative and liberal minded aspects of AI in the shaping of humanity. This demands that the future projects should target the safe-guarding of individuals' rights, autonomy, and wellbeing to ensure that AI systems are formed and utilized in such a way that they are respectful and preserve the dignity and worth of people. These, too, have emerged as key considerations for the future projects, which demonstrate that involving the local communities and the stakeholders is essential to ensure that AI solutions fit well within the local culture, they suit the context, and they are sensitive to local values, norms, and practices. Through the integration of local voices and visions in the process of AI design and implementation, the technologies can be more in tune with the community preferences and priorities therefore being adopted by the community.

Lastly, among many factors, cooperation and coordination of stakeholders are key elements for successful implementation of future humanitarian AI projects. Such initiatives seek to promote partnerships between governments, NGOs, academic institutions, and local communities, thus enabling them to bring in their combined expertise, resources, and networks for the same purpose of tackling the complex humanitarian issues much more effectively and sustainably. The ethical frameworks reviewed in this paper serve as a solid base for the realization and the use of AI technologies in humanitarian contexts. In doing so, the projects can equally achieve more positive impacts in humanitarian efforts, which in the end will help in advancing the shared goal of establishing a world that is more inclusive, equitable, and resilient for all.

REFERENCES

Anderson, M., Anderson, S. L., & Armen, C. (2018). *Ethics of Emerging Technologies: Scientific Facts and Moral Challenges*. Hoboken, NJ: John Wiley & Sons.

Borenstein, J., Byrne, E., & Iliev, R. (2021). Stakeholder communication strategies for implementing AI in health care: A systematic review. *Journal of Medical Internet Research*, 23(5), e25689.

Bourguignon, D., Francken, N., & Verwimp, P. (2019). Measuring the impact of AI on international development. *Development Informatics Working Paper Series*, 65(65), 39–52.

Cath, C. (2018). Governing artificial intelligence: Ethical, legal and technical opportunities and challenges. *Governing Artificial Intelligence*. https://doi.org/10.1098/rsta.2018.0080

Confludi, E., & Sanders, J. T. (2004). Risks to human dignity posed by the commercialization of the human genome and genetic services: The need for global health law and coordination. *Houston Journal of Health Law & Policy*, 4, 193.

Dabbish, L., Stuart, C., Tsay, J., & Herbsleb, J. (2012). Social coding in GitHub: Transparency and collaboration in an open software repository. In *Proceedings of the ACM 2012 Conference on Computer Supported Cooperative Work* (pp. 1277–1286). Seattle: ACM.

Donnelly, J. (2013). The concept of human dignity in human rights discourse. *Human Rights Quarterly*, 25(2), 445–487.

Floridi, L., & Sanders, J. W. (2004). The method of levels of abstraction. *Minds and Machines*, 14(2), 2004.

Floridi, L., & Taddeo, M. (2016). What is data ethics?. *Philosophical Transactions of the Royal Society A: Mathematical, Physical and Engineering Sciences*, 374(2083), 20160360.

Gebru, T., Morgenstern, J., Vecchione, B., Vaughan, J. W., Wallach, H., Daumeé III, H., & Crawford, K. (2018). Datasheets for datasets. *arXiv preprint arXiv:1803.09010*.

Geiger, F., & Piller, F. T. (2016). The market for open innovation: Increasing the efficiency and effectiveness of innovation. *California Management Review*, *59*(1), 86–111.

Gillespie, S., Menon, R., & Kennedy, L. (2016). Scaling up impact on nutrition: What will it take? *Advances in Nutrition*, *7*(3), 440–451.

Haklay, M., Basiouka, S., Antoniou, V., & Ather, A. (2020). AI for humanitarian action: How to get it right. *Nature Machine Intelligence*, *2*(5), 215–218.

Israel, B. A., Schulz, A. J., Parker, E. A., & Becker, A. B. (2018). Review of community-based research: Assessing partnership approaches to improve public health. *Annual Review of Public Health*, *19*(1), 173–202.

Jupyter Development Team. (2016). Jupyter notebooks—A publishing format for reproducible computational workflows. In F. Loizides & B. Schmidt (Eds.), *Positioning and Power in Academic Publishing: Players, Agents, and Agendas* (pp. 87–90). New York: IOS Press.

Lakhani, K. R., & Von Hippel, E. (2003). How open source software works: "Free" user-to-user assistance. *Research Policy*, *32*(6), 923–943.

Mittelstadt, B. D., Allo, P., Taddeo, M., Wachter, S., & Floridi, L. (2016). The ethics of algorithms: Mapping the debate. *Big Data & Society*, *3*(2), 2053951716679679.

Nissenbaum, H. (2011). A contextual approach to privacy online. *Daedalus*, *140*(4), 32–48.

Obermeyer, Z., Powers, B., Vogeli, C., & Mullainathan, S. (2019). Dissecting racial bias in an algorithm used to manage the health of populations. *Science*, *366*(6464), 447–453.

Pizzi, M., Romanoff, M., & Engelhardt, T. (2020). AI for humanitarian action: Human rights and ethics. *International Review of the Red Cross*, *102*(913), 145–180.

Resnik, D. B. (2011). *What Is Ethics in Research & Why Is It Important?* Research Triangle Park, NC: National Institute of Environmental Health Sciences.

Rudin, C. (2019). Stop explaining black box machine learning models for high stakes decisions and use interpretable models instead. *Nature Machine Intelligence*, *1*(5), 206–215.

Schuler, D., & Namioka, A. (1993). *Participatory Design: Principles and Practices*. Cambridge: CRC Press.

Sen, A. (2006). *Identity and Violence: The Illusion of Destiny*. London: Penguin UK.

Turilli, M., & Floridi, L. (2009). The ethics of information transparency. *Ethics and Information Technology*, *11*(2), 105–112.

Veale, M., & Binns, R. (2017). Fairer machine learning in the real world: Mitigating discrimination without collecting sensitive data. *Big Data & Society*, *4*(2), 2053951717743530.

Vinck, P., Pham, P. N., Baldo, S., Shigekane, R., & Hean, S. (2014). Conflict exposure and peacebuilding in fragile states: Findings from a global survey in 2014. *Journal of Conflict Resolution*, *61*(5), 950–976.

Ethical Considerations in AI for Humanitarian Context

A Case Study of the Palestine-Israel Conflict

Selene Roldán Ruiz and
Arturo Roman Cesar Sanjuan

INTRODUCTION

The chapter commences by giving the reader a brief introduction to the history of the Palestine-Israel conflict, followed by a nuanced analysis of how artificial intelligence

DOI: 10.1201/9781003479109-13

(AI) has been used in warfare throughout the ongoing conflict. Afterward, we will explore Susan Sontag's *Regarding the Pain of Others* (2003), where she analyzes the role of images in shaping the public perception of distant conflict and how we as an audience react to them. We will be applying Sontag's ideas to the Palestine-Israel conflict, particularly into the ethical implications of AI-generated imagery while questioning how these technologies mediate the public opinion and empathy of the global audience. Additionally, it will scrutinize the concept of the "inert spectator" in the context of the Palestine-Israel conflict and the social media age, delving into how the immediacy of videos and images of war create a visual overload, numbing audiences not only to the emotional impact of the content but to the human rights violations these images portray. This section will address the ethical considerations associated with the creation and proliferation of AI-generated images, and it will explore the questions of potential misinformation, the need for ethical guidelines in the creation of said images, and the urgency of accountability and responsibility in AI.

Subsequently, we will analyze attentiveness as understood in Simone Weil's philosophy and the importance of incorporating an ethic of attention into the design and implementation of AI technologies. This section will explore how AI systems can be designed to uphold the dignity, humanity, and agency of those affected in humanitarian contexts, particularly the Palestine-Israel conflict. Thus, attentiveness will appear as a response to the biases AI systems can perpetuate and amplify, especially when they are not adhering to principles of neutrality and impartiality. Furthermore, Weil's philosophy discusses the importance of understanding social and cultural context, allowing us to understand the importance of contextual awareness, intersectionality, and cultural sensitivity in the development of AI. This will bring into discussion the need for AI to be developed with human rights in mind.

A BRIEF HISTORY OF
THE PALESTINE-ISRAEL CONFLICT

The Palestine-Israel conflict is a problem that has contested the Middle East for nearly a century. During World War I, Britain pledged to establish an Ethnostate for Jewish people in Palestine; under the Balfour Declaration, British troops took the territory from the Ottoman Empire at the end of October 1917 (Chughtai, 2023). This declaration noted that it was "clearly understood that nothing shall be done which may prejudice the civil and religious rights of existing non-Jewish communities in Palestine" (Westfall, 2023).

In 1947, the United Nations General Assembly passed Resolution 181, dividing the land into two independent states, one Arab and one Jewish, while Jerusalem remained under special international administration. The Arab side refused for it to happen, arguing it was unfavorable to their majority population. There was a territorial dispute over the land between the Jordan River and the Mediterranean Sea, both considered an ancestral homeland to Muslims and Jews. This contested terrain has witnessed cycles of war, displacement, ethnocide, uprising, and genocide. Between 1918 and 1947, the Jewish population in Palestine increased from 6% to 33%.

A year later, Israel declared its independence, and this was followed by an attack of a coalition of Arab states against Israeli forces, the first of several Arab-Israeli wars. In the end, Israel gained control of a larger portion of territory, forcing 700,000 Palestinians to flee, and this is what Palestinians refer to as the *Nakba*[1] (Westfall, 2023). This should not be understood as a mere displacement, but as an ethnic cleansing.

In June 1967, amidst persistent tensions, the Six-Day War, also known as the 1967 Arab-Israeli War, erupted. Partially triggered by Egypt's blockade, the conflict worsens as Israeli warplanes launch strikes at Egyptian airfields, allowing Israeli ground forces to enter the Sinai Peninsula. Jordan joins the Egyptian forces; however, Israeli forces have the upper hand, nearly eradicating Egypt's air power. This resulted in Israel taking control of the Gaza Strips, Sinai, the West Bank, the Golan Heights, and East Jerusalem, predominantly inhabited by Palestinians. More than 300,000 Palestinians were displaced during the Six-Day War (Chughtai, 2023).

In September 1978, a pivotal diplomatic milestone was achieved through the Camp David Accords, a peace agreement brokered between Egyptian President Anwar Sadat and Israeli Prime Minister Menachem Begin under the patronage of U.S. President Jimmy Carter. This landmark agreement laid the groundwork for a subsequent peace treaty between Egypt and Israel the following year, which includes Israel's withdrawal from the Sinai Peninsula. Additionally, the Camp David Accords delineated a comprehensive framework for the initiation of a process aimed at establishing Palestinian self-governance in the territories of the West Bank and Gaza Strip. This allowed for discussions and proposals for potential Palestinian peace, whose implementation remained unacted.

Alarmed by the displacement of Palestinian people, a Palestinian uprising or intifada took place in December 1987; the disobedience and protests against the Israeli occupation of the West Bank, Gaza, and Israel – former Palestine – led to a harsh Israeli military response, resulting in many killed and injured on both sides.

In 1993, the inaugural phase of the Oslo Accords, comprising two seminal agreements, marked a relevant moment in the Israeli-Palestinian conflict. Signed between Israel and the Palestine Liberation Organization (PLO), these accords demarked a peace process grounded in prior United Nations resolutions, allowing for incremental Palestinian self-governance in the occupied territories of the West Bank and Gaza Strip. Subsequently reinforced by an accord signed in 1995, these agreements established the institutional framework for the Palestinian Authority, tasked with the administrative affairs within these regions. Even with this diplomatic breakthrough, unresolved challenges persist, notably concerning the Israeli settlements within the West Bank and the status of Jerusalem, the latter regarded by the Palestinians as the capital of any future state (Westfall, 2023).

In October 2023, following a surprise attack by Hamas militants, Israel declared war on Hamas: "Since 7 October 2023, over 29,313 Palestinians – including more than 12,000 children – have been killed in Gaza. By 7 January 2024, Israel had bombarded Gaza with 65,000 tons of explosives" (Al Jazeera Media Network, 2024).

USE OF ARTIFICIAL INTELLIGENCE DURING THE ONGOING PALESTINE-ISRAEL CONFLICT

The ongoing conflict in Gaza, which began on 7 October 2023, is a paradigm shift. Demonstrating that fifth-generation warfare is not just about bombs and bullets, instead, we are dealing with a concept that evolves with every new conflict. "It may include the use of, but not limited to, artificial intelligence, fully autonomous systems of social engineering through tools like social media, unethical cyber-attacks, and a plethora of misinformation and false news, which includes biased, misleading, deceptive, or hyper partisan news" (Lakhani, 2023, p. 2). AI has been around since the 1950s. The term was coined at a conference held at Dartmouth College in the summer of 1956 (Moor, 2006). According to Kaplan and Haenlein (2019), artificial intelligence is "a system's ability to correctly interpret external data, to learn from such data, and to use those learnings to achieve specific goals and tasks through flexible adaptation."

Among the different types of AI, the one we frequent the most is generative artificial intelligence. Harvard University's IT describes it as: "Generative AI is a type of artificial intelligence that can learn from and mimic large amounts of data to create content such as text, images, music, videos, code, and more, based on inputs or prompts" (Harvard University, 2024).

When users face this type of AI, it is hard to differentiate fake from real. This is because generative AI is trained to mimic data that already exist and selectively chooses bits and pieces of what is real or deemed correct and then creates something entirely different out of it, such as images, stories, and even videos. AI-generated information tends to be inaccurate and deceptive and is manipulated with malicious intent, even during humanitarian crises, like the one in Gaza.

Additionally, AI has been used to map battle space. Israel's bombing campaign in Gaza has been described by many news outlets as the deadliest and most relentless in recent history, and what seems surprising is how AI has made it possible. "Israel appears to be relying heavily on artificial intelligence to map out the battle space and inform tactical responses AI is being used to help with everything from identifying and prioritizing targets to assigning weapons to be used against those targets" (Marijan, 2024).

While AI has the potential to enhance military performance and efficiency, its use in warfare raises several ethical questions, particularly those about accountability and transparency. It also makes us aware of how dangerous AI can be when used in warfare, and the threat it becomes when humans rely fully on these systems and lose the ability to consider the risk of civilian harm and the damage to necessary infrastructures such as hospitals and refugee camps.

Generative AI and AI warfare systems are not the only forms in which AI has materialized in the Palestine-Israel conflict; there are also social media algorithms that can serve as a means of resistance and as a vehicle for misinformation and ideological biases. Palestinians have historically used social media as a territory for resistance: "Social media has become an essential factor in the development of, and an increasingly important element in, political action, as it helps to form citizens' political culture, and shape positive political awareness, if it's well utilized" (Abunahel, 2023, p. 89).

Over the last decade, social media platforms such as YouTube, Facebook, Instagram, and X – formerly known as Twitter – have been utilized to report and document events occurring in Palestine. Since October 2023, this has amplified, particularly on TikTok; the short videos and live streams have shown the world the practices of Israel, such as exploitation, confinement, humiliation, and military attacks. The exposure triggered international protests asking for a cease-fire. Palestinians have made social media a central weapon in the fight for the narrative, and it has opened a discussion regarding Palestinian identity.

Palestinians have used social media, especially TikTok (Sky News, 2023), to share their stories, to connect with others, to advocate for their rights, and, most important of all, to show the world the ethnic cleansing to which Palestinians are subjected. We are witnessing a genocide through our phone screen, we are watching Palestinians fleeing their homes and avoiding air strikes, and we are watching Palestinians mourn their loved ones through a live stream on TikTok:

> The power to see, to create images, and to control images is a crucial aspect of the struggle for cultural survival and political self-determination. Native Americans have been fighting against images and representations that disempower, dehumanize, and commodify them for centuries. Yet, at the same time, they have been creating images that empower, humanize, and decolonize their identities.
>
> *(Shehadeh, 2023, p. 9)*

Social media was created with hopes that it would educate, inform, encourage, and inspire people, becoming the backbone of modern media. It has now transformed the way we communicate, the way we consume information, and the way we access news. Social media has turned into a new propaganda tool; it tells its audience who to sympathize with, who to believe, who to defend, and who to scrutinize. This was worsened by the algorithms it deploys, all it takes is a single interaction, and the user is immediately immersed in a bubble with like-minded people. Social media stops being a place for critical thought and reflection and turns into an echo chamber.

Susan Sontag: Desensitization and the Spectacle of War

Nearly a century ago, Virginia Woolf argued that looking at pictures that reflected the atrocities of war was enough to make them stop or at least to bring out the best in people making them unite in goodwill. Woolf never imagined that every human with a smartphone would have unlimited access to photographs and footage of war, that there would be an app filled with more than a thousand videos of a war, and that we would live in a time where we are bombarded by so much media regarding the war that we cannot decide which one is important or worse and cannot differentiate real from fake.

Intellectuals have said that people in the digital age have seen things on their phones that they will never forget; especially since October 2023, people have witnessed a war and its atrocities in real time. The extent of the violence, the loss of life, and degradation is extraordinary and overwhelming, to the point where people cannot make a nuanced appreciation of the Palestine-Israel conflict; instead, they mindlessly blame one side or the other (Sky News, 2023).

Before the social media age, the memory of war, like most memories, was local, but when the spectator is looking at the war on Twitch, X, Instagram, and TikTok, it feels almost as if it was happening to them, and they too bear witness to it. Looking at war brings in "a shame as well as shock in looking at the closeup of a real horror" (Sontag, 2002, p. 83). This shame poses a relevant question, should we be allowed to look at such devastation and horror?

When we look at war from our dining rooms, bedrooms, public transport, and smartphones, we are always distancing ourselves from the conflicts that are occurring on the other side of the world; this is also how we understand war, from a distance. We have not experienced it firsthand; we get a choice, we can always choose to stop looking at annihilation, and we get to turn our eyes away from the destruction that has not touched us in any tangible way. "Narratives can make us understand. Photographs do something else: they haunt us" (Sontag, 2022, p. 94).

However, when we let the videos play, when we stare at the photographs, and when we interact with content from the Israel-Palestine conflict, we echo Susan Sontag (2002): "This is what war does. War tears, rends. War rips open, eviscerates. War scorches. War dismembers. War ruins." Pictures of war, videos of mutilated bodies, and the recorded wailings of a father who has just lost his son, all can be used to condemn war, to bring a part of their reality to those who have never experienced such horrors. We may begin to question:

> What is the point of exhibiting these pictures? To awaken indignation? To make us feel bad; that is, to appall and sadden? To help us mourn. Is looking at such pictures really necessary, given that these horrors lie in a past remote enough to be beyond punishment? Are we the better for seeing these images? Do they actually teach us anything?
>
> *(Sontag, 2002, p. 95)*

If images and footage of war stop circulating, we can begin to ignore what is happening to others, but if they circulate relentlessly across our social media, we become desensitized. An image is drained of its revolutionary force by the way it is used, where, and how often we look at it. When violence is everywhere, we dare to look and we become desensitized; it allows for a certain level of violence and sadism to become acceptable in mass culture. "Our capacity to respond to our experiences with emotional freshness and ethical pertinence is being sapped by the relentless diffusion of vulgar and appalling images" (Sontag, 2002, p. 97). We live in a world oversaturated with images, and the ones that should matter the most – such as war images – have a minor effect on their spectator; as a society, we are becoming increasingly insensible. We feel remorse, but cannot be fully moved into action; we are losing our ability to react; and we just keep scrolling.

Furthermore, Sontag (2004) argued that photographs are easier to memorize because it is a quick way of apprehending something and a compact form to memorize, but now that we have social media platforms such as Instagram, X, and TikTok – the latter being known for its short-format videos – they allow us to take in the worst horror humankind has to offer in mere seconds. We are haunted by the empty gaze of Palestinian children, the screams of a mother holding the corpse of her child, and the impotence of a sister trying to wake her brother from eternal sleep. These tragic videos are followed by entertainment, by an influencer advertising a product, or by some sort of entertainment; the line begins to blur and suddenly war and pain are no longer a shock to the spectator but another spectacle.

Furthermore, they demonstrate that war is not and should never be turned into a spectacle. Their suffering is real. They are real people who have been tortured, humiliated, degraded, killed, raped, displaced, and kept as prisoners. The Palestine-Israel conflict must be named as what it is, a war, an ethnocide, and a genocide, because as Sontag (2003) said words alter, words add, and words subtract. Looking at the pain of others and gazing at Palestinians bring us to an understanding that this war is not barbarism, and those at war are not animals but people, mirrors of ideology, and racism, who have chosen to refer to and treat others as less human, legitimating torture, displacement, and murder.

SIMONE WEIL: ATTENTIVENESS IN WAR

War is an order of the day; we live in constant expectation of it. In every epoch, war defines a new species of violence. Concerning the Palestine-Israel conflict, one must analyze how generative AI, AI-led systems, and social media algorithms are part of a particular form of violence that is characteristic of this war. It cannot be compared to any other war, never did we have a war playing as background noise on our phone screen, and we would have never imagined scrolling through horrific images and videos amidst advertising. In other words, modern war is completely different from anything designated by that name in universal history.

Simone Weil (1945) argued that in war, the essential point is the obliteration of the individual by a state-serving fanaticism. When fighting a war, this would imply barbarous oppression by crushing people under the weight of an even more barbarous massacre. Modern war is a struggle led by all the state apparatuses and their staff against anyone bearing arms; against children, women, and disabled people who have no way of defending themselves; and against civilians looking for refuge.

Now, what happens to the ones subjected by these soldiers? What are the implications of a human telling another human you do not interest me; I do not care for your life or your heritage? This is cruelty and a giant offense against justice and morals. All human beings expect to be treated with dignity, even when they are victims of crimes; even if they are tortured, they have a glimpse of hope remaining in them, hope that good and not evil will be done to them.

Palestinians have been tortured, displaced, and killed for nearly a century; when evil is done to them, it still evokes a cry of surprise and pain. They are not passive or inert matter; even if we gaze at their empty eyes, they are not quite dead, and they are simply unable to cry out. All they can do is lament. "But the cry 'Why am I being hurt?'

raises quite different problems, for which the spirit of truth, justice, and love is indispensable" (Weil, 2005, p. 93).

Therefore, attentiveness counteracts the desensitized gaze Sontag was concerned about, the anaesthetized reaction of the viewer. The quality of attentiveness is at risk in the digital age; we cannot concentrate fully; we cannot watch videos longer than 30 seconds; and if we are attentive to one thing, one person, and one's suffering, we form an ethical consciousness. If the spectator is attentive, or fully present in their interaction with others, they will be able to empathize fully and genuinely.

SLAVOJ ŽIŽEK: IDEOLOGY, SUBJECTIVE VIOLENCE, AND CYNICAL DISTANCE

Slavoj Žižek is critical of the position that affirms the existence of a 'pure' pre-ideological reality without any discursive bias, arguing on the contrary that such a notion is ideological par excellence (Žižek, 2013, p. 18). This means that, for him, our access to reality begins with subjective mediation involving interests and positions that allow us to approach it. The aim is to examine the relationship between ideology and the Palestinian-Israeli conflict to gain insight into how we approach political and social issues.

Barrett (2013) discussed the concept of the future, which arose from the impossibility of society. The term, derived from medical language, refers to the process by which the surgeons of hegemony attempt to treat the continual and permanent tearing of the body politics' skin, but ultimately fail to stop the bleeding and close the scar (Barrett, 2013, p. 273). The primary nature of suture, as an ideological tool to address the incapacity of society, is the ongoing attempt and perpetual failure: the dominant exertion to fully encompass the body politic is inadequate considering the latter.

In the Palestinian-Israeli conflict, both sides use AI-generated imagery as propaganda. Eisele noted that image-generating tools are used to depict fictional scenes of the conflict, which support narratives by appealing to empathy for civilian suffering or patriotism (Eisele, 2023).

The point of suture in this context is the graphic representation aligned with one party involved in the conflict, seeking to exhaust the war but excluding its counterpart. However, this attempt to hegemonize the phenomenon of war fails to acknowledge the suffering of the other side. Therefore, it represents an exercise of external violence that accompanies the fighting in the trenches.

The relationship between symbolic and subjective violence can be explained by the reversal of the lesson that Žižek acknowledges from discourse analysis. As noted earlier, all access to phenomena requires an ideological subjective mediation of political positions and interests. Therefore, objectivity free of bias does not exist (Žižek, 2013, p. 18). Regarding the conflict, the objective representations of symbolic violence, generated by AI, influence the side taken by each party. The question is whether this exercise of violence is bilateral or if one party exercises more violence than the other.

According to Henry Farid, a forensic professor of digital analytics at UC Berkeley, the use of AI to justify certain positions in the Palestine-Israel conflict is immoral. He argued that these events are exceptional and isolated and do not reflect the entire narrative construction of the war phenomenon (Eisele, 2023). However, is this not the quintessential description of a symptom? From a psychoanalytic-Marxist perspective, a symptom is an exception that subverts the logic of a system, a short circuit that exposes the usual state of affairs through its subversion (Žižek, 1992, p. 47).

Of these reasons, the last one caused the biggest stir among the audience, who, amidst shouts and boos, denounced the need for such a historical analysis, without considering that every speaker at the fair who addressed the topic did so from an Israeli point of view. The point here is not to find out whether Slavoj Žižek's position in presenting his lecture was genuinely neutral or whether his political position could be glimpsed between the lines. The crucial factor is whether the audience was aware of the absence of impartiality in his approach to the conflict or, in other words, whether their indignation was due to a lack of awareness of the bias, and therefore exclusion, of his position.

Thus, this research updates Marx's definition of ideology and applies it to the Israel-Palestine conflict. It is widely acknowledged that the conflict is complex, and any approach is inherently one-sided and incomplete. This is especially true when using an image generated by artificial intelligence with implicit political positions. Despite this, people continue to reproduce and disseminate these images and base their position on the conflict without considering the ideological background behind it.

CONCLUSION

When we are constantly gazing at images portraying horror, murder, war, and torture, we do so from a distance, a distance that makes it harder for us to empathize, to realize that those pictures had to be taken somewhere, that this is the real world and that there is suffering and war in the real world, even when we cannot face it, or better said, when we chose to put out attention somewhere else. Furthermore, the intersection of symbolic and subjective violence in the Israel-Palestine conflict reveals how AI-generated imagery serves as a tool for hegemonic discourse, perpetuating partial representations of the conflict that suppress the dimension of the other. Moreover, the dissemination of AI-generated imagery in the context of the Israel-Palestine conflict serves as a potent example of ideological manipulation, wherein partial representations of the conflict are used to justify and perpetuate violence. It is imperative that we take decisive action to halt all forms of warfare and conflict, recognizing the devastating human toll and suffering they inflict. In our pursuit of global peace and harmony, we must harness the transformative potential of artificial intelligence (AI) to uplift humanity and contribute to the betterment of the world. AI, with its unprecedented capabilities and advancements, holds immense promise in addressing pressing global challenges, from healthcare and education to environmental conservation and social justice.

NOTE

1   Nakba means catastrophe in Arabic; it refers to the mass displacement and dispossession of Palestinians.

REFERENCES

Abunahel, M. (2023). Where to go: Fake news, democracy, social media and artificial intelligence. *Trends in Interdisciplinary Research, 12*(1), 89–100.

Al Jazeera Media Network. (2024). Know their names: Palestinian children killed in Israeli attacks on Gaza. https://interactive.aljazeera.com/aje/2024/israel-war-on-gaza-10000-children-killed/

Ali, R. (2023). How is Israel using artificial intelligence in its deadly attacks on Gaza? https://www.aa.com.tr/en/middle-east/how-is-israel-using-artificial-intelligence-in-its-deadly-attacks-on-gaza/3088949#

Barrett, M. (2013). "Ideología, política, hegemonía de Gramsci a Laclau y Mouffe". In S. Žižek (Ed.), *Ideología: Un mapa de la cuestión* (2nd ed., pp. 263–235). Buenos Aires: FCE.

Bureau, N. P. (2024). Israel-Palestine conflict: AI warfare in action? https://www.nationalherald-india.com/international/israel-palestine-conflict-is-ai-warfare-being-used

Chomsky, N. (2008). *The essential Chomsky*. London: The Bodley Head.

Chomsky, N. (2011). *How the world works*. London: Hamish Hamilton.

Chughtai, M. H. (2023). Israel-Palestine conflict: A brief history in maps and charts. https://www.aljazeera.com/news/2023/11/27/palestine-and-israel-brief-history-maps-and-charts

Eisele, I. (2023). Fact check: AI fakes in Israel's war against Hamas. https://www.dw.com/en/fact-check-ai-fakes-in-israels-war-against-hamas/a-67367744

Haenlein, M., & Kaplan, A. (2019). A brief history of artificial intelligence: On the past, present, and future of artificial intelligence. *California Management Review, 61*(4), 5–14.

Harvard University. (2024). Generative Artificial Intelligence (AI). https://huit.harvard.edu/ai

Hull, J. (2023). What are the implications of Israel's reported use of AI in Gaza war? (R. G. Meron Rapoport). https://www.aljazeera.com/program/inside-story/2023/12/3/what-are-the-implications-of-israels-reported-use-of-ai-in-gaza-war

Kaplan, A., & Haenlein, M. (2019). Siri, Siri, in my hand: Who's the fairest in the land? On the interpretations, illustrations, and implications of artificial intelligence. *Business horizons, 62*(1), 15–25.

Laclau, E., & Mouffe, C. (1985). *Hegemony and socialist strategy: Towards a radical democratic politics*. London: Verso.

Lakhani, M. (2023). Fighting disinformation in the Palestine conflict: The role of generative AI and Islamic values. *Al Misbah Research Journal, 3*(4), 2–13. https://doi.org/10.5281/zenodo.10456052

Marijan, B. (2024). How Israel is using AI as a weapon of war. *The Walrus*. https://thewalrus.ca/israel-ai-weapon/

Moor, J. (2006). The Dartmouth College Artificial Intelligence Conference: The Next Fifty Years. *AI Magazine, 27*(4), 87–87.

Shehadeh, H. (2023). Palestine in the cloud: The construction of a digital floating homeland. *Humanities, 12*(75), 1–18.

Sontag, S. (2002). Looking at war. *The New Yorker*, 9(1), 82–98.

Sky News. (2023). Is TikTok the new battleground for the Israel-Palestine conflict? https://news.sky.com/story/is-tiktok-the-new-battleground-for-the-israel-palestine-conflict-13035547

Sloterdijk, P. (2003). *Crítica de la razón cínica*. Madrid: Siruela.

Sontag, S. (2002). Looking at war. *The New Yorker*. https://www.newyorker.com/magazine/2002/12/09/looking-at-war

Sontag, S. (2003). Courage and resistance. *The Nation*. https://www.thenation.com/article/archive/courage-and-resistance/

Sontag, S. (2004). *Regarding the pain of others*. New York: Picador.

Thomas, C. (2020). Simone Weil: The ethics of affliction and the aesthetics of attention. *International Journal of Philosophical Studies, 28*(2), 145–167. https://doi.org/10.1080/09672559.2020.1736127

Weil, S. (1945). Reflections on war. *Politics*, 12(3), 51–55.

Weil, S. (2001). *Oppression and liberty*. London: Routledge.

Weil, S. (2005). *An anthology* (S. Miles, Ed.). London: Penguin Books.

Welt. (2023). Buchmesse: Tumult bei Rede von Philosoph Slavoj Zizek. *Die Welt*. https://www.welt.de/kultur/article248057060/Buchmesse-Tumult-bei-Rede-von-Philosoph-Slavoj-Zizek.html

Westfall, S., Murphy, B., Taylor, A., & Pietsch, B. (2023). The Israeli-Palestinian conflict: A chronology. *The Washington Post*, 12–14.

Willmann, C. (2018). Empathy – Attentiveness – Responsibility: Milestones of humanity in the work of Edith Stein, Simone Weil, and Dag Hammarskjöld and their relevance in the world today. In T. C. Philosophy (Ed.), *Re-Learning to be human in global times: Challenges and opportunities from the perspectives of contemporary philosophy and religion* (pp. 151–161). Washington, DC: The Council for Research in Values and Philosophy.

Žižek, S. (1992). *El sublime objeto de la ideología*. Ciudad de México: Siglo XXI.

Žižek, S. (2009). *Sobre la violencia. Seis reflexiones marginales*. Buenos Aires: Paídos.

Žižek, S. (2013). *Ideología: Un mapa de la cuestión* (2nd ed.). Buenos Aires: FCE.

Žižek, S. (2019). *Sex and failed absolute*. London: Bloomsbury Academic.

Public and Private Partnerships

14

Merging the Best of Both Worlds for Social Change

Rajasekhara Mouly Potluri
and Yerzhan B. Mukashev

INTRODUCTION

The conventional boundaries between the public and private sectors are muddling in today's rapidly changing and developing knowledge economy. The urgency and necessity for collaboration are imperative, particularly for governments to get technical and financial support from the private sector. The governments are working extensively to collaborate with the private sector to bring about dynamic changes in every field of the economy and bring about expected and radical social change. These innovative collaborations bring together the strengths and resources of both sectors to drive economic growth and increase competitiveness. These PPPs catalyze sustainable development and show multiple ways to revolutionize the current knowledge-based economies. The core reason behind these PPPs is that both parties candidly realize that, individually, they lack the power, resources, and skills to "go it alone" and find the best solutions to the diverse challenges on their own. To bring about the expected social change, communities

                      DOI: 10.1201/9781003479109-14

must increasingly work together to accurately address every society's various societal and humanitarian requirements, which have an extraordinary variation in their requirements and nature.

The public and private sectors possess exceptional and substantial uniqueness and vast experience related to financial strength and technical and managerial know-how, which, adequately pooled, harbor considerable capability to make a difference. Around the globe, there is an increasing tendency to develop PPPs to synchronize all kinds of input factors, along with other managerial and technical capacities. Usually, these kinds of partnership collaborations are a widespread phenomenon in developing large-scale government projects, such as roads, bridges, or hospitals, and other infrastructure-related projects like railways, telecom, flyovers, and oil and gas pipelines to be completed with private funding. These kinds of projects have observed an encouraging inclination as businesses progressively exploit their main capabilities and connect forces with companies whose expertise complements each other. These partnerships work well when the private sector's technology, innovation, and financial support combine with the public sector's managerial support and incentives to finish work on time and within the stipulated budget. The world has witnessed this kind of collaboration only on infrastructure-related projects. PPPs enable governments to procure and deliver public infrastructure/services and leverage the resources and expertise of the private sector through risk-sharing arrangements (Mohammed et al., 2023).

CONCEPTUAL VIGOR ON PUBLIC AND PRIVATE PARTNERSHIPS (PPPS)

Public and private partnerships, called PPP, 3P, or P3, are long-term arrangements between a government and private institutions (Hodge & Greve, 2007; Roehrich et al., 2014). It generally involves personal capital financing government projects and services up-front and then drawing revenues from taxpayers and/or users for profit throughout the PPP contract (Caves, 2004). Much of the early infrastructure of the United States was built through what can be considered PPPs. This includes the Philadelphia and Lancaster Turnpike Road in Pennsylvania, initiated in 1792 (Buxbaum, 2009). PPPs have experienced a significant swing in recent years, from being unstated as a risk justification application for the public and private sectors to a broader view of structuring agreements that can bring overall development benefits—including incorporating the sustainable development goals (SDGs).

Alongside this evolution came a new generation of more resilient, regenerative PPPs that aim to leave no one behind. This conceptual transformation is examined alongside the Addis Ababa Action Agenda (Addis Agenda) and approaches to improve PPPs' flawed reputation and strengthen advocacy for this new generation of PPPs (Jean-Christophe, 2022). These partnership units are organizations responsible for promoting, facilitating, and assessing P3s in their territory. They can be government agencies or semi-independent organizations created with full or partial government support. Governments develop these units to respond to criticisms of implementing P3 projects in their country before starting the P3 unit (Siemiatycki, 2015). In 2009, 50% of Organization for Economic Cooperation and Development (OECD) countries had created a centralized PPP unit, and many more of these institutions exist in other countries (Lemma, 2013). A PPP is a contracted agreement between the governments and the respective countries' private sector partners in which the governments hold ownership of the projects. The political leadership should ensure public awareness of the relative costs, benefits, and risks of PPPs and traditional procurement. A popular understanding of PPPs requires active consultation and engagement with stakeholders and involving end-users in defining the project and, subsequently, in monitoring service quality. The OECD defines PPPs as "long-term contractual agreements between the government and a private partner whereby the latter delivers and funds public services using a capital asset, sharing the associated risks".

In contrast, the private partners have taken full responsibility for finishing the project, from day one to managing it. The rights over these projects mostly remain with the governments, based on the terms and conditions of the contractual agreements when it comes to the project's conclusion. These parties share the profits caused by the finished project, and PPP agreements can last for decades. The core features of PPPs are risk sharing and allocation, ample public notes, performance expenses, capacity to deliver, openness, and keen competition. This is an excellent time to develop PPPs for socially responsible infrastructure projects because the entire world urgently needs at least basic infrastructure.

However, according to the World Bank's blog, the world won't have basic infrastructure. For instance, nearly 675 million people have no access to electricity, about 2 billion people don't have safe drinking water, and 2.7 billion people, or roughly one-third of the global population, continue to be unconnected to the Internet (Nyirinkindi, 2023). The author of the World Bank Blog, Dr. Nyirinkindi, evidently enunciated five ways PPPs can deliver confident and significant influence for people and our planet: (a) do more with less: developing and underdeveloped countries witnessed substantial financial scarcity, which is the major constraint on their capacity to invest. Most governments in the said world find an amicable solution for the given economic scarcity only with the establishment of agreements between the private sector, where governments can do more productive work with less effort; (b) share risk to make projects bankable: well-structured and adequately designed with clear start and end dates, PPPs help the public and private sectors share risks in which both parties don't have to bear the entire burden; (c) improve public service delivery: governments primary responsibility is to govern with the objective of social welfare. However, with the lack of funds, these governments struggle to deliver water, healthcare, and education services (unproductive and essential sectors) that are imperative for the greater good of society (Çela, 2022). The proposed PPPs can provide assurance and expand access to these critical and cardinal services; (d) boost infrastructure resilience to climate change: most of the governments have successfully introduced innovative climate mitigation measures in their infrastructure PPPs, moving them closer to meeting their Paris Agreement goals; (e) PPP projects can bolster gender equality and economic inclusion by incorporating standards to ensure development gains reach women, youth, and underserved or marginalized communities.

Granting public works and services paid for through a fee from the government's budget, such as hospital projects, concessions may include the right to direct users' payments, for example, with toll highways. In cases such as phantom tolls for highways, costs are based on the authentic procedure of the service, and as far as wastewater treatment is concerned, payment is made with fees collected from users (Public-Private Partnership Knowledge Lab, 2020a). These partnerships primarily involve transport, municipal and environmental infrastructure, and public service accommodations (Public-Private Partnership Knowledge Lab, 2020b). The World Bank is intensely concerned about these challenges in fully leveraging private sector participation in infrastructure development. PPP transactions do not inevitably respect monitoring restructurings, as can be seen when contrasting outcomes.

Furthermore, the World Bank can provision countries address these tests by, for example, assessing existing binding limitations to private contribution in infrastructure through country diagnostics and supporting the formation of an allowing milieu for personal contribution in infrastructure through the espousal of custom-made PPP supervisory transformations; backing with the progress of a channel of PPP projects to marshal private investment, and assistance with handling infrastructure PPPs throughout the project life cycle comprising adequately reflecting their fiscal promises and depending liabilities as well underpinning the capacity of governments to manage PPP contracts (Jean-Christophe Barth-Coullare, 2022). In late 2008, the world witnessed a severe financial crisis, which forced many governments to consider PPPs as their best strategy to get private funding support. The book also precisely discussed partnerships, concentrating on the idea that PPPs include government partnerships with private sector organizations and non-profit organizations, along with diverse levels of PPPs like project, organizational form, policy, and governance symbol or tool, and located in a broader historical context what constitutes "public" and "private" in a given society (Greve & Hodge, 2013). Many governments in different parts of the globe increasingly depend on the private sector for the implementation of projects because the public sector can no longer afford significant investments, which stresses the importance of governance (Bult-Spiering & Dewulf, 2008). Most of the PPPs are exclusively for infrastructure development projects, which are meant for economic growth, development, and infrastructure delivery and to achieve quality service delivery and good governance. At the same time, clear identification of the changing economic, social, and political environment, coupled with globalization and budgetary constraints, has made PPPs inevitable and definitely required in many countries worldwide (Akintoye et al., 2015).

PEOPLE-FIRST PUBLIC AND PRIVATE PARTNERSHIPS (PPPS)

The term "people-first PPPs for the SDGs" (now shortened to PPPs for the SDGs) was coined in 2015, along with discussions around the Addis Ababa Action Agenda on Sustainable Development Goals of the Third International Conference on Financing for

Development. Emphasizing people as recipients was envisioned to highlight culpability, as referenced in paragraph 48:

> …Projects involving blended finance, including PPPs, should share risks and reward fairly, include clear accountability mechanisms and meet social and environmental standards. We will, therefore, build capacity to enter into PPPs, including planning, contract negotiation, management, accounting, and budgeting for contingent liabilities.
>
> *(Sustainable Development Goals Knowledge Platform, 2022)*

After the development mentioned above concerned PPPs for the SDGs, there was a sea change in the orientation of PPPs toward achieving SDGs throughout the globe. By understanding the infrastructure and service requirements of societies, many governments have initiated a myriad number of social change projects on a war footing basis. Many governments are now fully considering the design and development of PPPs to deliver confident results under the United Nations 2030 Agenda to achieve the prescribed set of 17 SDGs.

Undoubtedly, the Addis Ababa Agenda on SDGs confidently indulgences sustainable and robust infrastructure as a vital thematic zone, specifying that reserves in transportation, energy, water, and sanitation are prerequisites for attaining the SDGs, and the same agenda points out solidly the necessity for PPP capacity development in the mechanical, financial, societal, ecological, legal, and other aspects that are indispensable to appropriately channel PPPs that meet development goals (Jean-Christophe Barth-Coullare, 2022). Extensive research from Belgium emphasized the prerequisite to integrate sustainability considerations in infrastructure projects delivered through PPPs and found that these play a restricted role and that the social dimensions of sustainability are largely neglected. The same research highlighted that a compelling sustainability perspective appears fundamentally contradictory to the contractual PPP project structure, which requires measurable and enforceable performance indicators (Hueskes et al., 2017).

The problem has stimulated PPPs and the infrastructure community. The crucial question arises in the 6th Session of the United Nations Economic Cooperation of Europe (UNECE) Working Party on PPPs (UNECE, 2022). In the meeting, UNECE Executive Secretary Olga Algayerova called on investors to grab the prospect of opportunity in the channel of climate projects recognized to have a significant involvement in the 2030 Agenda in the UNECE region. Besides, the member states of the UNECE developed 12 new policy documents by the Working Party to develop the PPPs for the SDGs approach. These priority areas are: (a) digital transformation for sustainable development; (b) sustainable economic recovery and reconstruction; (c) sustainable PPP and infrastructure finance; and (d) green PPP procurement.

By promising the SDGs, countries covenant to follow progress on economic, social, and environmental targets in a stabilized and unified manner. The SDGs are crosscutting and determined, and they demand a shift in how we work in partnership. The SDGs push everyone in the world to radically alter the level of public and private investment (Mohieldin, 2018). Academicians like Gideon and Unterhalter (2020) posited that PPPs have increased in high, middle, and low-income countries since the middle of the new millennium, and most of these partnerships concentrated on achieving SDGs.

The world has witnessed the emergence of strategic cross-sector partnerships; keep in mind the millennium development goals (MDGs) eight challenges: (a) eradicate extreme poverty and hunger, (b) universal education, (c) gender equality, (d) child health, (e) maternal health, (f) combat HIV/AIDS, (g) environmental sustainability, and (h) global partnerships for development (Maurrasse, 2013).

SUSTAINABLE PUBLIC AND PRIVATE PARTNERSHIPS (PPPS)

Sustainability is the most crucial agenda item in many modern governments, and concentrating on social change and infra-related projects is the prime concern for these. Even though this is the core concern of many governments, particularly in developing and underdeveloped countries, the concept is not adequately extended to at least some basic infrastructure-related projects like electricity, drinking water, sanitation, housing, roads, telecommunications, and many more. To provide all these, governments essentially needed the support of the private corporate sector to make swift multi-criterion decisions. Researchers Dolla and Laishram (2020) emphasized a model of sustainability to evaluate the bid proposal that has been proposed, and the model is developed using an analytical network process with signs that are reputable on the four pillars of sustainability, namely economic sustainability, social sustainability, environmental sustainability, and institutional sustainability.

Another exciting piece of research from China highlighted that cognition, institutional, financial, and participation aspects are key barriers confronted by PPP sustainability, and governments play a dominating role in controlling factors causing sustainability-related problems in PPPs (Liu et al., 2024). Another astonishing study related to agriculture was initiated in India, another essential sector to change society by offering the required quantity and quality of agriculture-based production. The study from India stressed that PPPs are crucial for advancing agricultural sustainability, tackling issues related to enhancing global food security, and helping the farming community with advanced technology. As PPPs bring together public, private, and civil society efforts, they are commonly touted to boost productivity and foster growth in the agriculture and food sectors (Agarwal et al., 2023; Strang et al., 2022; Strang et al., 2020). Another exceptional research from Africa, especially Ghana, emphasized that contractual governance influences of PPP are more prominent than noncontractual ones for sustainable PPP projects and implied that PPP project managers should improve governance aspects for the sustainable development of PPP projects in Africa. The trifecta of black swan events over the last 3 years—the global COVID-19 pandemic, natural disasters, and geo-political events—has destabilized many countries' economies.

In the new millennium, the PPP business model has received considerable attention from many governments and private sector companies to promote infrastructure-related projects along with socially beneficial facilities to many societies in different parts of the globe and in the process of achieving sustainability development goals by improving its performance in developing countries required to build infrastructure projects to provide basic amenities to set right the lifestyle deficiencies of the public. PPPs are crucial to achieving sustainable goals in any country by concentrating on infrastructure and social change projects. It is contemplated that spreading the involvement in project investment between private and public sectors is one of the critical variables affecting the sustainability performance of PPP-type projects.

The research examines the impacts of the contribution distribution between public and private sectors on project sustainability performance and develops a model named the sustainability performance-based evaluation model (SPbEM) to assess the level of sustainability performance of PPP projects (Shen et al., 2016). The same study investigates the probability of succeeding in appropriate sustainability through an apt arrangement of the investment distribution between the two primary sectors in developing PPP-type infrastructure projects. Inarguably, the role of infrastructure projects is comprehensively significant in the socio-economic development of any country, irrespective of the nature of evolution, due to their contributions to their respective national priorities, competitiveness, and social welfare in underdeveloped, developing, and developed countries. In the last two to three decades, many researchers have extensively conducted sustainability-related research on the relationship between PPPs and sustainability. An extensive study offers a thorough understanding of the body of knowledge of the nexus between these two, their development, and the connections between their core topics. The study allows for integrating dispersed studies within a comprehensive PPP sustainability framework (Castelblanco et al., 2021). Around the globe, PPPs have become increasingly popular as an innovative model for developing social change and infrastructure. PPPs are generated based on the respective countries' requirements, which leads to their priority of achieving the SDGs. The study from China reviews the development of China's PPP and briefs on its characteristics through the theory of evolutionary economic geography. It also discusses four dimensions: driving force, subject, process, and object. The study results showed that the sustainability-oriented PPP framework explains the development process and trend of PPP, not only meeting the PPP development needs in China but also providing a reference value for other developing countries (Cheng et al., 2021).

Beneficial synergies are beleaguered by recommending a conjunction of hitherto parallel international happenings concerning (a) emerging better and more sustainable relationships for more productive construction project teams in general and (b) optimizing the necessarily long-term contractual arrangements of PPPs. Examples are drawn from Africa and Latin America to emphasize registered PPP encounters from other regions and build a case for injecting "relational contracting approaches" to develop more productive and sustainable PPPs. Strong and sustainable relationships are shown to be essential and complementary to appropriate contractual incentives that would empower PPP project teams to focus on developing sustainable infrastructure and overall sustainable development. These propositions are merged into a basic model that merits further investigation and development to ensure that planned PPPs benefit the community, concerning both present and future generations (Kumaraswamy et al., 2005). Most countries' governments prefer PPPs as the best route to develop social change and infra-related projects essential to their public because of their budgetary constraints and the efficiency gains the private sector provides.

Whenever the private sector is influenced chiefly by profit earning, even by entering PPP agreements, there is severe criticism against PPPs for focusing on economic and financial targets while giving less emphasis to achieving social objectives. As a result, both infra and socially responsible project development through PPP will fail to promote SDGs. The research paper argues the outcomes from a designated review of Indian PPP procurement, focusing on the weaknesses of infrastructure development through PPP in supporting sustainable development (Patil & Laishram, 2016). Another exciting book chapter by the academicians Alexander et al. (2021) emphasized that the mounting significance of PPPs indicates the necessity to evaluate their impacts on sustainability-related objectives. With a systematic appraisal of the business and public administration literature, this study expounds on whether pragmatic indication designates that PPPs are suitable instruments to achieve the sustainability objectives of governments and which success factors are crucial for this purpose. Results reveal that business research on PPPs rarely integrates sustainability concepts; findings about their contributions to sustainability remain inconclusive.

PUBLIC AND PRIVATE PARTNERSHIPS (PPPS) IN KAZAKHSTAN: AN OVERVIEW

Despite the PPP development initiated in the early 90s, just like other Russian CIS countries, Kazakhstan's slow progress and experience were much smaller from 2004 to 2005 (Mouraviev & Kakabadse, 2016). The core reasons are mainly the lack of interest in partnerships and the lack of signs of bureaucratic impediments. Just like other countries' governments, the government of Kazakhstan also evidently recognized the vital significance of PPPs for their economic development. The government website itself highlights the meaning, characteristics, main objectives, forms, and types of possible projects to initiate under this business model, the role of the Kazakhstan PPP center, objects that cannot be implemented, and the role of the National Chamber of Entrepreneurs (NCE) or "Atameken" in PPP (Government of Kazakhstan, 2021).

With a broader vision, the government of Kazakhstan established the JSC "Kazakhstan Center for Public-Private Partnerships" center for developing PPPs, which is essentially required to initiate various projects based on the nation's priorities from time to time. The center's core activities are conducting research and developing recommendations on PPP issues, examining tender documentation and business plans for republican PPP projects, evaluating the implementation of PPP projects, training specialists in the field of PPP, and maintaining a list of PPP projects planned for implementation. Keep in mind the commitment toward the public of Kazakhstan; the government never allows PPPs in the following list of society-required basic amenities and nation's treasure projects, viz., land, water, flora and fauna, specially protected natural territories, objects of cultural heritage, railways, water facilities of strategic importance (dams, waterworks), and depositories of pathogens of dangerous infections. The government of Kazakhstan and other stakeholders can get advice about partnerships of this kind at the NCE. Following Article 28 of the Law of the Republic of Kazakhstan "On Public-Private Partnership," NCE RK "Atameken" performs the following functions: (a) participation in the tender commission to determine a private partner, and (b) participation in monitoring the implementation of PPP projects.

The premier joint stock company, the NCE, persistently offers consultations and seminars on PPP issues, as well as legal support and protection of the rights and legitimate interests of business entities in the state bodies of the Republic of Kazakhstan. The Asian Development Bank (ADB) developed a comprehensive report on Kazakhstan's PPP environment by assessing the country's progress in creating better conditions for PPPs, increasing infrastructure funding, and improving service delivery. The comprehensive report was prepared after consolidating data from leading financial and legal experts. It includes more than 500 qualitative and quantitative indicators profiling the country's national PPP landscape, covers eight infrastructure sectors, and includes local government projects.

The pandemic has driven social infra to the forefront of policy and planning, and the report also focuses on healthcare, education, and affordable housing (Asian Development Bank, 2022). There is an enhancing trend among academicians to initiate more research on diverse issues of PPPs in Kazakhstan. The research study emphasized that the effectiveness of PPP projects is based on economic, social, human, political, and entrepreneurial factors (Abdymanapov et al., 2016). Kazakhstan has established a well-structured legal and institutional framework for preparing PPPs at national and regional levels. The government has prioritized PPPs as an economic and social infrastructure delivery mode. The central emphasis on PPPs had a strong impact at the regional level, with many relatively small projects signed in the past few years. The effect has been modest nationally, primarily due to financing challenges.

CONCLUSION

PPPs are imperative to take a comprehensive approach to create swift infrastructural development and, at the same time, social change projects by synchronizing the abilities and resources of governments and private parties. This chapter offers valuable insights. The spectrum of possible PPPs extends from conventional businesses to projects that would bring about social change. Whatever the commitments politicians give at the time of elections, it is imperative to introduce broader reforms to resolve underlying infrastructure governance issues. The design and development of mutually beneficial agreements between the public and private sectors must introduce sector-based strategies and reforms based on the emergencies of projects like the pandemic, natural calamities, and geo-political disturbances to create momentum for the nation's priorities and generate interest among all stakeholders. A solid framework that the government must develop, accompanied by sufficient institutional arrangements and well-resourced human resources backup, to design and complete PPPs. The bottom line is that, throughout the globe, many governments extensively use PPPs to collaborate with resourceful private sector companies to get the expected level of financial and technical support, particularly for socially responsible projects. Even though there are advantages and disadvantages to these partnerships, governments still use them specifically to finance transportation, municipal and environmental infrastructure, and other public service projects. Therefore, it is a must for governments and private sector companies who plan to enter PPPs exclusively for social change by synchronizing their resources, dexterities, and other competitive and core advantages.

REFERENCES

Abdymanapov, S. A., Toxanova, A. N., Galiyeva, A. H., Abildina, A. S., & Aitkaliyeva, A. M. (2016). Development of public-private partnership in the Republic of Kazakhstan. *International Electronic Journal of Mathematics Education, 11*(5), 1113–1126.

Agarwal, V., Malhotra, S., & Dagar, V. (2023). Coping with public-private partnership issues: A path forward to sustainable agriculture. *Socio-Economic Planning Sciences, 89,* 101703.

Akintoye, A., Beck, M., & Kumaraswamy, M. (Eds.). (2015). *Public-Private Partnerships: A Global Review*. London: Routledge.

Alexander, P., Nahid, R., & Julia, T. (2021). Public-private partnerships as instruments to achieve sustainability-related objectives: the state of the art and a research agenda. *Sustainable Public Management, 20*(1), 1–22.

Asian Development Bank. (2022). Public-private partnership Monitor: Kazakhstan. https://www.adb.org/publications/public-private-partnership-monitor-kazakhstan

Bult-Spiering, M., & Dewulf, G. (2008). *Strategic Issues in Public-Private Partnerships: An International Perspective*. Hoboken, NJ: John Wiley & Sons.

Buxbaum, J. N. (2009). *Public Sector Decision Making for Public-private Partnerships*. Washington, DC: Transportation Research Board (p. 9).

Castelblanco, G., Guevara, J., & Mendez-Gonzalez, P. (2021). Sustainability in PPPs: A network analysis. In *Proceedings of International Structural Engineering and Construction, Interdisciplinary Civil and Construction Engineering Projects. ISEC, 11* (pp. 1–6). Athens.

Caves, R. W. (2004). *Encyclopedia of the City*. (p. 551). Oxfordshire: Routledge. ISBN 9780415252256.

Çela, E. (2022). A summary of the national plan for European integration related with the development of education system in Albania during 2020–2021. *Euro-Balkan Law and Economics Review, 3*(1), 71–86.

Cheng, Z., Wang, H., Xiong, W., Zhu, D., & Cheng, L. (2021). Public-private partnership as a driver of sustainable development: Toward a conceptual framework of sustainability-oriented PPP. *Environment, Development and Sustainability, 23,* 1043–1063.

Dolla, T., & Laishram, B. (2020). Enhancing sustainability in public-private partnership projects through bid selection model. *Transportation Research Procedia, 48,* 3896–3907.

Gideon, J., & Unterhalter, E. (Eds.). (2020). *Critical Reflections on Public-Private Partnerships*. London: Routledge.

Government of Kazakhstan. (2021). What you need to know about public-private partnerships. https://www.gov.kz/situations/338/884?lang=en

Greve, C., & Hodge, G. (2013). *Rethinking Public-Private Partnerships: Strategies for Turbulent Times* (1st ed.). Routledge. https://doi.org/10.4324/9780203108130.

Hodge, G. A. & Greve, C. (2007). Public-private partnerships: An international performance review, *Public Administration Review, 67*(3), 545–558.

Hueskes, M., Verhoest, K., & Block, T. (2017). Governing public-private partnerships for sustainability: An analysis of procurement and governance practices of PPP infrastructure projects. *International Journal of Project Management*, *35*(6), 1184–1195.

Jean-Christophe Barth-Coullare. (2022). A short history of PPPs for development: The good, the bad, and the hopeful. https://blogs.worldbank.org/ppps/short-history-ppps-development-good-bad-and-hopeful

Kumaraswamy, M., Anvuur, A., & Rahman, M. (2005). Balancing contractual and relational approaches for PPP success and sustainability. In *Proceedings of the Conference on Public Private Partnerships: Opportunities and Challenges* (pp. 104–114). Hong Kong: The University of Hong Kong and Civil Division of HKIE.

Lemma, A. (2013). *Literature review: Evaluating the costs and benefits of centralized PPP units*. Overseas Development Institute, Economic and Private Sector PEAKS, April.

Liu, B., Li, J., Wang, D., Liu, H., Wu, G., & Yuan, J. (2024). Public-private partnerships: A collaborative framework for ensuring project sustainable operations. *Engineering, Construction and Architectural Management*, *31*(1), 264–289.

Maurrasse, D. (2013). *Strategic Public-Private Partnerships: Innovation and Development*. Northampton, MA: Edward Elgar Publishing.

Mohammed, N., Salem, Y., Ibanez, M., & Bertolini, L. (2023). *How can public-private partnerships (PPPs) be successful?* The World Bank. https://www.worldbank.org/en/region/mena/brief/how-can-public-private-partnerships-ppps-be-successful#

Mohieldin, M. (2018). *SDGs and PPPs: What's the connection?* The World Bank Blogs. https://blogs.worldbank.org/ppps/sdgs-and-ppps-whats-connection

Mouraviev, N., & Kakabadse, N. K. (2016). *Public-Private Partnerships: Policy and Governance Challenges Facing Kazakhstan and Russia*. London: Palgrave Macmillan by Springer Nature.

Nyirinkindi, E. (2023). *Five ways PPPs deliver impact*. The World Bank Bogs. https://blogs.worldbank.org/ppps/five-ways-ppps-deliver-impact

Patil, N. A., & Laishram, B. (2016). Public-private partnerships from sustainability perspective– A critical analysis of the Indian case. *International Journal of Construction Management*, *16*(2), 161–174.

Public-Private Partnership Knowledge Lab. (2020a). PPP contract types and terminology. https://pppknowledgelab.org/guide/sections/6-ppp-contract-types-and-terminology

Public-Private Partnership Knowledge Lab. (2020b). How PPPs are used: Sectors and services. https://pppknowledgelab.org/guide/sections/8-how-ppps-are-used-sectors-and-services

Roehrich, J. K., Lewis, M. A., & George, G. (2014). Are public-private partnerships a healthy option? A systematic literature review. *Social Science & Medicine*. *113*, 110–119.

Shen, L., Tam, V. W., Gan, L., Ye, K., & Zhao, Z. (2016). Improving sustainability performance for public-private partnerships (PPP) projects. *Sustainability*, *8*(3), 289.

Siemiatycki, M. (2015). Public-private partnerships in Canada: reflections on twenty years of practice. *Canadian Public Administration*, *58*(3), 343–362.

Strang, K. D., Che, F., & Vajjhala, N. R. (2020). Urgently strategic insights to resolve the Nigerian food security crisis. *Outlook on Agriculture*, *49*(1), 77–85.

Strang, K. D., Che, F. N., & Vajjhala, N. R. (2022). Agriculture business problems: Analysis of research and probable solutions in Africa. In Ferdinand Ndifor Che, Kenneth David Strang, & Narasimha Rao Vajjhala (eds), *Research Anthology on Strategies for Achieving Agricultural Sustainability* (pp. 1184–1209). Hershey, PA.

Sustainable Development Goals Knowledge Platform. (2022). *Addis Ababa Action Agenda of the Third International Conference on Financing for Development*. https://sustainabledevelopment.un.org/frameworks/addisababaactionagenda

United Nations Economic Cooperation of Europe (UNECE). (2022). UNECE sustainable development goals. Sustainable PPPs and infrastructure finance play important role in the 2030 Agenda. https://unece.org/economic-cooperation-and-integration/news/sustainable-ppps-and-infrastructure-finance-play

Halal Food Safety in the AI Era

New Horizons for Humanitarian Action

Md Mahfujur Rahman

15

INTRODUCTION

The global demand for halal food has surged, appealing not only to the Muslim population but also to a broader demographic seeking ethically produced and high-quality food options. Halal food production adheres to stringent standards, ensuring compliance with Islamic dietary laws by prohibiting any non-compliant ingredients or practices. This market has experienced rapid growth driven by an increasing Muslim population and a growing interest in halal practices among diverse consumer groups (Industry Research Co., 2023). Beyond religious observance, the concept of halal emphasizes food safety, hygiene, and reliability, earning the trust of both Muslim and non-Muslim consumers alike (Farhan & Sutikno, 2022). Halal food safety management systems, grounded in principles of accountability, cleanliness, traceability, and continuous improvement, not only align with but also enhance global food safety protocols, giving halal products a competitive edge in the international market (Demirci et al., 2016; Putri et al., 2022; Ali & Suleiman, 2018).

DOI: 10.1201/9781003479109-15

BACKGROUND

The integration of artificial intelligence (AI) into halal food safety practices heralds a new era of innovation within the industry. Halal Food Councils now leverage AI to analyze extensive datasets, enhancing the monitoring of production processes and swiftly identifying any compliance issues, thereby maintaining the integrity of halal certification. Additionally, blockchain technology has revolutionized the traceability of halal products, enabling transparent, real-time access for consumers to verify the halal status, origin, and journey of certified products (Halal Certification Services, 2023). Notable initiatives like the first halal blockchain slaughterhouse in Indonesia and Sreeya's pioneering efforts in chicken slaughterhouses, certified by Majelis Ulama Indonesia, highlight blockchain's role in bolstering consumer confidence and safety (Jati, 2020). Moreover, the introduction of virtual reality (VR) and augmented reality (AR) technologies has streamlined compliance checks through remote inspections, reducing costs and promoting sustainable practices. In ensuring the halal management of the food supply chain, it is imperative that every member of the chain serves as both a supplier and a customer. Perceptual discrepancies can lead to inefficiencies in the supply chain operations and marketplace, resulting in reduced halal quality or quantity (Rahman et al., 2023). This integration of AI and sustainable practices within halal food safety aims to improve operational efficiency and transparency, meeting the diverse needs of consumers, including those in pursuit of ethical and quality food options (Demirci et al., 2016; Bux et al., 2022).

This chapter explores how the successful incorporation of AI into halal food safety not only promises operational enhancements but also significant humanitarian and societal benefits. These range from ensuring higher food safety and quality, fostering traceability and transparency, empowering consumers, and reducing instances of fraud and mislabeling to addressing ethical considerations, facilitating global trade, and promoting public health and sustainability. As such, AI-driven innovations are poised to contribute substantially to a more transparent, efficient, and sustainable global food system.

REVOLUTIONIZING HALAL FOOD SAFETY: INTEGRATION OF AI

The integration of AI in the halal food industry represents a significant leap toward enhancing efficiency, transparency, and trust in food safety. Numerous advantages can result from the use of AI in halal food safety, such as real-time monitoring and analysis. Furthermore, the integration of AI technologies in the halal food industry can contribute to broader consumer groups' ethical and quality food options, as halal standards often require rigorous hygiene practices, stringent ingredient selection, and transparent labeling, ensuring that halal-certified products meet higher safety, hygiene, and quality standards. Table 15.1 provides an overview of various AI applications and their impact

TABLE 15.1 Enhancing halal food safety through artificial intelligence (AI) integration

BENEFIT	AI APPLICATION	IMPACT	FOOD SAFETY ISSUES	TECHNOLOGIES USED	REFERENCES
Enhanced halal compliance	Scanning product labels and ingredient lists, machine learning (ML) for monitoring processes	Prevents contamination, ensures standards, and proactive issue detection	Ensuring adherence to halal dietary laws and preventing non-halal contamination and mislabeling of ingredients to uphold halal food safety	ML, AI scanning	Ahmed (2022, 2023) and Halal Food Council USA (2024)
Optimized halal supply chain	Real-time information on inventory, production, shipping, and blockchain for a tamper-proof ledger	Reduces waste, optimizes inventory, improves efficiency	Maintaining halal integrity in the supply chain by minimizing disruptions in the cold chain and reducing risks of spoilage and contamination, thus safeguarding halal food safety	Blockchain, AI analytics	Ahmed (2022), Halal Food Council USA (2024), and Omar (2023)
Improved animal welfare	AI-powered sensors to monitor animal behavior in slaughterhouses	Detects distress in animals, allows for immediate action	Ensuring humane treatment in accordance with halal standards to mitigate stress-induced meat safety issues, thereby enhancing overall halal food safety	AI sensors	Ahmed (2022)
Guaranteed traceability and transparency	Blockchain for traceability from farm to fork, AI for food traceability and labeling	Enhances transparency, combats fraud, decentralized verification	Ensuring authenticity and halal compliance throughout the supply chain, combating mislabeling and fraud to maintain the highest standards of halal food safety	Blockchain, AI traceability systems	Ahmed (2022, 2023), Islamic Services America (2024), Halal Food Council USA (2024), and Omar (2023)
Ensured safety and compliance	Internet of Things (IoT) devices to track temperature, humidity, storage conditions	Ensures halal requirements, minimizes risk of non-compliance	Temperature abuses, improper storage conditions leading to spoilage	IoT devices	Ahmed (2023) and Islamic Services America (2024)

on addressing food safety within the halal food industry. Each row outlines a specific benefit of AI integration, the corresponding AI application, its impact on food safety, the associated food safety issues it addresses, the technologies used, and the relevant references. These insights shed light on how AI technologies contribute to ensuring compliance, optimizing supply chain operations, improving animal welfare, guaranteeing traceability and transparency, and ensuring safety and compliance standards are met within the halal food sector.

Enhancing Halal Food Safety through AI Certification

Halal certification processes may benefit from AI integration (Nusran et al., 2023). By utilizing AI for the scanning of product labels and ingredient lists, halal food safety may significantly improve. AI systems meticulously identify any elements that do not conform to halal standards, thereby mitigating the risk of accidental non-halal contamination. The application of machine learning (ML), an AI subset, enables the thorough analysis of extensive datasets, which helps in detecting irregular patterns and anomalies indicative of non-compliance. This vigilant, proactive approach not only facilitates early detection of potential issues but also strengthens the overall integrity of halal certification processes. Consequently, AI-driven methods offer a robust solution to guarantee the highest levels of safety and quality in halal food while also contributing to the establishment of a unified standard for halal certification. These advancements in AI applications in halal food safety underscore a commitment to upholding stringent halal guidelines across the food industry.

Optimizing Halal Supply Chain with AI

Advanced AI systems enhance the halal supply chain by delivering instantaneous data on inventory levels, production timelines, and delivery schedules. This real-time tracking capability aids in minimizing waste, refining inventory control, and bolstering overall operational efficiency. Complementing AI, blockchain technology plays a pivotal role in ensuring the integrity of the halal supply chain. It provides a secure, immutable record, giving stakeholders and consumers transparent access to the halal certification status, origin, and journey of halal products. This integration of AI and blockchain fortifies the halal supply chain against contamination risks and non-compliance, ensuring the safety and purity of halal food items from the source to the consumer (Ahmed, 2022; Halal Food Council USA, 2024; Omar, 2023).

AI-Enhanced Animal Welfare in Halal Processing

AI-powered sensor technology in slaughterhouses plays a crucial role in the ethical treatment of animals, which is a core tenet of halal food safety. These sensors monitor animals for signs of distress or discomfort, allowing for immediate intervention to ensure humane treatment in accordance with halal standards. The use of AI in this context not only aligns with ethical mandates but also improves the quality of meat by reducing stress-induced complications, thus preserving the halal integrity of the produce (Ahmed, 2022).

Halal Traceability and Transparency

Blockchain technology fortifies halal food safety by offering an immutable ledger system that tracks the journey of halal products from their origin to the consumer. This heightened traceability ensures that every halal item is verifiable, reducing the potential for fraud and mislabeling. The decentralized nature of blockchain hampers unauthorized alterations to halal certificates, thereby upholding the authenticity and safety of halal food items. In parallel, AI-infused traceability and labeling solutions work to maintain rigorous safety and quality (Qian et al., 2020) and may provide comprehensive oversight in the halal food industry.

Internet of Things (IoT) for Real-Time Halal Supply Chain Monitoring

Internet of Things (IoT) devices are integral to real-time monitoring within the halal supply chain. These devices continuously measure and report on essential parameters like temperature and humidity, crucial for preserving the halal status of food during storage and transport. By ensuring environmental conditions adhere to halal guidelines, IoT technology mitigates the risk of non-compliance and allows for prompt corrective measures, safeguarding the safety and integrity of halal food products (Ahmed, 2023; Islamic Services America, 2024).

AI Algorithms for Halal Compliance Determination

In the intricate realm of halal food production, adherence to strict dietary laws is paramount. AI algorithms emerge as vigilant guardians in this process, offering sophisticated solutions to swiftly identify and address non-compliance. From analyzing vast ingredient databases to real-time surveillance of production lines, AI systems are transforming the landscape of halal certification—ensuring that consumed food not only meets religious standards but also upholds the highest ethical production quality. Figure 15.1 illustrates the multifaceted application of AI algorithms in safeguarding halal food production, showcasing how ML identifies non-compliance in ingredient labeling while AI systems monitor real-time production deviations. Additionally, advanced detection of non-halal ingredients is emphasized, along with AI's role in combating food fraud to protect halal preparation and marketing principles.

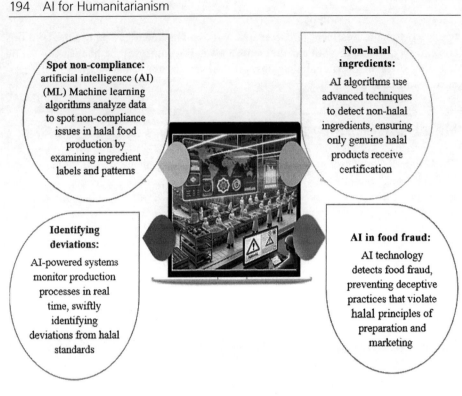

Spot non-compliance: artificial intelligence (AI) (ML) Machine learning algorithms analyze data to spot non-compliance issues in halal food production by examining ingredient labels and patterns

Non-halal ingredients: AI algorithms use advanced techniques to detect non-halal ingredients, ensuring only genuine halal products receive certification

Identifying deviations: AI-powered systems monitor production processes in real time, swiftly identifying deviations from halal standards

AI in food fraud: AI technology detects food fraud, preventing deceptive practices that violate halal principles of preparation and marketing

FIGURE 15.1   AI surveillance for halal product compliance.

Machine Learning (ML) for Non-Compliance Identification

ML algorithms are effective in detecting non-compliance in the manufacture of halal food, which is crucial for preserving the integrity of halal. In order to properly analyze ingredient labels and cross-reference them with huge halal databases, these algorithms are able to find trends and anomalies that may signal non-compliance. This is accomplished through the careful study of extensive datasets. This capability is crucial for flagging potential issues early in the production process, thereby maintaining the sanctity of halal certification and preventing the risk of non-compliance. These sophisticated algorithms are instrumental in the proactive monitoring of production processes, ensuring that halal standards are meticulously adhered to (Omar, 2023).

Real-Time Monitoring with AI-Powered Systems

AI-powered systems are indispensable for the real-time monitoring of halal food production processes. Their ability to facilitate the early detection of deviations from halal standards is paramount for implementing timely corrective actions. These systems enhance the oversight of production lines, offering instant analysis of product labels and ingredient lists. By identifying non-halal components quickly, they prevent the inadvertent contamination of halal products, thus playing a pivotal role in preserving the integrity and trust in halal food certification (Omar, 2023; Ahmed, 2022).

Detection of Non-Halal Ingredients and Contaminants

In the context of ensuring halal compliance in food production, the detection of non-halal ingredients and contaminants is of paramount importance. Specialized AI algorithms may be developed and deployed specifically for this purpose. These algorithms may be meticulously designed to analyze the composition of food products (Doherty et al., 2021). It may scrutinize every ingredient to identify any substances that are not compliant with halal dietary laws. Using advanced ML techniques, these algorithms can recognize patterns and anomalies in ingredient lists or contaminants that are present. This detection process is precise and efficient, allowing for thorough screening of food items to ensure they meet halal standards. This proactive approach to detecting non-halal ingredients and contaminants contributes to maintaining consumer trust and confidence in the halal food industry.

AI in Contamination Reduction

Vision AI, including VR and AR, is revolutionizing traditional food safety training techniques (Friedlander & Zoellner, 2020). By simulating real-world scenarios, these technologies provide immersive learning experiences for employees, covering essential practices such as handwashing, prevention of cross-contamination, and proper storage. This advancement not only fosters a robust halal food safety culture but also contributes to reducing the likelihood of product contamination, thereby earning consumer trust. Furthermore, these interactive training methods enable employees to engage more effectively with the material, leading to better retention and application of food safety practices in real-world scenarios. Additionally, Vision AI facilitates remote training sessions, allowing employees across different locations to receive consistent and standardized training, ensuring uniformity in food safety protocols across the organization. Through continuous reinforcement and practice in simulated environments, employees become more adept at identifying and addressing potential sources of contamination, thereby enhancing overall food safety standards within the halal food industry.

AI in Consistent Data Management

In response to the unique requirements of halal food safety, retailers may invest in new information technology and database management systems to collect, store, and share critical food safety information. Consistency in halal food safety practices across both physical and digital platforms is essential to meeting the personalized needs of halal consumers and participating effectively in multistate recall and outbreak response efforts. As described by Friedlander & Zoellner (2020), text AI services may play a vital role in achieving this omnichannel consistency by powering internal or industry-wide databases with advanced capabilities tailored specifically for halal food safety standards.

Personalized AI for Halal Food Safety

Customers are increasingly relying on voice assistant devices and chatbots to assist them with their grocery or food service shopping needs, as well as in their home kitchens for accessing information and setting reminders. Similarly, retailers can enhance their in-store food safety operations by harnessing interactive AI tools as personal food safety assistants (Friedlander & Zoellner, 2020). These innovative AI solutions can effectively engage with employees, suppliers, and consumers alike, providing real-time guidance and support in maintaining halal food safety standards.

AI in Proactive Halal Food Management

Analytical AI's predictive analytics play a crucial role in proactive halal food safety management. By analyzing data sets for patterns of environmental contamination and supply chain risks, these tools enable halal food businesses to design targeted environmental monitoring programs and make informed decisions to mitigate the risk of foodborne outbreaks. Furthermore, predictive analytics support strategic procurement by assessing supplier risks and forecasting potential safety issues with certain commodities (Horn & Friedrich, 2019; Vangay et al., 2014; Zoellner et al., 2019).

AI in Operational Efficiency

Functional AI, facilitated by robotics and IoT devices, has the potential to translate data analytics into actionable tasks, thereby significantly enhancing operational efficiency in halal food production. Robots are revolutionizing various processes in food processing, handling, palletizing, packing, and serving, offering increased speed, precision, and consistency compared to manual labor (Iqbal et al., 2017). For instance, robotic arms can automate repetitive tasks such as sorting, cutting, and packaging, reducing production time and minimizing the risk of contamination. Furthermore, IoT devices play a crucial role in ensuring optimal conditions during transportation, monitoring factors like temperature and humidity in real time to prevent spoilage and maintain product quality (Gillespie et al., 2023). By leveraging these technologies, halal food producers can streamline their operations, improve resource utilization, and enhance traceability throughout the supply chain. Ultimately, this integration of functional AI in halal food production not only increases efficiency but also upholds the integrity and safety standards of halal products, meeting the expectations of consumers and regulatory bodies alike.

AI in Food Hygiene

AI and ML are increasingly vital in addressing food safety and security concerns, revolutionizing various aspects of the food industry. With applications ranging from modeling to quality control and data analysis, AI plays a crucial role in maintaining hygiene standards and ensuring the safety of food products. For instance, AI-driven systems like self-optimizing clean in place contribute significantly to maintaining cleanliness in food processing facilities (Addanki et al., 2022). Furthermore, AI technologies are pivotal in optimizing farming practices to increase yields and address challenges posed by factors such as population growth, climate change, and pollution (How et al., 2020; Kleineidam, 2020). Techniques like Bayesian networks enable efficient decision-making in pest control management and pesticide usage, ultimately enhancing agricultural productivity and food quality (Addanki et al., 2022; How et al., 2020). By leveraging AI tools, the food industry not only ensures the quality and safety of its products but also improves manufacturing, packaging, and cleaning processes, thus contributing to overall food hygiene. AI and ML are increasingly vital in addressing food safety and security concerns, revolutionizing various aspects of the food industry.

LEVERAGING AI FOR HUMANITARIAN BENEFITS

AI enables real-time tracking of the entire supply chain, recording each step from ingredient sourcing to production and distribution (Maheshwari et al., 2023; El Jaouhari & Hamidi, 2024). By providing transparency, the halal food industry can ensure that ingredients are sourced ethically and responsibly, supporting fair trade practices and local communities. Additionally, AI algorithms may verify the authenticity of halal certifications, ensuring that ingredients come from ethical sources and promoting trust among consumers. Moreover, AI analyzes product labels and ingredient lists to detect discrepancies or mislabeling, thereby reducing the risk of fraud. By identifying non-halal components, AI helps ensure that consumers receive genuinely halal products. Furthermore, AI conducts real-time audits of suppliers, manufacturers, and distributors, promptly identifying non-compliant practices and enabling corrective actions to be taken (Koshiyama et al., 2021). This proactive approach not only protects consumers but also upholds ethical standards in halal sourcing.

Humanitarian Implications of AI for Promoting Responsible Consumption

Product safety is paramount as it directly impacts consumer health (Rahman & Razimi, 2023). AI technologies hold the potential to foster responsible consumption by enhancing safety measures. Additionally, AI aids in fostering consumer trust and acceptance by enabling independent verification of product authenticity (Spencer, 2024). Specific humanitarian implications of AI in promoting responsible consumption of halal food products may include:

1. Ensuring compliance with halal standards and regulations.
2. Building consumer trust and acceptance.
3. Providing increased transparency and traceability in the halal food supply chain.
4. Reducing the risk of food fraud and contamination.
5. Improving animal welfare through AI-powered sensors and monitoring systems.

Humanitarian implications of AI in halal food security

The advent of new AI and computer vision systems holds promise for leveraging extensive data resources for active training, leading to the development of smart machines capable of real-time operations and predictive modeling (Kakani et al., 2020). Within the halal food industry, AI serves as a cornerstone in bolstering the efficiency and reliability of production and supply chains, directly contributing to food security. Through optimized inventory management processes and precise demand forecasting, AI technologies ensure the resilience of halal food supply chains, adapting to evolving consumer preferences. Furthermore, with their real-time monitoring capabilities, AI systems uphold the integrity of halal food products, proactively mitigating the risks of contamination and spoilage. This technological intervention is particularly vital in regions where halal food holds cultural and dietary significance, as it aids in preventing food shortages and guarantees a steady supply of halal food to meet the needs of burgeoning populations. Through its multifaceted applications, AI emerges as a potent instrument for safeguarding food security within the halal food industry.

Humanitarian implications of AI on sustainable practices and environmental impact

The integration of AI and ML into sustainable agricultural practices heralds a transformative era in promoting environmental stewardship and humanitarian outcomes. These cutting-edge technologies are leading the advancement of nano-enabled agriculture, showing significant potential to enhance crop efficiency and sustainability. Already, several innovative methods have garnered regulatory endorsement, showcasing the tangible benefits of AI-driven agricultural practices (Zhang et al., 2021). This evolution underscores the pivotal role of AI in fostering sustainable halal food production systems that not only adhere to halal compliance but also contribute to reducing environmental footprints and supporting global food security efforts. Within the realm of halal food production, AI's predictive analytics and efficiency improvements offer promising avenues for fostering more sustainable practices and reducing the environmental footprint of food production. By optimizing processes and resource utilization, AI technologies can minimize waste and promote responsible stewardship of natural resources. This approach ensures that production methods not only comply with religious laws but also uphold principles of environmental sustainability, aligning with the global emphasis on eco-conscious practices.

Data Integrity and Privacy Concerns in AI Applications

The quality of the input data may significantly impact the efficacy of AI and ML algorithms in the halal industry. Data that is unreliable, partial, or erroneous may lead to erroneous decision-making procedures and negative consequences. When AI deploys public health resources and conducts inspections of food establishments using big data generated by consumers, a potential issue arises. This raises concerns about the potential for individual consumer biases to spread throughout the halal food industry. This bias may impact the enforcement of food safety regulations and consumer purchasing behaviors. Altenburger and Ho (2019) revealed that predictive analytics prompted by consumer complaints disproportionately targeted Asian-owned establishments. Conversely, when compared to prior inspection history, crowd-sourced information for a particular establishment had less predictive power, and these assessments did not significantly improve the ability to predict food safety violations when inspection records and restaurant data were already available (Altenburger & Ho 2019). Hence, to mitigate bias and improve decision-making processes, ongoing investments in digital data accessibility, connectivity, and infrastructure are imperative for ensuring data quality in the halal industry.

GLOBAL PERSPECTIVES AND CASE EXAMPLES OF AI APPLICATIONS

AI technologies, along with big data and blockchain, are revolutionizing the food safety domain, particularly in ensuring halal compliance. These advanced technologies play a crucial role in enhancing transparency, traceability, and trust in the halal supply chain. Here are some key insights:

AI and Machine Learning (ML): Halal Certification

The Department of Islamic Development Malaysia (JAKIM) is developing an AI system to simplify the approval process for halal certificate applications (The Star, 2024). AI and ML algorithms are being utilized to streamline the certification process by analyzing vast amounts of data, identifying non-compliance issues, and flagging potential (Winter et al., 2021; Maleki et al., 2020). These technologies may assist in conducting audits, analyzing ingredients, monitoring production processes, and detecting cross-contamination risks, ensuring greater accuracy, efficiency, and consistency in certifying products and services.

Blockchain Technology: Ensuring Integrity in the Halal Industry

Cutting-edge blockchain technology is employed to ensure halal compliance by providing a decentralized and secure halal certification system. For instance, the HalalChain (Qitmeer Network) offers a platform for manufacturers, processors, and retailers to verify the halal authenticity of their products. Blockchain allows for the secure recording of halal certification data, such as ingredient sources, production processes, and logistics information, instilling confidence in consumers about the authenticity of halal products. In Indonesia, the first halal blockchain-based slaughterhouse by Sreeya is a pioneer in chicken slaughterhouses with halal certification from Majelis Ulama Indonesia (Jati, 2020). This provides added value by ensuring safety and comfort in consuming fresh chicken products for consumers. In the UK, blockchain technology is being applied to ensure traceability in the halal meat industry, whereas iov42 is developing a data-sharing platform that provides secure records of compliance with halal standards, addressing concerns about fraudulent products that breach halal standards. Notably, fraudulent activities in this industry range from sole traders to international organized crime groups. In 2020, a Malaysian "meat cartel" scandal exposed the bribery of customs officials, the distribution of meat from uncertified slaughterhouses, and the mislabeling of kangaroo and horse flesh as halal beef (Macaulay, 2023).

Innovative AI in Halal Food Safety and Digital Solutions

AI is setting new benchmarks in enhancing halal food safety, offering innovative solutions that ensure the integrity and purity of halal products. From farm to fork, AI technologies may deploy to monitor, analyze, and optimize various aspects of halal food production, addressing the unique challenges of maintaining halal standards while meeting global demand. Table 15.2 outlines the integration of AI technologies in enhancing halal food safety, detailing various entities and their specific AI

TABLE 15.2 Innovative AI applications in halal food safety

TECHNOLOGY	ENTITY	APPLICATIONS IN HALAL FOOD	INVESTORS
Robotics, drones	Various startups	Monitoring halal crop health, ensuring produce purity through precise pesticide application	Tech and agricultural investment firms
Sensors	Sensor-based startups	Quality control in halal food production, ensuring environmental conditions meet halal standards	Investors focusing on environmental sustainability and tech
Precision agriculture and predictive analysis	Companies specializing in data analytics	Optimizing crop yields for halal produce, predictive analysis for halal food supply planning	Diverse groups from traditional agriculture to modern tech venture capitalists
Plant data analysis	Firms using ML	Genetic analysis of halal crops to ensure nutritional standards, analysis of growth conditions	Tech investors interested in agriculture and sustainability
Smart irrigation	Innovators in irrigation systems	Precision irrigation to maintain water supply purity in halal food production, reducing water wastage	Investors focused on sustainability, water conservation, and agricultural innovation

applications aimed at ensuring the halal integrity of food products. It illustrates the collaborative efforts between startups, tech companies, and investors to leverage AI for optimizing halal food production, from ensuring crop health to maintaining precise environmental conditions, thereby upholding halal certification and production standards.

Several innovative digital solutions are emerging to address various aspects of halal certification and management:

- *Halal Assurance System (HAS) Digitization:* The digitized version of HAS and traceability management system streamlines halal integrity processes, aiding companies in applying, renewing, and maintaining halal certification.
- *Halal Audit Digital Integrated System (HADIS™):* A mobile app used by halal certification bodies for conducting internal and external audits efficiently, facilitating evidence collection, reporting, and communication with auditees.
- *Certification Bodies Master System (CBMS™):* A user-friendly system for halal certification bodies to manage halal applications, track progress, and ensure data security through high-end cloud infrastructure.

- *Halal Centre Master System (HCMS™):* A user-friendly platform for halal centers to manage halal certification processes, client consultations, training services, and online training certificate generation.
- *Halal Digital Chain (HADIC™):* A blockchain-powered ecosystem aimed at creating an integrated and secure digital halal ecosystem, ensuring traceability, and eliminating fraud across the supply chain.
- *Verify Halal™:* A global halal search engine empowering authorities, industry players, retailers, and consumers to verify halal accreditation instantly, facilitating informed decision-making when purchasing halal products.
- *Global Halal Data Pool (GHDP™):* Powered by the GS1 standard, GHDP connects halal suppliers with buyers, retailers, and distributors globally, enhancing product traceability and market access for accredited halal producers.

CONCLUSION

In this chapter, we have embarked on a comprehensive exploration of the transformative role of AI in enhancing halal food safety, emphasizing its significant implications not only within the Muslim community but also for global food security, ethical consumerism, and sustainable practices. The integration of AI and blockchain technology has ushered in a new era of innovation in the halal food industry, providing advanced solutions for ensuring the integrity of halal certification, enhancing traceability and transparency, and fostering consumer trust and ethical sourcing. Notably, the adoption of technologies such as ML, IoT devices, and blockchain has facilitated the real-time monitoring of production processes, the detection of non-compliance issues, and the establishment of a tamper-proof ledger system that empowers consumers with valuable insights into the halal status and journey of certified products.

Moreover, this chapter has highlighted the humanitarian and societal benefits of AI integration in halal food safety, including the promotion of public health and safety, the reduction of food fraud and mislabeling, and the support of ethical considerations in global trade. These advancements underscore the potential of AI to contribute to a more transparent, efficient, and sustainable global food system, addressing the diverse needs of consumers and upholding the stringent guidelines that define halal food production. As we conclude, the successful incorporation of AI technologies in halal food safety practices promises not only operational enhancements but also significant contributions to humanitarian and societal welfare. These AI-driven innovations stand at the forefront of fostering a more inclusive, ethical, and environmentally conscious food industry. Future research and development in this field are essential for further optimizing halal food safety protocols and harnessing the full potential of AI to meet the evolving demands of consumers worldwide, ensuring that halal food continues to be a symbol of quality, safety, and ethical production in the global market.

ACKNOWLEDGMENTS

My profound gratitude is extended to the Institute of Halal Management and the Islamic Business School at Universiti Utara Malaysia, whose support has been instrumental in the fruition of this work. I am deeply appreciative of their commitment to advancing academic research and fostering our understanding of the intricate interplay between AI, halal food safety, and sustainability practices within a humanitarian framework.

REFERENCES

Addanki, M., Patra, P., & Kandra, P. (2022). Recent advances and applications of artificial intelligence and related technologies in the food industry. *Applied Food Research, 2*(2), 100126.

Ahmed, H. M. (2022, December 28). How can AI help the global halal industry? Retrieved January 2, 2024, from https://www.halaltimes.com/how-can-ai-help-the-global-halal-industry/

Ahmed, H. M. (2023, February 4). How to improve halal food safety by using AI? – The halal times. *The Halal Times.* Retrieved February 29, 2024, from https://www.halaltimes.com/how-to-improve-halal-food-safety-by-using-ai/

Ali, M. H., & Suleiman, N. (2018). Eleven shades of food integrity: A halal supply chain perspective. *Trends in Food Science & Technology, 71,* 216–224.

Altenburger, K. M., & Ho, D. E. (2019). When algorithms import private bias into public enforcement: The promise and limitations of statistical debiasing solutions. *Journal of Institutional and Theoretical Economics, 175*(1), 98–122.

Bux, C., Varese, E., Amicarelli, V., & Lombardi, M. (2022). Halal food sustainability between certification and blockchain: A review. *Sustainability, 14*(4), 2152.

Demirci, M. N., Soon, J. M., & Wallace, C. A. (2016). Positioning food safety in halal assurance. *Food Control, 70,* 257–270.

Doherty, A., Wall, A., Khaldi, N., & Kussmann, M. (2021). Artificial intelligence in functional food ingredient discovery and characterisation: A focus on bioactive plant and food peptides. *Frontiers in Genetics, 12,* 768979.

El Jaouhari, A., & Hamidi, L. S. (2024). Assessing the influence of artificial intelligence on agri-food supply chain performance: The mediating effect of distribution network efficiency. *Technological Forecasting and Social Change, 200,* 123149.

Farhan, F., & Sutikno, B. (2022). The acceptance of halal food products among non-muslim consumers in Indonesia. *Journal of International Food & Agribusiness Marketing, 36*(2), 125–146.

Friedlander, A., & Zoellner, C. (2020). Artificial intelligence opportunities to improve food safety at retail. *Food Protection Trends, 40*(4), 272–278.

Gillespie, J., da Costa, T. P., Cama-Moncunill, X., Cadden, T., Condell, J., Cowderoy, T.,.... & Ramanathan, R. (2023). Real-time anomaly detection in cold chain transportation using IoT technology. *Sustainability, 15*(3), 2255.

Halal Certification Services. (2023, May 29). Emerging technologies and their impact on halal certification. Retrieved December 15, 2023, from https://www.linkedin.com/pulse/emerging-technologies-impact-halal-certification

Halal Food Council USA. (2024, January 17). The growing role of technology in halal food councils in 2024. Retrieved February 5, 2024, from https://halalfoodcouncilusa.com/the-growing-role-of-technology-in-halal-food-councils-in-2024/

Horn, A. L., & Friedrich, H. (2019). Locating the source of large-scale outbreaks of foodborne disease. *Journal of the Royal Society Interface, 16*(151), 20180624.

How, M. L., Chan, Y. J., & Cheah, S. M. (2020). Predictive insights for improving the resilience of global food security using artificial intelligence. *Sustainability, 12*(15), 6272.

Industry Research Co. (Ed.). (2023, August 2). Exploring the halal food market: A global perspective till 2030. Retrieved February 1, 2024, from https://www.linkedin.com/pulse/exploring-halal-food-market-global-perspective-till/

Iqbal, J., Khan, Z. H., & Khalid, A. (2017). Prospects of robotics in food industry. *Food Science and Technology, 37*, 159–165.

Islamic Services America. (2024, January 18). From bytes to bites: The digital transformation of halal food verification. Islamic Services of America. Retrieved February 2, 2024, from https://www.isahalal.com/news-events/blog/bytes-bites-digital-transformation-halal-food-verification

Jati, S. (2020). Halal blockchain testimonial. Retrieved February 5, 2024, from https://www.sreeyasewu.com/en/technology/halal-blockchain

Kakani, V., Nguyen, V. H., Kumar, B. P., Kim, H., & Pasupuleti, V. R. (2020). A critical review on computer vision and artificial intelligence in food industry. *Journal of Agriculture and Food Research, 2*, 100033.

Kleineidam, J. (2020). Fields of action for designing measures to avoid food losses in logistics networks. *Sustainability, 12*(15), 6093.

Koshiyama, A., Kazim, E., Treleaven, P., Rai, P., Szpruch, L., Pavey, G.,... & Lomas, E. (2021). Towards algorithm auditing: A survey on managing legal, ethical and technological risks of AI, ML and associated algorithms. *Royal Society Open Science, 11*, 1–33. https://royalsocietypublishing.org/doi/pdf/10.1098/rsos.230859

Macaulay, T. (2023, June 5). Finally, a useful blockchain application: Tracing halal meat. Retrieved February 12, 2024, from https://thenextweb.com/news/blockchain-tracing-halal-meat-iov42-startup-gets-wales-government-funding

Maheshwari, P., Kamble, S., Belhadi, A., Venkatesh, M., & Abedin, M. Z. (2023). Digital twin-driven real-time planning, monitoring, and controlling in food supply chains. *Technological Forecasting and Social Change, 195*, 122799.

Maleki, F., Muthukrishnan, N., Ovens, K., Reinhold, C., & Forghani, R. (2020). Machine learning algorithm validation: From essentials to advanced applications and implications for regulatory certification and deployment. *Neuroimaging Clinics, 30*(4), 433–445.

Nusran, M., Nasution, E. N., Prayitno, M. A., & Sudarmanto, E. (2023). Halal certification in the digital age: Leveraging online platforms for enhanced transparency and accessibility. *Jurnal Ekonomi, Akuntansi Dan Manajemen Indonesia, 2*(1), 105–115.

Omar. (2023, May 12). Halal assurance in food supply chains: Strengthening verification methods through audits and laboratory analysis. Retrieved January 5, 2024, from https://www.linkedin.com/pulse/halal-assurance-food-supply-chains-strengthening-methods-farhad-omar

Putri, N. T., Kharisman, A., Arief, I., Talib, H. H. A., Jamaludin, K. R., & Ismail, E. A. (2022). Designing food safety management and halal assurance systems in mozzarella cheese production for small-medium food Industry. *Indonesian Journal of Halal Research, 4*(2), 65–84.

Qian, J., Ruiz-Garcia, L., Fan, B., Villalba, J. I. R., McCarthy, U., Zhang, B.,... & Wu, W. (2020). Food traceability system from governmental, corporate, and consumer perspectives in the European Union and China: A comparative review. *Trends in Food Science & Technology, 99*, 402–412.

Rahman, M. M., & Razimi, M. S. A. (2023). Halal biotechnology product: Halal supply chain compliance and integrity risk. In Nina Naquiah Ahmad Nizar, Siti Aimi Sarah Zainal Abidin & Aishah Bujang (eds.), *Innovation of Food Products in Halal Supply Chain Worldwide* (pp. 195–204). Cambridge, MA: Academic Press.

Rahman, M. M., Razimi, M. S. A., Khan, I., & Chowdhury, Z. Z. (2023). Corporate social responsibility in the halal food industry: Application of supply chain perspective. *International Journal of Islamic Business, 8*(2), 34–43.

Spencer. (2024, January 17). Humanitarian AId?: Considerations for the future of AI-use in humanitarian action – World. Retrieved February 1, 2024, from https://reliefweb.int/report/world/humanitarian-aid-considerations-future-ai-use-humanitarian-action

The Star. (Ed.). (2024, January 18). Jakim developing AI system to simplify halal certification approval. Retrieved February 12, 2024, from https://www.thestar.com.my/tech/tech-news/2024/01/18/jakim-developing-ai-system-to-simplify-halal-certification-approval

Vangay, P., Steingrimsson, J., Wiedmann, M., & Stasiewicz, M. J. (2014). Classification of Listeria monocytogenes persistence in retail delicatessen environments using expert elicitation and machine learning. *Risk Analysis*, *34*(10), 1830–1845.

Winter, P. M., Eder, S., Weissenböck, J., Schwald, C., Doms, T., Vogt, T.,.... & Nessler, B. (2021). Trusted artificial intelligence: Towards certification of machine learning applications. *Machine Learning. arXiv preprint arXiv:2103.16910.*

Zhang, P., Guo, Z., Ullah, S., Melagraki, G., Afantitis, A., & Lynch, I. (2021). Nanotechnology and artificial intelligence to enable sustainable and precision agriculture. *Nature Plants*, *7*(7), 864–876.

Zoellner, C., Jennings, R., Wiedmann, M., & Ivanek, R. (2019). EnABLe: An agent-based model to understand Listeria dynamics in food processing facilities. *Scientific Reports*, *9*(1), 495.

Future Directions and Responsible AI for Social Impact

16

Adeyemi Abel Ajibesin, Eriona Çela, Narasimha Rao Vajjhala, and Philip Eappen

INTRODUCTION

Artificial intelligence (AI) has emerged as a transformative technology across various domains, including humanitarian efforts (Beduschi, 2022; Efe, 2022). As AI technologies continue to evolve, their potential to address complex humanitarian challenges becomes increasingly significant. However, the deployment of AI in these contexts necessitates a careful consideration of ethical, social, and operational factors. As the world continues to deal with increasingly complex humanitarian challenges, the potential of AI to revolutionize humanitarian efforts is becoming more evident (Pizzi et al., 2020; Rodríguez-Espíndola et al., 2020; Van den Homberg et al., 2020). AI technologies, including machine learning (ML), deep learning (DL), and natural language processing (NLP), have shown remarkable promise in enhancing the efficiency and effectiveness of disaster response, education, healthcare, and legal systems (Abdul et al., 2024; Jung et al., 2020). However, the integration of AI into humanitarian contexts must be approached with a strong emphasis on ethical considerations, transparency, and accountability to ensure that its deployment benefits those most in need without exacerbating existing inequalities. This chapter summarizes the key findings covered in the previous chapters in this book and explores future research directions and action points

DOI: 10.1201/9781003479109-16

for leveraging AI responsibly for social impact, focusing on transparency, accountability, and collaboration among stakeholders.

The preceding chapters of this book have examined a wide array of applications of AI in humanitarian work, showcasing its transformative potential across various domains. Chapter 1 was the introductory chapter providing the foundation for this book and explaining the organization of the various chapters in this book. In Chapter 2, the focus shifted to data collection and analysis, emphasizing how AI can enhance the efficiency and effectiveness of humanitarian actions by leveraging advanced data analytics. Chapter 3 provided field perspectives on the integration of AI in emergency preparedness and response, highlighting innovative strategies for utilizing AI in real-world humanitarian crises. Chapters 4 and 5 explored AI's role in alleviating poverty, discussing its impact during the Fourth Industrial Revolution and its contribution to sustainable development. These chapters illustrate AI's capacity to address economic disparities and promote inclusive growth. Chapter 6 examined the intersection of AI and informal m-health use, emphasizing how AI can improve healthcare access in humanitarian contexts, while Chapter 7 discussed the social-legal impact and innovations in digital hospitals and m-health. Chapters 8 through 11 explored specific healthcare applications of AI, from disease prediction to the diagnosis of cardiovascular diseases and Alzheimer's. These chapters underscore AI's potential to revolutionize healthcare delivery, particularly in underserved areas. Chapter 9 introduced a fair resource-sharing AI algorithm for humanitarian camps, demonstrating how AI can optimize resource allocation in critical situations. Chapters 12 and 13 tackled the ethical dimensions of AI in humanitarian contexts, discussing the challenges of ensuring transparency, safety, and ethical considerations, particularly in conflict zones like the Palestine-Israel conflict. These chapters highlighted the importance of addressing ethical challenges to harness AI's full potential responsibly. Chapter 14 explored the role of public-private partnerships in leveraging AI for social change, emphasizing the synergies that can be achieved by combining resources and expertise from both sectors. Finally, Chapter 15 discussed the application of AI in ensuring halal food safety, presenting new horizons for humanitarian action. Together, these chapters illustrate AI's capacity to address some of the most pressing humanitarian issues of our time, from predicting natural disasters and optimizing resource allocation to enhancing education and healthcare delivery. However, alongside these advancements, significant ethical challenges must be addressed to harness AI's full potential responsibly. This chapter will provide a set of future research directions and action points for policymakers to reflect on, based on the findings of the chapters in this book.

BACKGROUND

AI is a transformative technology that is having an impact in several domains, such as healthcare, finance, education, law, and humanitarian efforts (Morrow et al., 2023; Pizzi et al., 2020; Wamba et al., 2021). AI involves the application of several computational technologies that mimic the human brain in problem-solving and task performance

(Makudza et al., 2024). The advancements in AI and its enabling technologies have seen key breakthroughs in the last 5 years. AI technologies could learn and perform cognitive tasks, including speech recognition and visual analysis (Deng, 2018; Kumar et al., 2024; Sarker, 2022). AI is an experience-driven technology, and the decision-making is based on the machine's ability to recognize patterns and learning processes (Makudza et al., 2024). The rapid pace of development in AI means that while several areas are newly explored, there are still areas where the researchers have not fully tapped the possibilities of leveraging AI and associated technologies. For example, there is still room for examining the potential of AI in humanitarian work (Efe, 2022; Pizzi et al., 2020; Rodríguez-Espíndola et al., 2020). The availability of large amounts of data is an asset and a challenge for humanitarian organizations.

ML technologies are considered as a subset of AI and can enable machines to learn independently based on available data patterns (Garg et al., 2022; Kumar et al., 2024). ML algorithms also offer several benefits for humanitarian applications. AI relies on ML to enhance its functions by enhancing performance through learning from experience. ML algorithms can detect patterns and connections within datasets that may not be obvious to humans (Schmidt-Erfurth et al., 2018). DL is a subset of ML in which the system is trained to identify patterns in text, pictures, and sounds (Singh, 2024). NLP is another field of AI that enables machines to comprehend language facilitating more natural interactions between systems and users (Khurana et al., 2023). AI is a game changing technology that has the capacity to improve productivity, precision, and scalability across industries (Wamba et al., 2021). For example, AI can be utilized to create models that notify international aid agencies of potential disease outbreaks so that these organizations can tailor recovery and relief plans (Malik et al., 2021). The recent COVID-19 outbreak underscored the importance of identifying outbreaks, which could potentially save countless lives and enable governments to implement preventive measures. AI algorithms could also find application in industries, such as finance for detecting money laundering and other forms of activities (Khan et al., 2024). AI programs might also be beneficial in the field of education providing tailored learning experiences and aiding educators in pinpointing students requirements (Luan & Tsai, 2021).

Humanitarian efforts have faced increased challenges due to a range of factors such as disasters, pandemics, climate change, and conflicts. The fundamental values of humanitarian work include humanity, neutrality, impartiality, and independence serving as the foundation for humanitarian initiatives (Slim, 1997). Natural calamities, like earthquakes, floods, and hurricanes lead to destruction and force communities to relocate. Additionally, armed conflicts contribute to community displacement and significant loss of life creating scenarios with risks for efforts. Global pandemics such as the COVID-19 crisis underscore the necessity of coordinated responses to mitigate public health impacts and economic repercussions. Conventional methods of aiding are frequently hindered by issues related to resource distribution and decision-making processes (Hansen et al., 2019). Allocating resources can be quite intricate since it involves factors such as prioritizing resources and ensuring the delivery of assistance in an efficient way, which usually depends on getting precise and timely information (Yinusa & Faezipour, 2023). Therefore, it is important to leverage technologies, like AI to offer creative solutions, for tackling intricate problems (Beduschi, 2022; Van den Homberg et al., 2020).

CONVERGENCE OF AI AND HUMANITARIANISM

The convergence of AI and humanitarianism represents a significant leap forward in addressing complex global challenges. AI's ability to process vast amounts of data, recognize patterns, and make predictions offers unprecedented opportunities for enhancing humanitarian efforts (Beduschi, 2022). This convergence can transform disaster response, improve education systems, and streamline legal processes, thereby creating a more efficient and effective framework for humanitarian work. One of the most promising areas where AI and humanitarianism intersect is in disaster response and management (Pizzi et al., 2020). Traditional methods of disaster preparedness and response often rely on human expertise and historical data, which can be slow and inefficient. AI, on the other hand, can analyze real-time data from various sources, such as satellite imagery, social media feeds, and seismic sensors, to predict and respond to disasters more effectively. For instance, ML algorithms can examine weather patterns and seismic activity to provide early warnings for natural disasters such as hurricanes and earthquakes (Goswami et al., 2018). This predictive capability allows humanitarian organizations to mobilize resources and coordinate evacuations more efficiently, potentially saving countless lives. Moreover, AI can optimize resource distribution during disasters (Sun et al., 2020). ML models can analyze data on affected populations, infrastructure damage, and available resources to recommend the most efficient allocation of aid (Dhakal & Zhang, 2023). This ensures that resources are delivered to where they are most needed, reducing waste and improving the overall effectiveness of humanitarian responses.

Being ready for disasters is crucial for responding to emergencies. AI can bring benefits to this field since current conventional approaches to disaster readiness and reaction depend on information and human knowledge (Fan et al., 2021). ML algorithms have the capability to examine sets of weather data and seismic behavior to identify early warnings of calamities. This information is crucial for taking steps, such as organizing evacuations and mobilizing resources effectively (Dimililer et al., 2021; Jiao & Alavi, 2020). AI systems can also assist in distributing resources to areas and averting any deficits during emergency situations (Sun et al., 2020). International aid groups are utilizing AI technology to examine climate information and forecast food security threats. This enables them to position food provisions, in regions to natural calamities, like droughts and floods (How et al., 2020).

There are several examples of the successful use of AI technologies for offering humanitarian assistance. One such example is the case of the AI-supported disaster mapping tool that helped humanitarian agencies to provide emergency assistance in Mozambique in 2019 (Beduschi, 2022). Another example is that of Project Jetson under which the United Nations High Commissioner for Refugees (UNHCR) uses predictive analytics to forecast the forced displacement of people (Beduschi, 2022). The World Food Program (WFP) has developed an AI model using predictive analytics to forecast food insecurity in conflict zones (Beduschi, 2022). AI technologies can play a role in supporting work, particularly in the field of logistics. For example, ML algorithms can be utilized to develop solutions that aid organizations, in enhancing the efficiency of their aid delivery logistics and managing their supply chains effectively (Akbari & Do, 2021). AI programs are useful for improving travel routes, anticipating issues, in the supply chain and aiding in inventory management (Abaku et al., 2024). In times of calamity, relief agencies are frequently overwhelmed, with inquiries from those displaced and their worried loved ones. During instances, AI-driven chatbots and virtual assistants can provide responses to the queries and collect details about specific requirements in the affected areas (Peña-Cáceres et al., 2024).

AI's impact on education is another critical area where it converges with humanitarian efforts (Slimi & Carballido, 2023). Educational systems in disaster-prone or conflict-affected regions often struggle with limited resources and infrastructure (Peters, 2021). AI can help bridge this gap by providing scalable and adaptable educational solutions. Recent educational transformations have highlighted the necessity for new curricula, reshaping traditional teaching methods and tools by incorporating technological advancements (Burbules et al., 2020). Digital platforms, social networks, and computers have become integral to modern education, offering fresh perspectives and enhancing the educational experience. The adoption of these new curricula and tools has significantly improved student engagement and the quality of education. Moreover, the recent utilization of AI in education has introduced new skills for teachers and students, revolutionizing various industries and providing solutions to complex societal problems. In this context, the relationship between AI and humanitarianism is particularly significant, as these tools are applied by and for humans in fields that directly impact human lives.

The utilization of AI tools has significantly enhanced the efficiency of educational institutions, enabling the rapid collection and analysis of data at a reduced cost. These tools facilitate insights across various disciplines addressing behavior and violence, including historical events, mathematical assignments, and social sciences. Automating tasks through AI contributes to this increased efficiency by delivering quicker results. AI tools and techniques are invaluable for researchers and scientists in enhancing their efforts to improve quality of life. In the areas of education and scientific research, governments are significantly investing to enhance curricula and teaching processes. Notably, the Global Learning XPrize has allocated $15 million to incentivize the development of software that empowers students to take control of their own education (Huntington et al., 2023). The integration of AI tools into educational curricula, particularly in online tutoring and teacher training, is enhancing various educational aspects. Given the rapid advancements in education, AI adoption was projected to grow at a compound annual rate of 32% from the present until 2024, reaching approximately $6 billion by 2022, a growth trajectory that has already surpassed expectations (Agarwal et al., 2024).

FUTURE RESEARCH DIRECTIONS

The enhancement of decision support systems (DSS) for humanitarian organizations is a critical area for future research, aiming to significantly improve the effectiveness and efficiency of response strategies during crises (Gupta et al., 2022). There is a need for integrating AI algorithms with real-time data streams, advanced analytics, and predictive modeling techniques, as these systems can provide decision-makers with actionable insights and recommendations, ultimately leading to more informed and timely decisions (Agbehadji et al., 2020). Humanitarian organizations face numerous challenges in making quick and effective decisions during crises, including data over-load, data quality, issues with real-time analysis, and lack of predictive capabilities. The large volume of data from various sources, such as social media, satellite imagery, and ground reports, can overwhelm decision-makers, apart from issues in ensuring the accuracy, relevance, and timeliness of data (Joseph et al., 2018). Also, traditional DSS often struggles to analyze data in real-time, which is essential for timely decision-making during emergencies. Apart from these issues, many existing systems lack advanced predictive capabilities, which are necessary for anticipating future scenarios and preparing appropriate responses. Hence, future research must focus on issues related to real-time data integration by utilizing diverse data sources, including satellite imagery, sensor networks, social media feeds, weather reports, and on-the-ground assessments. There is also a need to develop techniques for fusing data from these sources into a unified framework that allows for comprehensive situational awareness. Researchers must also focus on implementing mechanisms for continuous data quality assessment and improvement to ensure that decision-makers are working with accurate and reliable information.

As AI becomes increasingly integrated into humanitarian operations, ensuring that AI systems are transparent, accountable, and trustworthy is quite important (Afroogh et al., 2023). Explainable AI (XAI) techniques address these needs by making AI algorithms and their decision-making processes understandable to human users (Arrieta et al., 2020). XAI in humanitarian context focuses on developing interpretable AI models that enhance transparency, accountability, and trust in AI-driven decision-making processes within humanitarian contexts (Andres et al., 2020). This is a key future research direction because AI systems, particularly those based on DL and other complex algorithms, often operate as black boxes meaning their internal workings are not easily interpretable by humans. This lack of transparency can lead to several challenges, including trust issues, accountability, bias and fairness, and regulatory compliance (Akinrinola et al., 2024). The trust issues facing stakeholders, including humanitarian workers and affected communities, may result in hesitancy to rely on AI systems if they do not understand how decisions are made. There are also issues about accountability as without clear explanations, it is difficult to hold AI systems accountable for their decisions, particularly if those decisions have negative consequences. Bias and fairness also need to be investigated because unexplainable AI systems may perpetuate biases present in the training data, leading to unfair outcomes without stakeholders understanding why these biases occur (Mehrabi et al., 2021). Also, many policymakers and international legal experts are demanding regulations that require that AI decisions be explainable, particularly in sensitive areas such as healthcare, humanitarian efforts, finance, and law. Future researchers need to focus on developing and implementing the key components to enhance explainability in AI systems used in humanitarian operations, including creating interpretable models, using post hoc explainability techniques, causal explanations, and interactive explanation systems.

Future research work could focus on developing AI models that are inherently interpretable, such as decision trees, linear models, and rule-based systems, which are easier for humans to understand, while at the same time balancing the complexity and performance of AI models with their interpretability, ensuring that high-performing models do not compromise transparency (Mahbooba et al., 2021). Future research work could also focus on implementing methods that identify and rank the importance of different features (inputs) in making predictions. Techniques such as SHAP (SHapley Additive exPlanations) and LIME (Local Interpretable Model-agnostic Explanations) can be used to explain individual predictions (Assegie, 2023). Also, developing visualization tools that help users understand the decision-making process of AI models by including visual representations of decision boundaries, feature contributions, and model behaviors could be quite useful. Researchers should also focus on developing causal models that explain not just correlations but causations, as well as understanding the cause-and-effect relationships in data, leading to more meaningful explanations. The emphasis on XAI techniques represents a critical area for future research in the integration of AI into humanitarian operations because by developing interpretable models, post hoc explainability techniques, causal explanations, interactive explanation systems, and robust evaluation methodologies, researchers can significantly enhance the transparency, accountability, and trustworthiness of AI systems (Andres et al., 2020; Ghaffarian et al., 2023). These advancements will ensure that AI-driven decision-making processes in humanitarian contexts are ethical, fair, and effective, ultimately leading to better outcomes for vulnerable populations and more resilient humanitarian responses.

The intersection of AI and humanitarian efforts provides opportunities for transformative solutions to complex global challenges. As AI technologies advance, future trends in this intersection will increasingly involve partnerships and collaborations across various sectors, including academia, government, the private sector, and civil society organizations (Ulnicane et al., 2021). There is a need for future researchers to focus on cross-sector partnerships, with an emphasis on developing collaborative frameworks, joint research and development (R&D) activities, capacity building, as well as monitoring and evaluation. Future researchers could focus on developing effective models for collaboration that define roles, responsibilities, and mechanisms for coordination among stakeholders by establishing governance structures that oversee the collaboration, ensuring transparency, accountability, and equitable decision-making. Researchers could also focus on the efficacy of creating innovation hubs or labs where stakeholders can co-develop AI solutions, as these hubs can serve as incubators for new ideas and technologies promoting the sharing of resources, including data, technology, and expertise, to accelerate the development of AI-driven solutions. There is also a need for future research work on developing training programs and educational initiatives to build capacity among stakeholders, particularly in AI literacy and skills by engaging local communities in the development and implementation of AI solutions, ensuring that they have the knowledge and tools to utilize these technologies effectively. Future research work could also focus on developing methodologies for monitoring and evaluating the impact of AI-driven solutions with regular assessments helping identify best practices and areas for improvement. A practical example of the benefits of cross-sector collaboration can be seen in the development and deployment of AI for disaster response. In such collaborations, academic researchers may develop predictive models to forecast natural disasters, such as floods or earthquakes. These models are then refined and tested in partnership with tech companies that provide the necessary infrastructure and technological support. Governments can facilitate access to relevant data and provide funding, while NGOs and civil society organizations implement these solutions on the ground, ensuring they are culturally and contextually appropriate. By working together, these diverse stakeholders can create a robust and scalable AI-driven disaster response system that saves lives, reduces suffering, and enhances resilience in vulnerable communities.

As AI technologies become increasingly integrated into humanitarian efforts, the development of robust ethical frameworks and governance models is essential to ensure their responsible and equitable use (Coppi et al., 2021). These frameworks must address various ethical implications, including data privacy, consent, bias, and accountability, to prevent harm and promote fair outcomes. AI systems can perpetuate or exacerbate existing biases if not carefully designed and monitored. Hence, future research work must focus on governance models to ensure that AI applications are fair and do not disproportionately impact certain groups. There is also a need for future research work to focus on transparency and accountability to build trust among stakeholders, including affected communities, humanitarian organizations, and donors. Many countries have stringent regulations regarding data privacy and AI use, hence there is a definite need for robust governance models to help organizations comply with these legal requirements, avoiding penalties, and encouraging international cooperation (Singh, 2024). Future research work can focus on privacy by design by incorporating data privacy considerations into the design of AI systems from the outset by implementing encryption, anonymization, and secure data storage practices. Also, there is a need for developing mechanisms to obtain informed consent from individuals whose data is being collected and used and ensuring that consent is freely given, specific, informed, and revocable.

Future research work could also focus on enhancing data integration and interoperability for AI applications in humanitarianism focuses on developing techniques and standards to seamlessly incorporate diverse data sources, such as satellite imagery, social media, and local reports, into AI systems. Researchers can aim to improve the accuracy, efficiency, and reliability of AI-driven decision-making by addressing challenges related to data fusion, real-time processing, standardized formats, privacy, and security (Gupta et al., 2022). This will facilitate better collaboration and data sharing among humanitarian organizations, leading to more informed and effective responses to crises, ultimately supporting more ethical and impactful humanitarian efforts.

ACTION POINTS FOR POLICYMAKERS

Policymakers need to ensure that regulations and frameworks are in place for AI deployment in humanitarian contexts by establishing clear ethical guidelines, regulatory frameworks, and standards (Akinrinola et al., 2024). These frameworks should be designed to ensure that AI technologies are developed and utilized in a manner that respects fundamental ethical principles and human rights. This includes creating policies that mandate transparency in AI algorithms and decision-making processes, enabling stakeholders to understand how AI-driven conclusions are reached. Additionally, accountability mechanisms must be embedded within these frameworks to ensure that AI developers and operators can be held responsible for the outcomes of their technologies. Fairness should be a cornerstone of these guidelines, requiring that AI systems do not perpetuate biases or lead to discriminatory practices. Privacy protections are also essential, given the sensitive nature of the data often used in humanitarian AI applications.

In developing these ethical and regulatory frameworks, a collaborative approach is essential. Policymakers should engage with a broad range of stakeholders, including AI researchers, humanitarian organizations, affected communities, and international bodies, to gather diverse perspectives and ensure comprehensive guidelines (Madianou, 2021; Van den Homberg et al., 2020). These frameworks should be adaptable, allowing for updates as AI technologies evolve and new ethical challenges emerge. Furthermore, these frameworks should include provisions for regular audits and assessments to monitor compliance and effectiveness, ensuring that AI technologies in humanitarian contexts are not only innovative but also ethical and just. Policymakers must also focus on establishing comprehensive and forward-thinking guidelines that will help safeguard human rights, promote fairness, and build public trust in AI-driven humanitarian efforts. Governments have an important role in developing partnerships and collaborations between various sectors, including government agencies, humanitarian organizations, academia, and the private sector. Governments can leverage the unique strengths and resources of each sector to develop and implement AI-driven solutions for humanitarian preparedness and response by actively promoting and facilitating these partnerships (Madianou, 2021). Government agencies can provide policy support, funding, and access to critical data, while humanitarian organizations bring on-the-ground insights and experience in crisis management. Academia contributes cutting-edge research, innovative methodologies, and rigorous testing of AI technologies, ensuring that solutions are scientifically sound and effective. Meanwhile, the private sector offers technological expertise, advanced tools, and scalable solutions that can be rapidly deployed in crisis situations (Henriksen, 2024). By creating platforms for collaboration, such as joint research initiatives, public-private partnerships, and multi-stakeholder working groups, governments can ensure that these diverse contributions are harnessed effectively to enhance the overall impact of AI in humanitarian efforts.

Such cross-sector collaborations are crucial for developing holistic and scalable AI solutions that can address the multifaceted challenges faced during humanitarian crises (Henriksen, 2024). For instance, during a natural disaster, an integrated AI system developed through cross-sector collaboration can combine satellite imagery (provided by private tech companies), predictive models (developed by academic researchers), and real-time data from humanitarian organizations to create accurate, actionable insights for government agencies coordinating the response. This synergy allows for more efficient resource allocation, faster decision-making, and improved outcomes for affected communities. Government-led initiatives to promote such partnerships can include creating funding programs that require multi-sector involvement, establishing innovation hubs where stakeholders can co-create solutions, and facilitating knowledge-sharing platforms where best practices and lessons learned are disseminated (Henriksen, 2024). Ultimately, by enabling an environment of collaboration, governments can significantly enhance the effectiveness and sustainability of AI-driven humanitarian interventions.

AI developers have a crucial role in advocating for responsible AI practices within the AI community (Golbin et al., 2020). They should take an active stance in raising awareness about the potential risks and ethical implications of deploying AI technologies in humanitarian settings. This involves highlighting issues such as bias, privacy concerns, and the need for transparency in AI decision-making processes. By engaging in open dialogues and sharing knowledge about the challenges and opportunities of AI in these sensitive contexts, developers can contribute to a more informed and conscientious community. This advocacy is not limited to technical aspects but also extends to the social and ethical dimensions of AI applications, ensuring that the benefits of AI are realized without compromising human rights or exacerbating inequalities.

Humanitarian organizations should proactively allocate resources and funding toward research and innovation in AI technologies specifically tailored for humanitarian purposes (Beduschi, 2022). This investment is crucial for developing advanced tools and methodologies that can enhance the effectiveness and efficiency of humanitarian efforts. By dedicating funds to AI research, organizations can support the exploration of new algorithms, data integration techniques, and predictive models that address the unique challenges faced in humanitarian contexts (Henriksen, 2024). Additionally, such investments can promote partnerships with academic institutions, private tech companies, and research organizations, leveraging their expertise to drive innovation forward. Through targeted funding, humanitarian organizations can accelerate the development of AI solutions that improve disaster response, resource allocation, and overall crisis management.

Policymakers must continue to encourage a mindset that values experimentation, learning, and adaptation can lead to the discovery of novel approaches and best practices in the use of AI (Stix, 2021). This involves creating environments where teams feel empowered to explore new ideas, pilot innovative projects, and learn from both successes and failures. Organizations can establish innovation labs or centers of excellence that focus on integrating emerging technologies into their operations. By promoting continuous learning and adaptability, humanitarian organizations can stay at the forefront of technological advancements, ensuring they are prepared to leverage AI's full potential in addressing future humanitarian challenges.

Humanitarian organizations should prioritize the facilitation of knowledge sharing, collaboration, and networking among AI developers, researchers, and other relevant stakeholders (Bealt et al., 2016). This can be achieved through the creation of dedicated platforms, events, and initiatives that bring together diverse groups to exchange ideas and experiences. For instance, organizing conferences, workshops, and hackathons focused on AI in humanitarian contexts can provide valuable opportunities for stakeholders to collaborate and learn from one another. These events can highlight innovative projects, share best practices, and address common challenges, building a community of practice that is committed to leveraging AI for humanitarian good. There is also a need for promoting the exchange of ideas, experiences, and lessons learned is essential for enhancing the collective understanding and application of AI in humanitarian efforts. This can be achieved by creating repositories of knowledge, such as online forums, databases, and publications. Humanitarian organizations can ensure that valuable insights and innovations are accessible to all stakeholders. This collaborative approach helps to avoid duplication of efforts and allows for the scaling of successful AI solutions across different contexts and organizations. Additionally, encouraging partnerships with academic institutions, technology firms, and other humanitarian organizations can facilitate the co-creation of AI tools and frameworks that are informed by a broad range of perspectives and expertise. Through these concerted efforts, the humanitarian sector can build a robust ecosystem of knowledge and collaboration that drives the effective and ethical use of AI in addressing global humanitarian challenges.

CONCLUSION

This chapter presented future research directions and action points highlighting the critical need for a multifaceted approach to integrating AI into humanitarian efforts. As AI technologies continue to evolve, they hold immense potential to revolutionize the way humanitarian organizations respond to crises, manage resources, and support vulnerable populations. However, realizing this potential requires addressing several key areas: enhancing DSS, developing explainable AI techniques, promoting cross-sector collaboration, creating robust ethical frameworks, ensuring data integration and interoperability, and promoting responsible AI practices. The enhancement of DSS through the integration of AI algorithms with real-time data streams and advanced analytics can provide actionable insights that significantly improve crisis response strategies. Also, there is a need for emphasizing explainable AI techniques to ensure that these systems are transparent and trustworthy, which is essential for gaining stakeholder confidence and ensuring accountability. Furthermore, promoting cross-sector collaboration between government agencies, humanitarian organizations, academia, and the private sector leverages the diverse strengths and resources of each sector, leading to more comprehensive and scalable AI solutions.

Policymakers must focus on developing robust ethical frameworks and governance models to ensure that AI applications adhere to principles of transparency, accountability, fairness, privacy, and human rights. This approach not only prevents harm but also ensures equitable outcomes for all affected communities. There is also a need for enhancing data integration and interoperability by developing standardized data formats and protocols, which facilitates better data sharing and collaboration among humanitarian organizations, ultimately leading to more effective and informed decision-making. Researchers must also work on promoting responsible AI practices within the AI community and advocating for guidelines and standards is essential for mitigating risks and maximizing the benefits of AI in humanitarian contexts. Similarly, investing in innovation and research will help in developing a culture of continuous improvement, enabling humanitarian organizations to adapt to emerging technologies and best practices.

Finally, facilitating knowledge sharing and collaboration through platforms, events, and initiatives enhances the collective understanding and application of AI, driving forward the effectiveness and impact of humanitarian efforts.

REFERENCES

Abaku, E. A., Edunjobi, T. E., & Odimarha, A. C. (2024). Theoretical approaches to AI in supply chain optimization: Pathways to efficiency and resilience. *International Journal of Science and Technology Research Archive*, 6(1), 092–107.

Abdul, S., Adeghe, E. P., Adegoke, B. O., Adegoke, A. A., & Udedeh, E. H. (2024). AI-enhanced healthcare management during natural disasters: Conceptual insights. *Engineering Science & Technology Journal*, 5(5), 1794–1816.

Afroogh, S., Mostafavi, A., Akbari, A., Pouresmaeil, Y., Goudarzi, S., Hajhosseini, F., & Rasoulkhani, K. (2023). Embedded ethics for responsible artificial intelligence systems (EE-RAIS) in disaster management: A conceptual model and its deployment. *AI and Ethics*, 23(1), 1–25.

Agarwal, P., Swami, S., & Malhotra, S. K. (2024). Artificial intelligence adoption in the post COVID-19 new-normal and role of smart technologies in transforming business: A review. *Journal of Science and Technology Policy Management*, 15(3), 506–529.

Agbehadji, I. E., Awuzie, B. O., Ngowi, A. B., & Millham, R. C. (2020). Review of big data analytics, artificial intelligence and nature-inspired computing models towards accurate detection of COVID-19 pandemic cases and contact tracing. *International Journal of Environmental Research and Public Health*, 17(15), 53–76.

Akbari, M., & Do, T. N. A. (2021). A systematic review of machine learning in logistics and supply chain management: Current trends and future directions. *Benchmarking: An International Journal*, 28(10), 2977–3005.

Akinrinola, O., Okoye, C. C., Ofodile, O. C., & Ugochukwu, C. E. (2024). Navigating and reviewing ethical dilemmas in AI development: Strategies for transparency, fairness, and accountability. *GSC Advanced Research and Reviews*, 18(3), 050–058.

Andres, J., Wolf, C. T., Cabrero Barros, S., Oduor, E., Nair, R., Kjærum, A., Tharsgaard, A. B., & Madsen, B. S. (2020). Scenario-based XAI for humanitarian aid forecasting. In *Extended Abstracts of the 2020 CHI Conference on Human Factors in Computing Systems*. Honolulu, HI, USA.

Arrieta, A. B., Díaz-Rodríguez, N., Del Ser, J., Bennetot, A., Tabik, S., Barbado, A., García, S., Gil-López, S., Molina, D., & Benjamins, R. (2020). Explainable Artificial Intelligence (XAI): Concepts, taxonomies, opportunities and challenges toward responsible AI. *Information Fusion*, 58, 82–115.

Assegie, T. A. (2023). Evaluation of local interpretable model-agnostic explanation and shapley additive explanation for chronic heart disease detection. *Proceedings of Engineering and Technology Innovation*, 23, 48–59.

Bealt, J., Fernández Barrera, J. C., & Mansouri, S. A. (2016). Collaborative relationships between logistics service providers and humanitarian organizations during disaster relief operations. *Journal of Humanitarian Logistics and Supply Chain Management*, 6(2), 118–144.

Beduschi, A. (2022). Harnessing the potential of artificial intelligence for humanitarian action: Opportunities and risks. *International Review of the Red Cross*, 104(919), 1149–1169.

Burbules, N. C., Fan, G., & Repp, P. (2020). Five trends of education and technology in a sustainable future. *Geography and Sustainability*, 1(2), 93–97.

Coppi, G., Moreno Jimenez, R., & Kyriazi, S. (2021). Explicability of humanitarian AI: A matter of principles. *Journal of International Humanitarian Action*, 6(1), 19.

Deng, L. (2018). Artificial intelligence in the rising wave of deep learning: The historical path and future outlook [perspectives]. *IEEE Signal Processing Magazine*, 35(1), 180–177.

Dhakal, S., & Zhang, L. (2023). A social welfare–based infrastructure resilience assessment framework: Toward equitable resilience for infrastructure development. *Natural Hazards Review*, 24(1), 04022043.

Dimililer, K., Dindar, H., & Al-Turjman, F. (2021). Deep learning, machine learning and internet of things in geophysical engineering applications: An overview. *Microprocessors and Microsystems*, 80, 103–113.

Efe, A. (2022). A review on risk reduction potentials of artificial intelligence in humanitarian aid sector. *Journal of Human and Social Sciences*, 5(2), 184–205.

Fan, C., Zhang, C., Yahja, A., & Mostafavi, A. (2021). Disaster city digital twin: A vision for integrating artificial and human intelligence for disaster management. *International Journal of Information Management*, 56, 102–117.

Garg, S., Sinha, S., Kar, A. K., & Mani, M. (2022). A review of machine learning applications in human resource management. *International Journal of Productivity and Performance Management*, 71(5), 1590–1610.

Ghaffarian, S., Taghikhah, F. R., & Maier, H. R. (2023). Explainable artificial intelligence in disaster risk management: Achievements and prospective futures. *International Journal of Disaster Risk Reduction*, 98, 104123.

Golbin, I., Rao, A. S., Hadjarian, A., & Krittman, D. (2020). Responsible AI: A primer for the legal community. In *2020 IEEE International Conference on Big Data (Big Data)*, 10–13 December 2020, Atlanta, GA.

Goswami, S., Chakraborty, S., Ghosh, S., Chakrabarti, A., & Chakraborty, B. (2018). A review on application of data mining techniques to combat natural disasters. *Ain Shams Engineering Journal*, 9(3), 365–378.

Gupta, S., Modgil, S., Bhattacharyya, S., & Bose, I. (2022). Artificial intelligence for decision support systems in the field of operations research: Review and future scope of research. *Annals of Operations Research*, 308(1), 215–274.

Hansen, J. W., Vaughan, C., Kagabo, D. M., Dinku, T., Carr, E. R., Körner, J., & Zougmoré, R. B. (2019). Climate services can support african 'farmers' context-specific adaptation needs at scale. *Frontiers in Sustainable Food Systems*, 3(1), 21–34.

Henriksen, S. E. (2024). Finding the "Sweet Spot": The politics of alignment in cross-sector partnerships for refugees. *Business & Society*, 63(1), 145–184.

How, M.-L., Chan, Y. J., & Cheah, S.-M. (2020). Predictive insights for improving the resilience of global food security using artificial intelligence. *Sustainability*, 12(15), 62–72.

Huntington, B., Goulding, J., & Pitchford, N. J. (2023). Expert perspectives on how educational technology may support autonomous learning for remote out-of-school children in low-income contexts. *International Journal of Educational Research Open*, 5, 100263.

Jiao, P., & Alavi, A. H. (2020). Artificial intelligence in seismology: Advent, performance and future trends. *Geoscience Frontiers*, 11(3), 739–744.

Joseph, J. K., Dev, K. A., Pradeepkumar, A., & Mohan, M. (2018). Big data analytics and social media in disaster management. In *Integrating Disaster Science and Management* (pp. 287–294). Amsterdam: Elsevier.

Jung, D., Tran Tuan, V., Quoc Tran, D., Park, M., & Park, S. (2020). Conceptual framework of an intelligent decision support system for smart city disaster management. *Applied Sciences*, 10(2), 666.

Khan, H. U., Malik, M. Z., & Nazir, S. (2024). Identifying the AI-based solutions proposed for restricting money laundering in financial sectors: Systematic mapping. *Applied Artificial Intelligence*, 38(1), 2344415.

Khurana, D., Koli, A., Khatter, K., & Singh, S. (2023). Natural language processing: State of the art, current trends and challenges. *Multimedia Tools and Applications, 82*(3), 3713–3744.

Kumar, A., Krishnamoorthy, B., & Bhattacharyya, S. S. (2024). Machine learning and artificial intelligence-induced technostress in organizations: A study on automation-augmentation paradox with socio-technical systems as coping mechanisms. *International Journal of Organizational Analysis, 32*(4), 681–701. https://doi.org/10.1108/IJOA-01-2023-3581

Luan, H., & Tsai, C.-C. (2021). A review of using machine learning approaches for precision education. *Educational Technology & Society, 24*(1), 250–266.

Madianou, M. (2021). Nonhuman humanitarianism: When "AI for good" can be harmful. *Information, Communication & Society, 24*(6), 850–868.

Mahbooba, B., Timilsina, M., Sahal, R., & Serrano, M. (2021). Explainable artificial intelligence (XAI) to enhance trust management in intrusion detection systems using decision tree model. *Complexity, 2021*(1), 6634811.

Makudza, F., Jaravaza, D. C., Makandwa, G., & Mukucha, P. (2024). Disruptive artificial intelligence: Augmenting consumer experience through chatbot banking. In N. Singh, P. Kansra, & S. L. Gupta (Eds.), *Digital Influence on Consumer Habits: Marketing Challenges and Opportunities* (pp. 1–18). Leeds: Emerald Publishing Limited. https://doi.org/10.1108/978-1-80455-342-820241001

Malik, Y. S., Sircar, S., Bhat, S., Ansari, M. I., Pande, T., Kumar, P., Mathapati, B., Balasubramanian, G., Kaushik, R., & Natesan, S. (2021). How artificial intelligence may help the Covid-19 pandemic: Pitfalls and lessons for the future. *Reviews in Medical Virology, 31*(5), 1–11.

Mehrabi, N., Morstatter, F., Saxena, N., Lerman, K., & Galstyan, A. (2021). A survey on bias and fairness in machine learning. *ACM Computing Surveys (CSUR), 54*(6), 1–35.

Morrow, E., Zidaru, T., Ross, F., Mason, C., Patel, K. D., Ream, M., & Stockley, R. (2023). Artificial intelligence technologies and compassion in healthcare: A systematic scoping review. *Frontiers in Psychology, 13*, 97–104.

Peña-Cáceres, O., Tavara-Ramos, A., Correa-Calle, T., & More-More, M. (2024). Integral chatbot solution for efficient incident management and emergency or disaster response: Optimizing communication and coordination. *TEM Journal, 13*(1), 50–61.

Peters, L. E. (2021). Beyond disaster vulnerabilities: An empirical investigation of the causal pathways linking conflict to disaster risks. *International Journal of Disaster Risk Reduction, 55*, 102092.

Pizzi, M., Romanoff, M., & Engelhardt, T. (2020). AI for humanitarian action: Human rights and ethics. *International Review of the Red Cross, 102*(913), 145–180.

Rodríguez-Espíndola, O., Chowdhury, S., Beltagui, A., & Albores, P. (2020). The potential of emergent disruptive technologies for humanitarian supply chains: The integration of block-chain, Artificial Intelligence and 3D printing. *International Journal of Production Research, 58*(15), 4610–4630.

Sarker, I. H. (2022). AI-based modeling: Techniques, applications and research issues towards automation, intelligent and smart systems. *SN Computer Science, 3*(2), 158–167.

Schmidt-Erfurth, U., Sadeghipour, A., Gerendas, B. S., Waldstein, S. M., & Bogunović, H. (2018). Artificial intelligence in retina. *Progress in Retinal and Eye Research, 67*, 1–29.

Singh, C. (2024). Artificial intelligence and deep learning: Considerations for financial institutions for compliance with the regulatory burden in the United Kingdom. *Journal of Financial Crime, 31*(2), 259–266. https://doi.org/10.1108/JFC-01-2023-0011

Slim, H. (1997). Relief agencies and moral standing in war: Principles of humanity, neutrality, impartiality and solidarity. *Development in Practice, 7*(4), 342–352.

Slimi, Z., & Carballido, B. V. (2023). Systematic review: 'AI's impact on higher education-learning, teaching, and career opportunities. *TEM Journal, 12*(3), 1627.

Stix, C. (2021). Actionable principles for artificial intelligence policy: Three pathways. *Science and Engineering Ethics*, *27*(1), 15.

Sun, W., Bocchini, P., & Davison, B. D. (2020). Applications of artificial intelligence for disaster management. *Natural Hazards*, *103*(3), 2631–2689.

Ulnicane, I., Knight, W., Leach, T., Stahl, B. C., & Wanjiku, W.-G. (2021). Framing governance for a contested emerging technology: Insights from AI policy. *Policy and Society*, *40*(2), 158–177.

Van den Homberg, M. J., Gevaert, C. M., & Georgiadou, Y. (2020). The changing face of accountability in humanitarianism: Using artificial intelligence for anticipatory action. *Politics and Governance*, *8*(4), 456–467.

Wamba, S. F., Bawack, R. E., Guthrie, C., Queiroz, M. M., & Carillo, K. D. A. (2021). Are we preparing for a good AI society? A bibliometric review and research agenda. *Technological Forecasting and Social Change*, *164*(1), 120–133.

Yinusa, A., & Faezipour, M. (2023). Optimizing healthcare delivery: A model for staffing, patient assignment, and resource allocation. *Applied System Innovation*, *6*(5), 78–92.

Index

Note: **Bold** page numbers refer to tables and *italic* page numbers refer to figures.

Printed in the United States
by Baker & Taylor Publisher Services